the Poison River

Steve Raymond

with

Mal Karman

New Amsterdam Press
Amsterdam
New York
San Francisco

Steve Raymond

Published by New Amsterdam Press
Suite 120, 666 Fifth Ave., New York, N.Y. 10103
A division of New Perspectives/Global Academics/Acolyte Press
Amsterdam, Holland

Printed in the United States of America
Address queries regarding rights and permissions to:
New Amsterdam Press, Suite 120, 666 Fifth Ave., New York, N.Y. 10103

First Edition. January 1995.
Cover concept and design by Jim Surine & M. M. Karman.

Publisher's Cataloging in Publication

Raymond, Stephen D.
        The poison river / by Steve Raymond with Mal Karman.
        p. cm.
        Includes biographical references and index.
        Preassigned LCCN: 94-67470
        ISBN 0-9642533-8-0(Softcover)
        ISBN 0-9642533-9-9(Hardcover)

        1. Raymond, Stephen D. 2. Tourist trade—Thailand—Biography.
3. Tourist trade—United States—Biography. 4. Businessmen—United
States—Biography. 5. Businessmen—Thailand—Biography. 6. Sex
oriented businesses—Thailand. 7. Sex-oriented businesses—United
States. 1. Karman, Mal. II. Title.

G154.5.R39 1994   338.4791'092
                                         QBI94-1957

This book is dedicated to the memory of

Lillian "Bill" Lundy

the Poison River

River

is a true story

Contents

Foreword

In his book "The Poison River", Steve Raymond performs a valuable service to those working for the reform of prison conditions in Thailand, and to those seeking accountability within the embassy system, by bearing witness to the abuse of inmates in Thai prisons, detention centers and police lock-ups.

Amnesty International has been concerned for years that prison conditions in Thailand do not meet minimum international standards for the treatment of prisoners. In 1989, part of the period of Steve Raymond's detention, Amnesty International received a number of reports of the mistreatment of Thai prisoners, including beatings and 30 suspicious deaths while in custody.

Earlier this year, Amnesty International conducted interviews with refugees and asylum-seekers who had been subject to ill treatment and detention by Thai authorities, and in some cases forced to return to the country from which they fled to face serious risk of human rights violations. Many had been detained in the Bangkok Immigration Detention Center (IDC), where Steve Raymond spent considerable time.

Amnesty International once again expressed concern that "conditions of detention at the IDC fall far short of basic international minimum standards and in some cases amount to cruel, inhuman and degrading treatment."

According to the Amnesty International report, "Thailand: Burmese and Other Asylum-Seekers at Risk", released September 8, 1994, "There is often chronic overcrowding in Bangkok IDC, to the point where inmates cannot lie down at the same time. At times, certain detainees have had to sit with their knees bent for several months at a time, and when they were finally released, they were unable to walk. There is no provision for exercise at all. Overcrowding leads to health problems, particularly fungal infections of the skin, which occur frequently. Detainees are fed twice a day, but the rations are inadequate. Children detained with their mothers do not qualify for food, as there are no charges against them. Mothers are forced to share their own scant rations, and malnutrition is the result. Nor do children under five years get fresh air or exercise. Amnesty International also received reports of beatings at the IDC... One prisoner said, 'I was beaten because I had no money'. Lack of money is a major problem for detainees. Anyone without a passport, who is convicted of 'illegal immigration' must pay the cost of travel outside the country; those without money may stay long beyond the period of sentencing. Amnesty International welcomes reports that a new leadership team in charge of the Bangkok IDC is eager to improve the conditions of detention, but the organization remains gravely concerned over the practice of indefinite detention in very harsh conditions. A number of recommendations have been made to the Thai authorities including, 'Ensure that ill-treatment of detainees in the Bangkok IDC, police lock-ups and all other places of detention ceases, and that independent inquiries are held into allegations of ill-treatment. The results of such inquiries should be made public and any police or other authorities found responsible for ill-treatment should be brought to justice'."

—Southeast Asia Coordination Group
Amnesty International, USA

Prologue

It was the second day of the hot season, nearly 100 degrees with suffocating humidity, a typical sweltering afternoon in March that made the city into an inferno baking with exotic smells and the fumes of cars, buses, trucks and tuk tuks. Traffic was twisted in a Gordian knot and I was in the middle of it, sopping wet with perspiration, my clothes matted to my body which leaked from every pore. It felt as if there were no oxygen in the air.

The Toyota crawled through congested Bangkok streets for 25 minutes, and finally pulled to the curb on Sri Ayudhaya Road. I was ordered out of the car, quickly marched into police headquarters and down a long open hallway to an auditorium. Having just experienced the most surreal 24 hours of my life, I was not prepared for more — but evidently I had very little say in the matter.

"In there!" a police officer said sharply. "In there!" I peered through the doorway. Television equipment was lined up and down an area in front of a stage and dozens of people anxiously milled around. "Reporters!" I shrieked, starting to bolt away. Two officers grabbed me and propelled me into the hall.

Suddenly I was face-to-face with still cameras, video cameras, microphones, photographers, newsmen — and I was dumbstruck. My mind was thrown into overdrive, trying to understand what was happening. Nothing was logical. Nothing made sense.

At the front of the auditorium were three tables and I was ordered to sit at one. Dozens of photographs of naked babies and young children were spread out before me. I glanced at them in disbelief, then leapt up at the English-speaking officer who had brought me from Din Daeng Police Station and demanded to know what was going on and why I was there.

"You know why," he said, gesturing at the photographs.

"What do these have to do with me?" I cried. "I've never seen these pictures in my life!" My heart was racing so feverishly I could feel my pulse pounding in my temples like a jackhammer. I turned to the reporters and repeated myself in Thai. "Mai koei hen ni!" I shouted again and again.

Colonel Khongdej Choosri, a man built like a bulldog with a bulldog's scowl, seized me by the arm and tried to pull me back to the chair. I resisted. "Mai koei hen ni!" I yelled, gesturing wildly, "I have never seen these!"

One of the taboos of Thai culture, considered the epitome of bad manners and always counterproductive, is raising one's voice in public. In fact, social dictates allow for any number of ways to avoid confrontation. I was definitely providing a media event for the reserved and impassive Thai people. With television cameras rolling and tape players recording, in a matter of hours the gyrations of this madman would be witnessed by millions of people across the Pacific Rim.

Now the highest-ranking officer at the press conference, Police General Manas Krutchaiyan, walked up to me and thrust a photograph in my face. Speaking in an unnaturally loud voice so that not one journalist would miss it, he roared, "This is a picture of you in bed with a young boy!!"

I looked aghast at the snapshot. "No it isn't, this is not me!!" I cried. "Why are you doing this?"

The general then turned to his subordinate and said, "It's him, isn't it?" The officer nodded his head in agreement.

The photo was not shown to any of the reporters in the auditorium nor did any ask to see it. It revealed a white foreigner (a "farang" as

2

we are called in Thailand) with a Thai boy, but the farang did not even remotely resemble me.

As a uniformed officer began distributing press releases to the media, I was near tears with helplessness. I sank into a chair and covered my face with a large manila envelope into which my money and passport had been placed. Colonel Choosri snatched it away, leaving me glaring at a copy of the press release. It was written in Thai, which I can't read, but in English was my name and the names of two friends — David Groat, my neighbor; and Mark Morgan, who operated the Bangkok Children's Shelter.

General Krutchaiyan addressed the assembled reporters while Colonel Choosri leafed through several photo albums on the table. I looked at them in stunned disbelief. Inside were pictures of babies, at most a year or two old.

Although I was too shocked to understand, the journalists were being told that I operated a sex tour business — that I brought pedophiles from around the world to Thailand, presented them with photographs of these infants whom the police claimed were from Mark Morgan's children's shelter, and then charged them to have sex with a child of their choosing. Mark's shelter, the press release stated, was nothing but a front for child prostitution.

The reporters were avaricious. Hungry for a scandalous story that would induce readers to buy papers and viewers to tune in, they seemed to eagerly accept what the police were telling them without question. But this was my life they were preparing to blast across their air waves and front pages like a three-headed dog in the National Enquirer.

I sprang to my feet and cried out again. Instantly, General Krutchaiyan roared that the press conference was over. To my utter astonishment, the entire assembly of journalists dutifully turned off their recorders and started packing up their cameras. This debacle ended with my relentless shrieks of protest filling the hall while the

General's obedient newsmen filed out the door without a single suspicious question dangling within their collective brains.

Thirty minutes later, I would be locked in a jail cell reeking with urine and vomit, and charged with the heinous crime of selling children in Thailand for sex.

* * *

I opened Tour Service (Thailand) Ltd. a little more than four years before this nightmare began. At the time I was still president and the major stockholder of a San Francisco tour company that dealt with all segments of the travel industry. As a result, I was getting stretched too thin. I did not want the same kind of pressure in Thailand — there I hoped to deal strictly with corporate incentive programs, building to one or two lucrative programs a month, and simply relax in between clients.

Travel industry colleagues in both America and Thailand doubted the wisdom of the idea. A Thai tour operator told me that if I was planning to handle only American incentive programs in Bangkok, I might as well declare bankruptcy before setting up shop. An American tour operator asked where I expected to find corporate clients crazy enough to take their valued employees half way around the world "just to visit Thailand".

During the first year of business at the Bangkok office, I had spent thousands of dollars more than I had anticipated; Thailand had withstood a military coup; and John Robbins, my sales manager, had been rushed back to America for a liver transplant. By the end of the second year, David Wood, my office manager, had died unexpectedly of a heart attack, and I had been forced to sell stock in the company to keep from going under.

But I was determined. I loved Thailand with a passion and told anyone who would listen to my ravings that the country would soon become the world's next major incentive destination. After David Wood died, I hired a Thai named Tone to be general manager. A few months later, I met Mark Morgan, an American who had recently moved to Thailand, and hired him as a sales manager.

As time went on, however, it became increasingly obvious that I could not successfully run two companies on different sides of the world. So, in 1987, I sold most of the stock in my San Francisco company and took up permanent residence to concentrate on the business in Bangkok.

One

The Eye of the Storm

February 13, 1989

Thai people have a knack for transforming the mundane into the exotic; they take ordinary fruit and carve it into artistic sculptures; they turn simple taxi rides into thrilling adventures aboard motorized samlors; they even celebrate the changing of seasons with spectacular pageants in the Temple of the Emerald Buddha, the most glittering square mile on earth. This celebration occurs three times a year, as Thailand has but three seasons.

Rather than confuse the issue with nondescript titles, Thais simply refer to their seasons as hot, cold, and rainy. Visitors from temperate climes may wonder about the term "cold", but those of us who lived year-round in Thailand did perceive an occasional cool breeze during the so-called "cold" season.

February is officially part of the cold season. But I found it difficult to think of it that way each day, as I turned on the air-conditioner in the office seeking relief from the 90-degree temperatures.

The office was located on the eighth floor of a drab apartment building, dubbed Victory Monument Condominium by the developers. The edifice had been constructed in the early 1980's, at the beginning of a building boom that was responsible for thoroughly changing the skyline of Bangkok, seemingly overnight. Since the condominium complex was erected, the city had sprouted hundreds of high-rise buildings, many exceeding 20 stories. The architects hadn't used a tremendous amount of creative genius. The box-like cement structure was similar to thousands of unimaginative, but functional buildings in dozens of developing tropical nations. The first floor allowed open-air parking, topped by eight floors of simple rectangular units, each exactly like the other. My office consisted of two of these units, thus it was twice the size of my apartment down the hall.

A twisting alley and an arched cement bridge across a putrid, polluted canal connected the building with its namesake, Victory Monument, which was a monolithic World War II memorial to Thai soldiers, sailors and airmen who died defending their King and country. At the base of the monolith were bronze statues of military figures encompassed by a traffic circle consisting of somewhere between 10 and 20 lanes, depending upon how many of Bangkok's two million plus vehicles were jammed into the roadway at any given time.

On the periphery of this enormous swarm of trucks, buses, automobiles, motorcycles, samlors and push carts were sidewalks packed with humanity cueing up to board buses that labored through the congested streets spewing black choking fumes into the already densely-polluted air.

Beyond the bus stops were small swards of swamp grass and a few struggling trees, which gave way to alleys clogged with street vendors, attempting to hawk everything from chicken fried over portable grills to ceramic piggy-banks and counterfeit name brand shirts and watches. Next to the alleys were western-style buildings with shops, restaurants, and, across the canal from my condominium, Robinson's Department Store.

The humid tropical air was filled with the stench of the canal water, the fumes from the hundreds of vehicles waiting for traffic signals to change, and the pungent odors of Kway Teeoh soup and fried rice — cooked and served at portable stalls lining the banks of the murky waterway.

I had decided to locate my office in the midst of this delicious chaos because I liked the neighborhood. I was introduced to it by a Thai consultant who owned the condominium unit and offered to lease it to me for a "reasonable price". It was only later that I learned I was paying more than anyone else in the building.

David Wood and John Robbins loved Thailand as much as I did. We loved it enough to disregard the monumental frustrations that accompanied the opening of a foreign business in the "Land of Smiles". Just because the company had been registered with the American Embassy and the office had officially been set up with the help of a corporate lawyer in accordance with the dictates of the Thai government didn't mean that we could start doing business right away. It took six months to get the telephones and telex installed, and that was only after the proper people had been "coerced" to move things along. The national motto of Thailand is "Jai yen yen" which loosely translated means "Cool down, relax, and have a drink". Thais are also fond of the word "prunee" which means "tomorrow" or, perhaps more appropriately, "Some time in the future... maybe".

But my faith in the country as an incentive market was beginning to pay off. The Tourism Authority dubbed 1987 "Visit Thailand Year" and it drew visitors in record numbers. We had handled 17 corporate incentive programs in the formative years including Federal Home Life Insurance, American Life Insurance, and GNB Battery Corp., and now had twice that many for 1989 and 1990 — clients such as Glaxo Pharmaceutical, National Travelers Life Insurance, Unisys Computer Corp., and DBE Facsimile Co. Things were beginning to happen.

I arrived at the door to my apartment and was surprised to see it closed. Normally, the two Thai boys who shared the unit with me were home from school by this time and the door was usually wide open so that afternoon breezes could flow through. I wasn't fond of air-conditioners and hadn't installed one in the apartment. I turned the door handle, but it wouldn't budge. It had been locked from inside. As I reached in my pocket for the key, the door swung open. Chat stood in the doorway with a rather sheepish grin on his face. He was a slightly stocky boy of 17, just over five feet with dark hair, dark skin and a ready smile. When he stepped aside, I saw a group of his friends in the same school uniform of white shirts and black shorts sitting on the floor in a circle. Nu, the other boy who shared my apartment, was on the couch in his school colors of white and blue shuffling cards.

"I hope you're not playing for money again", I exhorted in broken Thai, knowing full well that they had closed the door so that no one could see that they were gambling. Immediately, all the boys placed their hands in front of their faces as if they were praying. I acknowledged the "wais" directed at me, and walked past the partition into the bedroom.

During a business trip to Bangkok when I was still running the San Francisco office, I met Chat after inviting my neighbor's children and their friends to a day outing at an amusement park. I had organized these kinds of things as long ago as my college days when I drummed up donations from local merchants and put together afternoons for kids from low-income minority families. In Thailand such excursions were ridiculously cheap. I could foot the bill for 10 of them, bring a tremendous amount of joy to their lives, and it would cost less than renting a car for a day.

Chat was one of the youths who joined us that afternoon, and the only one in the group not in school. When I asked him why, he replied that his family had no money to support him. After completing elementary school in 1983, he came to Bangkok to work with his sister, selling her prepared foods in the street.

I came from a family of idealistic "bleeding heart" liberals who believe everyone should have an education. I hadn't spent enough time in Thailand to become hardened to the fact that Chat's fate was

9

typical of thousands of poor Thai children. I asked how much it would cost to get him back into school. His reply was 500 baht, a figure so unbelievably low that I offered without hesitation to pay for his schooling. Soon after, Chat, his sister Rekha, and I drove to their mother's house in Ubon to get her approval and retrieve his school records.

By the time I relocated myself full time to Bangkok, I had been sponsoring Chat for over a year. His brother had come from Ubon to replace him in the food stall, and because his sister could not house both him and his brother comfortably, Chat moved into my apartment at Victory Monument Condominium.

Not long after I started to sponsor Chat, another boy knocked on my door. A shy neatly-dressed round-faced kid of 13 stood before me and nervously said that his mother forced him to come over and tell me that he had just completed elementary school but could not afford to be sent to secondary school. He said she barely made $3 a day as a laborer. They wondered if I could help. Nu seemed almost fragile. As he looked up at me with imploring huge brown eyes that resembled those of a waif in a Walter Keane painting, my resistance crumbled and I agreed to pay for his schooling as well. The tuition for both boys was not much of a financial burden, amounting to something like $40 a semester.

At first, Nu lived at home while attending secondary school. Later, however, he went to the Bangkok Children's Shelter, the home Mark Morgan had created to help street kids. Mark had rented a large house on Lardprao Soi 66, about five miles from Victory Monument and equipped it with bunk beds, a TV, stereo, VCR, and ping pong table. It also had a huge yard with a trampoline, a garden with homegrown vegetables, and a dog, chickens, rabbits and a monkey. When Nu moved in, he was one of 16 children. But by late 1988, the population had grown to 29 boys and a girl (almost all street kids in Thailand were boys) and Nu grew weary of the crowd. He appeared on my doorstep one afternoon beseeching me to let him move in.

Though there were enough sofas and floor space to accommodate them, I thought it might get a bit cramped. But Chat was ecstatic about the idea of having a "younger brother" — so I gave in.

I grew to love both boys. They gave me a sense of family and made me feel like I was doing some good. As with most Thai children, they were extremely polite and well-mannered. Compared to the average American teenager, they were angels. I imposed a 9 PM curfew on weeknights because I wanted them to be clear-headed in class. I also gave them weekly chores around the apartment and, in exchange, an allowance. The only problem that developed was as a result of their gambling. Chat continually lost and Nu continually won. So, Chat, the elder by three years, was always broke. I asked them not to gamble for money because of the ill feelings it caused, but they didn't always listen.

"Cocktails?" a voice called out from the front. My American neighbor, David Groat, poked his head in to ask if I would join him for a drink.

"Is dinner included with the offer?" I joked.

"Yeah, I can probably throw something together," he said, "if you'll go down and pick up a video."

The apartment David lived in down the hall had a wet bar built into the wall between the rear of the unit and the balcony. He enjoyed playing bartender and preparing dinners. As my culinary abilities left much to be desired, I encouraged him as often as possible.

While I was sipping gin-and-tonic and ruminating on the probability that I would have to drag myself to a video store during rush hour, Ot, one of the boys from the slum next to our building, poked his head in the door and asked for Chat. He had a Thai language newspaper in his hand and he looked excited. I told him that Chat was home even though the door was closed. He disappeared down the hall.

A couple of minutes had passed when Chat, Nu and their friends rushed into the apartment. "Look at this," Chat cried. "It's about farangs at Victory Monument." He spread the Matichon daily on a table and read to us slowly so that we would understand. The headline trumpeted something about a foreign sex gang, followed by a story that a Thai orphan had been taken to a foreigner's home packed with Thai children, had been raped and sodomized, but had managed to escape following the attack.[1]

"You're the only foreigners who live in the neighborhood," Ot exclaimed in Thai. "Is this story about you?"

"Mai chai! It isn't about us!" I chuckled at the absurdity of the thought.

"I want to show this to the `soi'," Chat said, referring to the alleyway in the adjacent shantytown where his sister and Nu's family and many of his friends lived. The entourage then departed as abruptly as it had arrived.

"Have you noticed any farangs around who might be living in the neighborhood?" I asked David. The only others we knew about were those in our building. Donald, a Brit, lived down the hall with his Thai lover, and Bob, an American, was staying alone in my former apartment on the sixth floor. Although Victory Monument covers a large area, our building was the nicest within a half mile radius, and I couldn't imagine a "gang" of foreigners living in one of the rundown spartan Thai-style buildings.

"I haven't seen anybody," David said.

I shrugged and wondered what video to pick up.

February 14, 1989

The sun was just beginning to filter through the early morning haze as Nu opened his eyes. Feeling a slight chill, he reached over to turn off the fan. The temperature had dipped into the low 70's overnight. Nevertheless, the humid morning air hung over the city like a damp blanket. Everything was still, as if the elements were bracing for the imminent turmoil of the awakening masses. The sputter of a motorcycle or motorized samlor racing down Phaholyothin Road pierced the silence and announced the beginning of the commute.

Nu stretched just as his alarm went on. He reached over Chat to shut off the noise, then quietly rose and stumbled into the bathroom. He wasn't fully conscious. His body was reacting as if he were an automaton programmed into a morning routine. A half hour later, impeccably dressed and fully awakened, he emerged from the bathroom in his mandatory once-a-week boy scout uniform, went over to Chat and nudged him awake, then headed out the door to catch the bus for school.

Chat opened his eyes for a second, just enough time to register the time on the clock, then rolled over and closed them again. His school was much closer than Nu's and he could afford to sleep in a bit. A half hour later, he suddenly jerked awake, rushed into the bathroom, sprinkled some water on his body, threw on his school uniform, grabbed his books and darted out the door.

I was only vaguely aware of his departure, but instinctively I knew it was now my turn to wrest myself from a deep sleep. I thought of the previous night and the newspaper article. Its tone seemed strangely American/Christian to me, rather than Thai/Buddhist. Thais are much more tolerant of anything sexual. While prostitution is officially frowned upon, it is blatant around Patpong, Sapan Kwai, Soi Cowboy and other areas of the city. Even the rape of a child — shocking by our standards — would not necessarily provoke a hysterical reaction the way it would anywhere in America.

As usual, David Groat was at the computer in my office before I opened the door. The previous year he had programmed it for my business. In return, he was given an office key and access to my office equipment and came in regularly to play on the keyboard. Like many computer hacks, he sometimes seemed addicted to the screen. Mark Morgan asked if David would update mailing lists of donors and financial records for his ever-growing home for street children and I allowed him to use the equipment for that purpose too. What David got out of the deal was an excuse to continually have his visa renewed. He didn't have regular employment and spent much of his time either sitting at the computer or sitting in his apartment. His idea of an outing was to go to Marbohn Krohn Shopping Mall, have a steak dinner and pick up groceries for the week. I poured myself a cup of coffee and walked to my desk to check the calendar. A prepayment for one of my upcoming incentive programs was due and it hadn't yet arrived. I headed for the telex machine.

While I was typing the message requesting payment, Kenji came in. He was a very thin, small, half-Japanese half-Thai man in his early 20's. Despite his extreme timidity and shyness, he had a ready smile and always seemed calm no matter how turbulent things became. He had been working with me for about a year. Even though he was born in Thailand, he had grown up in Australia, spoke with an Australian accent and hadn't used Thai since he was six years old. So, when he returned to his native country, he took a Thai language class at the YWCA to re-learn the language.

Mark Morgan, who was studying at the same school, invited Kenji to apply for a job with my company as one of a number of Thai men and women whom I used as tour directors. But I had a greater need for an operations manager who could speak English well and Kenji seemed like he could handle the job. I hired him.

While I was still at the telex, another of my employees arrived. Like Kenji, Kachon had been working with the company since early in 1988. Although his English wasn't wonderful and he was constantly hyper, he was energetic and pleasant and could talk a cat out of eating a sparrow.

In fact, he seemed to have ongoing affairs with at least five women, some of whom would wait for him outside the office in order to castigate him for his indiscretions. His finer traits more than made up for his language deficiencies. Even though he was 10 years older than Kenji, he cheerfully accepted Kenji as a supervisor. Because of the status hierarchy in Thailand, older people often will not accept younger Thais in positions above them, so Kachon's attitude was unusual and refreshing.

I completed the telex message and pushed the "SEND" button. Nothing happened. I turned to Kenji. "There's something wrong," I said. "It won't connect to an outside line."

The telephone lines had been a continual source of frustration. The first year we had to wait, often for five or 10 minutes, just to get a dial tone. When I purchased a fax machine, the lines were so primitive the machine wouldn't connect with its computerized counterpart overseas. The telex, therefore, had become our lifeline.

Kachon picked up the phone and called C.A.T., the Communication Authority of Thailand, to tell their agent about our problem. "She say the lie is goos," Kachon said in his monstrous English after he hung up. "She sen the man come our offit to look at lie here."

"When?" I asked.

Knowing that no one could predict when anyone in Thailand would do anything, Kachon just shrugged.

I moaned. "Jai yen yen," I thought. It wouldn't do any good to call and demand immediate action. Being demanding or visibly irritated with a Thai never produced results. This was particularly true in my dealings with the government.

I settled down to finish my coffee when Kachon came around the corner to announce that the police were at the front door. "They wan Chat," he said.

"Chat? What do the police want Chat for?" I stood up and walked out to the reception area. Standing in the office doorway and spilling into the hallway were six of the largest Thai men I had ever seen. They could have been the offensive line for the San Francisco 49ers.

"Poleet say guard tell he Chat lif in offit," Kachon said. "I don'no. The poleet say he come becau he fine the story in Matichon newpaper."

"Come in," I offered. "Sit down."

15

Two of the officers stepped in and sat on two chairs facing Kachon's desk. The others remained standing outside the door.

"Chat's in school," I told them in Thai.

"Does he live here?" the first officer asked, also in Thai.

"No." I gestured around the room. "This is an office. Chat is one of the two boys who live in my apartment down the hall. Is there something wrong? What has Chat done?"

"Who is the other boy?" the second officer said, ignoring my question. I walked in front of Kachon's desk and squatted down in front of the officers to keep my head level with theirs — this is a sign of respect in Thailand. The Thais are very status conscious and little gestures are important.

"His name is Nu," I answered. "He is in school now as well. Both boys return from school at around 4:30. If you want to talk to them, you should come back then."

"Thank you, we will come back" the second officer said, rising to his feet. "Thank you," the other repeated, and the two of them stepped out the door to join their colleagues in the hallway.

When they had left, I turned to Kachon. "If you see Chat and Nu before I do, tell them that the police want to talk to them."

I walked back to my desk, sat down and picked up a now-cold cup of coffee. "What was that all about?" David Groat wondered aloud.

"Something to do with a newspaper story," I said. I picked up a travel trade magazine and started reading a story on the increase in Bangkok's hotel rates.

Before I finished my cold coffee, Kachon announced that Mark Morgan was on the line. David snapped up the phone. After I moved to Thailand in 1987, Mark had turned a project to help a few homeless street kids into a full-time job and had quit working as sales manager for my company. It took all of his time and then some just to raise enough money to keep the home operating. His resignation was

16

fortuitous, as my company was only allowed one work permit for a foreigner and I needed it myself.

The shelter was an hour away on the bus, so we had not seen much of each other lately. I visited the home once or twice a month and at Christmas when I played Santa Claus and brought gifts for all the kids, but Mark's visits to the condominium had become few and far between. A tall slender man of about 30 who wore glasses and straight blond hair as if it were cemented on his head, he had expanded the Bangkok Children's Shelter from a modest beginning to employ a Thai house father, a Thai house mother, a full time cook, three volunteer students from one of the universities, and occasional volunteer stewardesses from Northwest Airlines.

David hung up the phone and turned to me. "Mark says that a reporter from Matichon newspaper called him. She wanted to know what he knew about the story in her paper. He told her he didn't know anything and hadn't seen the article." David continued, "I told him that the police had just been here and wanted to talk to Chat about a newspaper article too. He's worried. He thinks that somebody is trying to ruin the home by getting it involved in a scandal. He wants to come over and talk."

The article did mention that a "home packed with Thai children" was run by a foreigner but it also said that the home was near Victory Monument. Mark's shelter was half-way across town. Why would the news reporter call him? The whole thing seemed very strange.

When Mark Morgan arrived later that afternoon, I was working on an incentive proposal for one of my American clients from San Diego.

He looked decidedly worried — in contrast to his usual outgoing and affable manner. "The whole thing has something to do with some Thai Catholic social workers," he said. "The reporter said that while they were teaching some street children out on the grass near People's Department Store, a farang walked right into the class, ignored the Catholics, told one of the boys to follow him and the two of them walked away. The boy returned the next day and told the story to the social workers who told a reporter at Matichon newspaper. I don't know how the home or Chat, for that matter, became involved. It's possible that the street children had been to the home and the stories got mixed up. I've asked the Thai volunteers at the home to go and talk to the Catholics to straighten the whole thing out."

While Mark was talking, I continued working on my proposal. I really didn't see how this bizarre incident could involve either one of us, so I was only half listening. I certainly didn't believe that there was any kind of crisis brewing.

"Mai pen arai" is an expression which captures the essence of the Thai attitude about life. Translated literally, it means "no be what" — or, more correctly, "it doesn't matter." To the Thai, nothing matters enough to become visibly irritated. I liked trying to adopt that attitude. I believed, like Voltaire's Candide, that I lived in the best of all possible worlds and that nothing could disrupt my somewhat charmed existence.

Two

Mysterious Clouds

*"What one does not know, one could utilize;
and what one knows, one cannot use."*

— Goethe

February 15, 1989

I slept late this morning and didn't get a chance to ask the boys about their conversation with the police. When I arrived in the office, Kachon and Kenji were already at their desks. Following my ritual cup of coffee, I asked Kenji to go to the security office with me and act as a translator.

"What did the police say to Chat?" we asked the guard. "Do you know why they wanted to talk to the boys?"

"I didn't hear the conversation," he said to me through Kenji. "They didn't tell me what they wanted, but they did say that they didn't find what they were looking for. They weren't regular police anyway. They were from the child welfare department."

When Kenji and I returned to the office, I was more confused than ever.

"Khun Sateef," Kachon cried looking over some correspondence he had just retrieved from the day's mail delivery. "Letter come from Labor Deparmen. He say your permit finit an he say no gip any more."

I frowned. "Why would they refuse to extend my permit?" I asked rhetorically. I had invested the proper amount of money — a requirement for operating in the country — and had followed all the guidelines. I had paid my taxes on time and my company was bringing the type of business into Thailand that the government wanted. I had personally been responsible for a number of corporate executives deciding to bring their incentive qualifiers — their top planners and managers and sales people, for example — to Thailand.

"Call Khun Phisan's office, Kachon. He'll straighten it out for me." The Permanent Secretary of the Interior was a personal friend of my former sales manager, John Robbins, who had brought me to the Department of the Interior specifically to introduce us. I was extremely impressed with the reception we had received. Although the waiting room was overflowing, we were whisked into the inner office immediately. Khun Phisan spent 45 minutes with us and told me to come see him if I ever had any problems. I had only done so once since then, and my reception had been just as cordial as it was on the first visit.

Kachon hung up the phone and said, "Sectary of Khun Phisan say you muss write the letter to make appoinmen."

This I couldn't believe! Had my relationship with the Permanent Secretary suddenly gone sour? Khun Phisan was the highest-ranking official I knew. Without his help this was going to be problematic.

"Thank you for trying, Kachon," I said glumly and sat back in my chair wondering what might have caused the sudden difficulties. I remembered an encounter I had had with a competitor the previous month in Bangkok's Ancient City. I arrived ahead of one of my groups scheduled to have lunch there and spotted Khun Anan, the owner of one of the oldest tour companies in Thailand, seated at a table. I greeted him warmly and he wheeled around at me, his eyes filled with cold fire. "Why did you write to my client?" he said angrily.

"What client?" I replied feebly, after rebounding from the unexpected assault. I had no idea what he was talking about.

"You know what client!" he hissed.

Then it hit me. I had written to an incentive company that had brought a group to Thailand the previous year. When the incentive was originally up for bid, my company made a proposal, but Anan's company had been awarded the contract. Then the incentive group came to Bangkok and I learned that their itinerary included some of the events I had suggested, so I sent the company a short telex asking that they allow me to continue to bid on future programs. I didn't believe there was anything unethical about this, but evidently Anan did.

"That is not the way we do business in Thailand!" he snapped as he turned and walked away. Then, without looking back at me, he muttered, "You don't know who I am!"

I stood in shock for a few moments, unable to believe my ears. I returned to my office that day and faxed Anan an extensive apology. But now I wondered if the apology had been unacceptable and Anan was secretly behind the rejection of my work permit or the rebuff from Khun Phisan's office. He came from a fairly influential family, and I assumed he was able to use it to influence government policy.

"Maybe the governor of tourism will help," I said aloud, as if someone were waiting for my idea. I had known the previous governor, but I really didn't know the man who had replaced him in 1987. I picked up the phone and called the director of the Thailand Incentive Convention Association (T.I.C.A.).

"Khun Sawalee" I said to her. "I have a problem with my work permit. It was rejected this year. Could you ask Governor Dharmnoon to intercede on my behalf?"

While I was on the phone, Kachon popped his head around the corner. As soon as I hung up, he announced that the Telephone

Organization of Thailand (T.O.T.) had sent three men to find the break in our telex line. "But," he continued, "he say the lie is cut off. He cannot fine where is. Sombody cut inside condo."

Was I getting paranoid or did it seem as if someone really was trying to sabotage my company? I wondered if the bizarre article in the Matichon daily newspaper was in any way connected with my problems with the telex and the Department of Labor. "It's just a coincidence," I said, putting it out of my mind, and went out to the soi to find something to eat.

On my way, I ran into the doctor from the local clinic. He told me that a man had been in to see him asking a number of questions about me, about Chat and Nu, and about the other foreigners in the condominium. He said he didn't know who the man was, but that he wasn't a Thai policeman. I decided I would have to make time to sit down and talk to Chat. Something was happening that I didn't understand.

Chat sometimes exhibited uncharacteristic behavior for a Thai. In addition to harnessing their tempers, most Thai people are not demonstrative in public. It's usually considered bad manners. But Chat was a bit of a non-conformist. Every day after school, he would traipse into the office, head for my desk, drop his books, throw his arms around me and hug me, pick up his books and leave without a word. It was his way of expressing gratitude for the things he felt I had done for him.

When he came into the office this day, I asked why the police had questioned him. He said they simply asked about his relationship to me and that he explained I was like a father to him.

I asked Chat to find Ot and retrieve the Matichon newspaper article from the other evening. Mark had just called to report another strange detail: his staff met with the Catholic social workers and they denied having spoken to a Matichon reporter. Yet, according to the Matichon reporter who had called Mark, the story in the newspaper had come from the Catholics. I wanted to see the article again. It seemed as if somebody was trying to create an incident and to implicate me and my associates. I hoped the article might provide a clue.

Chat returned a few minutes later with the paper. I asked Kachon to translate the story. His version provided no further clues. I had understood most of what Ot had previously read to us in Thai.

"What do the rest of the articles in this newspaper say?" I asked Kachon. I wondered if Matichon were the Thai version of the National Enquirer. "Who reads this newspaper?"

"Matichon welly poplar for people workeen in govermen," Kachon replied. He began to give me an overview of the rest of the articles. I noticed that four of the major stories were about foreigners and they were all negative. One concerned foreigners bringing AIDS to Thailand; another was about foreigners who had been caught illegally purchasing land in Pattaya; a third was about the negative effect of tourism on the environment; and the fourth was the front page salvo about the foreigner who had raped a boy. The slant of every article seemed to be geared toward exciting xenophobic passions. "Did this signal a change in government policy toward foreigners?" Nothing Kachon read provided any answers.

Nu arrived while Kachon was reading the newspaper. "What did the police ask you?" I said. His response was essentially the same as Chat's.

It was getting late. Chat, Nu and I left the office together and went back to the apartment. I needed a drink so I popped my head through David's doorway.

"I don't want to sound like an alarmist," I said, "but something very strange is happening." I told him about the work permit, the brush-off at Khun Phisan's office, the doctor, and the report from the telephone workers about the telex line.

He casually dismissed the telex problem and the revocation of my work permit as simply Thai inefficiency. However, he was concerned about the newspaper article and wondered what effect xenophobic stories might have on his future in the country.

23

David was a secretive man. We had met in Bangkok and I had not known him long. He never offered much about himself and I didn't prod, but he did say that he had lost several teeth in an American jail when savagely beaten by other prisoners. Small, thin, but with a developing beer belly and a scraggly receding hairline, he walked hunched over, dressed shabbily, and often went about without his dentures making him look twice as old as his 35 years.

Although the xenophobia was distressing, I accepted it as inevitable. Almost every society in the world is xenophobic. I believed that the attitude of most Thais would turn this into a tempest in a teapot. The friendliness of the Thai people, the acceptance of most of my colleagues in the tourism industry allowing me to cut a niche for myself in their country, the official slogans, were all signals that the welcome mat was out. Perhaps this was just a periodic spasm, a cleansing of the Thai soul. It wouldn't prevail. I wanted to believe it would blow over. I didn't want to accept that Thailand was anything but perfect.

February 16, 1989

The repairmen from the Telephone Organization of Thailand returned to try to find the exact location of the break in our telex line. Mid-morning, they walked into the office to announce that the break was somewhere between the first floor and our office, but because the lines in the building are on private property, they would not be able to fix them. It took three repairmen two days to tell us they could do nothing.

We had not dealt often with T.O.T. Most of our line problems had previously been solved by C.A.T., the Communications Authority of Thailand. The two organizations were like AT&T and the regional Bell companies after the breakup of the U.S. telephone monopoly. Both seemed to delight in blaming the other for any problems. And since we couldn't get anywhere with the T.O.T. people, I told Kachon to call our representative at C.A.T.

"She say the lie is not belon to C.A.T. Is mean you haf to contac with the T.O.T.," he explained.

"Tell her that the T.O.T. repairmen are here and they refuse to fix the line. Tell her that since we aren't able to use the telex line we don't feel we should have to pay the bill until it's repaired." That will induce some action, I hoped.

"She say if you not pay the bill, win cut your lie and when you wan connet, you haf to pay. Reely! No goos!" Kachon was holding the phone and waiting for my next volley.

"Thank her and tell her we'll call T.O.T.," I said shaking my head. `They'll fix it,' I thought, `if we decide to grease the right palms.'

Kenji and Kachon spent the rest of the day trying to get somebody to come out and fix the line without offering a bribe. I was ethically opposed to payoffs of any sort. Because I had refused to bribe immigration officials, I was paying income taxes from the highest tax bracket — the same bracket, they had told me, as the country's prime minister. I paid a monthly tax three times what I paid my employees, and I paid Kenji and Kachon much more than they might have made from a Thai employer.

"Corruption is tearing this country apart," I had once said to a friend. "I care too much for Thailand to let that happen without doing my part to resist it." I was sure that my feelings did not make me very popular with certain government employees. Perhaps the problem with my work permit was a result of my attitude.

Finally, in the late afternoon, Kenji came to tell me that the T.O.T. official said "if we want telex service, we have to buy a cable and connect it to the main cable ourselves."

"Great!" I thought.

In the meantime, the C.A.T. representative would allow us to pick up any incoming telex messages at the Main Post Office on Charoen Khrung Road.

When I went to David's for cocktails, he mentioned that a few days earlier a man on a ladder had been playing with the telephone lines outside the elevator shaft. He hadn't thought anything about it at the time. Residents were constantly moving phone lines in and out of apartments. The lines weren't buried in the walls. Rather, they were simply stapled to the outside of the walls. "Maybe the guy cut the line to your office by mistake," he theorized.

"Maybe so," I said. "By the way, did you talk to Mark today?" I had been so busy trying to get the telex connected and the work permit renewed that I had forgotten about him and the call from the newspaper reporter. I hadn't broken any laws and certainly wasn't concerned about myself. But if a scandal was being created by Matichon newspaper with sensationalized stories splashed across the front page as fact, I worried that Mark's shelter might receive negative publicity.

February 17, 1989

The Society of Incentive Travel Executives is the largest and most prestigious incentive travel association in the world. Its membership is comprised of top management personnel from some of the largest multi-national corporations as well as many of the world's finest hotels, incentive travel companies, destination management companies, airlines, theme parks, and others that serve the incentive travel industry.

In September of 1988, I had been elected president of the Thailand chapter of S.I.T.E.. Although it was an honor and it brought a tremendous amount of prestige, I was only awarded the position after a number of other influential members had turned it down. So although it gratified my ego to be elected to the post by such an august body of travel professionals, the truth was that I really became president because no one else wanted the job. Bert Van Walbeek, the Director of Sales from the Sheraton Royal Orchid Hotel had held the post prior to me until The Sheraton Corporation promoted him to the job of Director of Marketing for the Middle East and moved him and his wife to Cairo. He had initiated a program of seminars to teach people in the travel industry in Thailand what made up an incentive program and how it should be operated. When I succeeded him I also inherited his seminar schedule. I had just taught a class in Pattaya and another was scheduled for Hua Hin on the Malay Peninsula.

The seminars, however, were only trial heats for what I hoped would be the big event — the opportunity to host the first "University of Incentive Travel" ever held outside the United States.

I had called the executive board of S.I.T.E. Thailand to an afternoon meeting. As president I had to attend, even though I was knocked out from a cold and had to drag myself to the top of the Bangkok Bank building pumped full of sinus relief medicines. The session went on for more than two hours, centering around an essay contest and a plan to send the winner to S.I.T.E.'s next conference in Las Vegas.

We also discussed the upcoming training seminar in Hua Hin and then I announced my intention to try to bring the "University" to Thailand in 1990. "Hong Kong had an international seminar last year and Singapore has just been selected for this year's. So that clears the way for us to host it next year," I said. The University would bring incentive planners from around the world for weeklong classes and, once they landed here, I was sure they would agree with my claim that Thailand was the finest incentive travel destination in the world.

After the meeting, Sandy Ferguson, the publicity chairman, invited me for a drink. We took the elevator down to the fifth floor parking garage, jumped into Sandy's car and joined the Silom Road rush hour traffic. Actually, the word "traffic" is a misnomer because it implies slow vehicular movement. The vehicles on Silom Road at 5:15

27

PM do not move at all. They simply sit and wait while pedestrians are forced to endure the choking fumes caused by thousands of motors idling without smog devices or unleaded gasoline. We eventually arrived at the Dusit Thani Hotel at six o'clock, three short blocks and 45 minutes later.

En route, Sandy said, "You know, Tim Smucker is a friend of mine. He wasn't very happy about your letter to the editor in response to his article in the Bangkok Post. It made him look bad."

"It should," I snorted. "It was not at all a story I would expect to read in a respected newspaper."

I remembered the piece very well because I thought it so distorted and appealed to western sexual phobias. First it talked of street kids who prostituted themselves in the Patpong night life area, the point being that, somehow, being prostitutes made them sniff paint thinner. It then went on to claim that there were one million Thai prostitutes in the country, with all the dangers that that implies. In my letter to the editor I said I found that figure preposterous and stated that, unfortunately, street children all over the city sniffed paint thinner and particularly singled out my neighborhood around Victory Monument. Their addiction, however, did not mean that these kids were prostitutes.

"Tim is just trying to make a living," Sandy explained. "He writes articles that the newspaper will pay for. So what if it's a little distorted. It's his livelihood. Tim should be at the Press Club. He hangs out there. If he's around, I'll introduce you. He's not a bad guy."

The club sat atop the Dusit Thani Hotel and offered a spectacular view of the city. I ordered a lemonade and we sat at a window talking as the lights came on across the city and along Silom. The new Rama IX Bridge with its illuminated suspension cables reminded me of a view of the Bay Bridge from San Francisco, with the lights of Thonburi across the river resembling those of Oakland.

By 8 o'clock, Tim Smucker had not appeared. I bade Sandy farewell, took the elevator to the first floor and walked across Silom to catch a tuk tuk, my favorite form of transportation. The motorized samlor got its name from the sound its two-stroke engine makes while maneuvering through the streets. The Japanese-owned Thai company that created the unique but ubiquitous machine was now manufacturing them for export to neighboring countries. It had been David Wood's fantasy to buy one and bring it back to America. Unfortunately, he hadn't lived long enough to see his fantasy come true.

February 18, 1989

Even though it was Saturday and he didn't have to get up for school, Nu's internal alarm clock wouldn't allow him to sleep past 6 AM. His eyes popped open and he reached up to turn on the television. Within seconds, however, he was back asleep, while cartoon characters dashed across the screen. The uneven sounds of the English-version sound track and the louder, overdubbed Thai translation, blasted from the front room and jarred me into consciousness. Though both boys were sleeping, if I went in to turn off the set they would wake up and object vehemently. I grabbed a pillow, covered my head, and fell back to sleep.

The next thing I heard was a knock on the front door. The clock registered 10 AM. I peeked around the corner just in time to see Birt enter the apartment. "Sawatdee Khrap," he said, and he placed his two hands together in front of his face as if to pray. Although it is not required by custom to return a teenager's wai, I returned his. He was an orphan, about Chat's age, a very sensitive boy easily hurt by the slightest rejection. His mood regularly shifted between bubbly and sullen. When I first met him, he had been living with a group of musicians who had used him as their go-fer. Later, Mark Morgan took him in to the shelter at Lardprao Soi 66.

During one unfortunate incident, some radios and cameras disappeared. Ulit, the Thai house father, accused Birt and asked him to explain their disappearance. Birt ran away and was not heard from for months. In November, Mark fired Ulit and Birt came back, but no one was sure if he had actually been responsible for the theft.

"I got a job!" Birt cried. "I am an apprentice in Pakred." Although Mark insisted that all the kids go to school, I think he gave up that hope for Birt, who had never been particularly adept at it.

I went into the front room and sat down. "That's great, Birt! Tell me about your job," I said to encourage him. "How much do you get paid?"

"Nothing. I'm just learning a trade." he replied. "I really like working there."

Young people often "train" for months, or even years in Thailand without pay. King Chulalongkorn had abolished slavery in the country a century ago, but "trainees" evidently did not fall under the "slave" category.

"Dee mak. Very good," I said. If it made him happy I was happy for him. I just didn't want to see him taken advantage of. I got up and headed for my shower. When I emerged, Chat said he was going ice skating and asked if I'd join him.

"No, Chat. I'm expecting Maureen to call today. But if Birt wants to go, I'll pay his way." I hadn't accompanied Chat the last three times and I was feeling a bit guilty, a vestige, I'm sure, of my Christian upbringing as guilt didn't seem to have much of place in either Thai culture or in Buddhism.

My sister's daughter, Maureen, and her husband, Ken(West), had come to Thailand two weeks earlier for an extended honeymoon. They left Bangkok three days after their arrival in the country with a promise to call so I could arrange a visit to a game preserve near the River Kwai. They hadn't, and I was getting worried. I decided to stay near the phone.

Chat left with Birt and Nu went to visit a friend. I took advantage of the peace and settled down to read. A couple of hours later, the phone rang. I hoped it was Maureen. Instead, a male voice blurted, "Birt just got back. He told me a very interesting story." It was Mark Morgan.

"Birt?" I looked at my watch. He had only left a couple of hours earlier to go ice skating. It would have taken him at least that long to get a bus back to the shelter. "Why is he home so early?"

Ignoring my question, Mark went on. "Birt ran into Ulit on the street. Ulit asked how I was and when Birt told him I was fine, he told Birt that, in a few days, I wouldn't be fine. Do you think Ulit had anything to do with the Matichon thing?"

"I don't know, Mark, but I wouldn't worry too much about it. Ulit just lost face when you fired him and he's trying to stir up some shit. What can he do?" Ulit was friendly with all the local police from Din Daeng Station, but he really didn't have any pull with the government.

To fire a Thai from a job is always a bit risky. It's hard for us as westerners to understand how terrible it is for a Thai to lose face. I had learned that the year before when I fired Tone, my office manager. He took me to court and the judge awarded him two months severance pay.

While working for Mark, Ulit had contacted some of the shelter's local sponsors and asked them for personal loans and donations. He didn't repay the loans and had pocketed some of the donations. Although Mark knew about the incidents, he didn't want to fire Ulit. He agonized over the decision for months because Ulit had been his first employee. He had been a wonderful teacher and house father and the only child he ever alienated was Birt. But finally, in November, when Mark learned that Ulit had been forging his signature on checks, Mark let him go. Ulit swore revenge. He called the shelter's sponsors and claimed that Mark owed him money, that he hadn't been paid, and that he needed money to support his family.

31

"It's just sour grapes," I said, and hung up.

Chat returned from ice skating late in the afternoon. "Did Birt go skating with you?" I asked.

"No. When we left here, he said he wanted to use the money on something else. I went ice skating alone," Chat said rather resolutely, insinuating that I should have gone with him.

February 19, 1989

The honeymooners still hadn't called. I was getting quite worried, but there was really nothing I could do.

The president of an American air conditioning company, his wife, and a female corporate executive were scheduled to arrive at the airport so I had to concentrate on business and hope that my relatives were having such a good time they had simply forgotten. Since opening my company, I had spent much of my time giving site inspections. Most incentive planners were familiar with San Francisco, but very few knew Thailand. Before they would offer a destination as an inducement to reward outstanding work, the incentive planner had to be familiar with the product. It was my job to sell them on the merits of the country.

When the time came to go to the airport, I rented a car, stopped at the local florist to pick up flower garlands, then headed for the terminal, where I greeted my clients by laying a garland across each of their shoulders in a typical Thai welcome. We arrived at the Oriental Hotel in a respectable 45 minutes. I knew the accommodations would be impressive and the next day I'd be able to wow my guests with the delights of exotic Bangkok.

February 20, 1989

I still hadn't heard from the honeymooners, the telex line hadn't been repaired, and — five days after placing the call — Governor

Dharmnoon had yet to respond to my request for help with the work permit. In addition, there were no explanations as to why police had questioned Chat and Nu, or why some stranger was asking the local doctor about me and the boys.

However, with clients in town I could only concentrate on one thing — the selling of the program. Without it, I would have no income. And without an income I couldn't maintain the office, make the payroll, pay the suppliers. In short, I'd be out of business.

Although it would have been quicker to walk, I drove the rented Toyota to the hotel to meet my clients. I took them to a nearby dock, hailed the owner of one of the long-tailed speedboats, haggled with him about the cost of the morning's cruise, then helped my guests aboard.

The boat is similar to a large canoe. The owner sits on the rear seat and steers the propeller which is secured to the end of a 10-foot shaft extending from the back end of the vessel. According to rumor, they are powered by large engines cannibalized from trucks used by the American military during the war in Southeast Asia.

As the boat knifed through the water, passing under the Sathorn Bridge to the mouth of the Thonburi Canal, the banks of the "Mother Water" Chao Phraya bustled with life. At once, the modern skyscrapers of the Oriental and Shangri-La Hotels gave way to centuries-old warehouses and decrepit shacks. Workers on the docks scurried around to unload rice, vegetables, or any of the myriad of goods that constantly flowed up and down the river in large wooden barges and small family-owned boats. Children, happily cavorting in the brown water of the canal, waved as we passed by while their heads bobbed up and down.

"Everybody smiles all the time," one of the ladies observed. "They always seem to be so happy."

"This is fabulous," the company president said. "I usually despise tours, but this is so different. It's hard to describe, it's an experience instead of a tour. It's just so... exotic."

Thailand had infected them. It had taken hold as it seemed to with everyone who entered its mesmerizing aura. I never really had to sell Thailand. It sold itself. An American executive could never be convinced that ancient Siam was the perfect incentive destination while seated in an office on the 15th floor of a downtown building. He or she had to come and feel it. When I had first visited Thailand in November 1981, the country took hold of me and refused to let go. From that moment on, I was convinced I would never be the same living anywhere else. This had become my home.

The banks of the canal continued to expose its treasures — rickety wooden shacks, ornate ancient temples, tropical foliage, eventually waterfront shops and even a warehouse of Chinese caskets. Everyone was smiling. Everyone was happy among these omnipresent ebullient smiles.

As the boat swung back into the Chao Phraya River, suddenly looming above us was the spectacular Temple of Dawn. We disembarked, entered the compound and climbed up the increasingly precipitous stairway. Shaped like the Eiffel Tower, this porcelain-covered Khmer style pagoda was once the tallest structure in the city. Even though some of the city's skyscrapers are now much taller, it is still an awesome sight as it stands like a sentinel above the "River of Kings".

The guests were wide-eyed as I led them down to the boat and across the river to the Grand Palace and its Temple of the Emerald Buddha. No one is quite prepared for the jewelled splendor of this place. It's like driving to the edge of the Grand Canyon and, for the first time, looking out over its expanse. The first time one sees either the moment is never forgotten.

I had arranged for a limousine to meet us at the entrance of the compound and, from there, we drove around Sanam Luang, a grassy mall that extends for a half mile in front of the Grand Palace. Dozens of young men were engaged in the serious business of kite flying in the center of the sward as we continued past an art deco monument to

Democracy, then onto Ratchdamnoen Avenue, a tree-lined boulevard flanked by government offices. At the end of the boulevard, we passed the statue of King Chulalongkorn and his throne room, then stopped at the Golden Teakwood Palace. Fortunately, the traffic was relatively light in this area, so my guests had yet to experience The Bangkok Gridlock.

Following a guided tour through King Chulalongkorn's palace, I instructed the driver to take us to the Dusit Thani. This meant traveling along some of the busiest boulevards in the city, but I distracted my guests by keeping the conversation going during the 45-minute, six-mile drive. They had been so awed by the morning's activities that it wasn't hard to do. Then, returning them to the womb of a familiar western-style deluxe hotel, I seated my guests at a table in the penthouse bar where they could survey the city below and went in for the kill.

"Now let's talk about your program," I began. I then went on to outline an incentive program of Bangkok and asked if they would like me to block the hotel space. The sale was made. Thailand had won hands down over its closest competitors, Kenya and Hong Kong. The charisma of my adopted homeland had worked its magic once again.

February 21-23, 1989

Time is an abstract concept whose passing is inconsequential when one is happy and laborious when one is not. I enjoyed the time I spent showing off my country, so 10-hour outings with clients didn't phase me. I didn't know it then, but very soon time would pass very slowly. Instead of ignoring hours, I would count minutes and look back upon these days as if they had been part of a carefree adolescence long gone.

February 24, 1989

The site inspection completed, I slept in this morning. When I finally crawled into the office, I asked Kenji if the telex had been repaired while I was out with the clients.

"Not yet," he said apologetically. "Kachon hasn't had a chance to get the cable. We've been busy working on Glaxo." A Glaxo Pharmaceutical meeting was due to arrive at the Dusit Thani in a couple of weeks. The British incentive house operating Glaxo's programs had previously worked with my San Francisco company, but this was the first time we had ever handled a program for them in Thailand. I was very anxious that everything go well.

A longtime friend of David Groat's named Dan had come to Thailand to perform with the Bangkok Symphony. He was a violinist with the Netherlands Philharmonic Orchestra and was staying with David. It had struck me that it might be a wonderful touch to hire him, if I could, as a strolling violinist for a river cruise we were planning.

"David talked to him and he said he'd stay over and do it for us," Kenji reported.

I was delighted. "Has Khun (Governor) Dharmnoon called about my work permit?"

"Not yet," he said.

I had to do something to get things moving so I grabbed a cup of coffee, went to my desk in the next room, and dialed the director of the Thailand Incentive and Convention Association (T.I.C.A.) "Khun Sawalee?" I said, "have you talked to Khun Dharmnoon about my work permit?"

"I asked someone to get the forms for you to fill out," she replied.

"But I've filled out all the forms," I cried. She was treating me like I had just arrived in the country. "I called you because my request for this year's renewal has been rejected. I need to talk to somebody who has some pull with the Labor Department. I don't need to fill out any forms, I need to talk to Khun Dharmnoon."

"He's been out of the country," she said. "Why don't you just fill out the forms and try to apply again."

I hung up the phone exasperated. Thai people are always reticent about approaching their superiors, a result of cultural conditioning which emphasizes respect for those with higher status. Khun Sawalee's reaction is symptomatic of a problem that often translates into governmental inaction.

I heard some noises in the front of the office and a voice that I recognized. I quickly jumped up and walked around the partition. Standing in front of Kachon's desk were my two relatives, looking very bedraggled.

"What happened to you?" I asked sharply. There was no hiding my irritation, though I was relieved they were alive and well. "I thought the plan was for you to call me from Kanchanaburi last week."

"We only stayed at the River Kwai one night," Maureen replied. "Then we went to Chiang Mai and took a trek through the mountains and a river raft cruise. We had a great time and I'm sorry we didn't call, but we really haven't been around any phones."

I said rather forcefully, "You could have called from Chiang Mai. I've been terribly worried. I was about to call the tourist police to have them begin looking for you!" As much as I had wanted to be a guide for them, I knew that they were on their honeymoon and surmised that was really why they hadn't phoned.

"A friend from New England is visiting and asked me to take him to the Monkey Temple in Lopburi tomorrow. Would the two of you like to come along?" I asked, hoping they would give me the chance to show them some things.

"Sure," Maureen said, probably more to appease me than out of any real interest. "Sounds great!"

February 25, 1989

I picked up my friend, my niece, and her husband Ken in the rented Toyota and headed north. As I had done with my clients just two days earlier, I took them to the summer palace at Bang Pa-In, then hired a speedboat to run them to Ayudhaya. Once the most spectacular city in the world, Ayudhaya was a metropolis larger than any in Renaissance Europe. Then in 1767, it was totally destroyed by an invading Burmese army. Its golden idols were melted down and its jewelled treasures carted away.

The Thais opted to rebuild their capital to the south, across the river from the little village of Ban Kok, now this enormous metropolis of over eight million inhabitants. But the ancient capitol was still a place of wonder. We stood in its ruins and looked out at the deteriorating pagodas and crumbling statues and felt a sense of history as real as earth and sky.

After visiting the ruins and then the Monkey Temple in Lopburi, Maureen said, "This has been interesting, but I wouldn't want to do this kind of thing every day." I had so much wanted her to share the exuberance I felt about my "real magic kingdom" that her comment stung me. When she made another offhand remark, I snapped back at her. She stared at me in disbelief, then stopped talking and sank into her seat. Her eyes reddened and filled with tears.

After dropping my guests at their hotels, I went to David's for a gin-and-tonic. While we were discussing the day's activities, the phone rang. David grabbed it. A second later, he put his hand over the mouthpiece. "Bob is calling from Phuket. He wants to check the contents of the envelope he left with us. Would you run down to the office. I put it in the safe."

When Bob, the American who was staying in my former apartment, had left Bangkok a few days earlier, he gave David an envelope full of cash and airline tickets for safekeeping. I went to the office and opened the safe. The envelope was missing. I rushed back to David's apartment.

"Where did you put it?" I asked. "I can't find it!"

"You must be mistaken," he said. "It was there just a few days ago when I was in the office."

I picked up the phone. "What's the problem?" Bob asked.

"I don't know," I said with a weight in my voice. "David will talk to you in a minute."

"There has apparently been a theft," David told Bob.

"What are you saying?" Bob asked. "Somebody has taken my money?"

"I don't know," David replied.

I took the phone. "That's a lot of money," Bob cried. He was talking about nearly $2,000 in U.S. currency.

"I don't know what to say. I'm sorry. On Monday, we'll go to the police."

Bob hung up, indicating he would call back on Monday night. I felt a sense of loss, as if I had, in some way, been violated. Even though the money wasn't mine, it had been left in my office.

"Who could have taken it? You and I are the only ones with keys," I said to David.

February 26, 1989

I called my niece Maureen and apologized for my rotten behavior. David agreed to cook an American meal for all of us and I went shopping for the groceries. I hoped she and Ken would enjoy it but I wasn't sure. After all, they had only been away from home for three weeks.

"A green salad! This is great!" Maureen exclaimed as she sat down at the table. The evening was wonderfully warm, the hostile exchange of the previous day forgotten. We shared a bottle of Cabernet

Sauvignon that I had been saving for months and ended the evening with heartfelt hugs.

Maureen and Ken were bound for Koh Samui in the south the following morning. I wished them a pleasant trip and returned to my apartment grateful that we had patched things up.

Except for the disturbing incident with Bob's money, everything around me again appeared peaceful. I was not yet aware of the gathering clouds, or that I was living in the eye of a hurricane.

February 27, 1989

David suggested that everyone who may have had access to the safe be fingerprinted. So he, Kachon and I jumped into a tuk tuk and rode to Din Daeng Police Station to file a police report.

Inside a fenced compound and behind a parking lot sat a four-story building whose facade was once white, but whose walls were now caked with black soot from the exhaust of tens of thousands of vehicles which roared by every day. The first floor consisted of an open-air reception area where uniformed officers were perched behind wooden desks, recording on antiquated typewriters complaints by citizens reporting one incident or another.

After waiting a couple of hours, an officer grudgingly heard our story. As he typed, he grew more and more irritated, obviously believing we were wasting his time. "How do I know who took your money?" he exclaimed with exasperation. "You have the keys to the safe. You should know!"

After several persuasive arguments by Kachon, the officer completed the complaint and agreed to take our fingerprints, then send a team to the office to dust for fingerprints on the inside of the safe. If anyone besides David and me had gotten into the safe, his or her fingerprints would be found and I would have my culprit.

Suddenly everyone in the room leapt to their feet and stood at attention. I turned to see a well-decorated uniformed officer march in and glare at us. He was a stocky man in his mid-40's, with olive-brown skin and a regal air that crossed the line into pomposity.

"Why are the farangs here?" he snapped at one of his men. I couldn't quite interpret the answer, but it seemed to satisfy him. He sat down and opened a log book to check that day's reports. The others continued to stand. I got the feeling that he considered us impolite because we hadn't greeted him at attention, but he was just a police officer. It didn't make sense.

Before leaving the station, an officer suggested I send other employees in for fingerprints. I would ask Kenji and Mark Morgan, who had gone to the office the previous week to work on the mailing list for the children's home. It was late afternoon by the time we returned to the office. The lab technicians had already gone through and dusted for fingerprints inside the safe. Their efficiency was surprising, in contrast to the nearly eight hours we had spent at the station simply to file a report and get fingerprinted.

The hassle of completing the police report was exhausting. David did not have the energy to cook, so I invited him, Chat and Nu to dinner at their favorite haunt, the Foremost Ice Cream Shop. Predictably, David refused but the boys were eager. Hardly a week passed when we didn't eat lunch or dinner there. I didn't know it, but this would be our last.

After dinner, the boys returned to the apartment and I went searching for my favorite dessert, khao neo mamuang — mangoes and sticky rice topped with coconut milk. I bought several bags to share with everyone and returned gleefully to the condominium as if I had just robbed a bank.

February 28, 1989

"I don't want to have my fingerprints taken," Mark complained into the receiver. "It's too much like Big Brother. I'll wait until the report returns on the others."

"The police want you to go down there immediately," I said, "so they can match them with any that may have been in the safe."

"I have to finish my mailing list," he snapped. "I'll see you this afternoon and we can talk about it."

We hung up. "Thou protesteth too much," I thought to myself.

When he arrived, I confessed that I "feel so guilty about suspecting any of my friends. But this makes the third theft in the past three months. Each time, it's like I've been raped." When money had disappeared before, perhaps foolishly I didn't even care about it. It had only been a few thousand baht and I had more important things to attend to. But I wanted to know who the thief was, so that I wouldn't mistrust everyone. "Not being able to trust my friends is almost worse than the thefts themselves," I said. "But this time, it's different. This time, the money wasn't mine."

"I know the feeling," Mark replied, referring to the disappearance of the radios and cameras from the shelter, and to the donations that Ulit had kept for himself.

Chat was waiting for me when I arrived home later in the day. "I want to talk to you," he said.

"What is it?" I asked.

"It's about Nu," he replied. "He has been acting funny. He's been swearing too much."

"Yes, I noticed that." Some of the first words I had learned to speak in the Thai language were obscenities. They were not expressions that the boys ordinarily used. But something had changed since the police questioned Nu.

"I'll have a talk with him," I told Chat.

When Chat got up to go, I felt a great deal of paternal love toward him. His sensitivity was very heartening. What a tremendous feeling it gave to me to have a part in influencing positively the future of this gentle, caring person. I made a promise to myself to see that he got through college so that he might have a chance to do what he wants with his life.

Three

Justice Perverted, Virtue Condemned

*"I have done no harm. But I remember now
I am in this earthly world; where to do
harm is often laudable; to do good,
sometimes accounted dangerous folly."*
— Shakespeare *Macbeth*

March 1, 1989

The most unsettling day of my life began like any other day. The boys got up and went to school before I was awake. I didn't hear them leave. When I finally awoke, it was after 8 AM. I went to the office thinking that it would be an uneventful day. The Glaxo program was 11 days away and the preliminary arrangements had all been made. The office was still locked when I arrived. I fumbled for the odd-shaped key that fit an enormous padlock I had put on after the last robbery. The room was already hot and muggy. The sun had been shining through the sliding glass doors that faced a balcony. I reached over to turn on the air conditioner, then walked into the kitchen to make some coffee. David arrived looking ragged. "What's the matter?" I asked.

"I don't feel well, but I'll be better after a cup of coffee." He grabbed a cup, spooned out two heaps of instant, drowned it in lukewarm water and headed for the computer. At the desk, he propped up his favorite cardboard Garfield-the-Cat greeting card which displayed the message, "Don't bother me under penalty of death."

Kenji came in before the coffee started to boil. "Good morning," he cheerily remarked, substituting the Australian "G'Day" with the

43

American equivalent. I responded in kind. David grumbled something inaudible.

It was 9:30 by the time Kachon wandered in. He was habitually late and, over the months, I must have threatened to fire him half a dozen times. He always managed to charm me out of it and I would end up laughing. "The traffic again?" I asked skeptically. Kachon nodded and sat down at his desk. Kenji walked over, gave him an assignment, then left to inspect a boat that we were planning to charter for the Glaxo program. Just after he left, the phone rang.

Kachon answered and fed the call to me. "This is Khun Noo's secretary," the voice on the line reported. "The letters acknowledging the 10 finalists for the S.I.T.E. essay contest are ready for you to sign."

"I'll be right down." I hung up the phone, left the office, and strolled by Victory Monument as the fruit vendors were setting up their stalls for the day. I passed Robinson's Department Store and took the pedestrian bridge to the bus stop. Khun Noo's office was in Charn Issara Tower on Rama IV, about three miles away. The morning traffic was at its usual standstill and the ride lasted nearly an hour.

After signing the S.I.T.E. letters, I climbed aboard the returning coach. At Marbohn Krohn, I considered stopping for lunch, but decided instead to get back to the office. I wished later that I had made that stop.

David was still at the computer when I returned. And he still looked like hell. "I think I'm going to bed," he moaned. "Do you mind if Dan practices his violin in your apartment? I can't sleep when he's playing that damn thing."

An obvious lover of the arts. "Of course, no problem," I replied, handing him the key to my front door. He left and I sat down in front of the IBM clone.

A few minutes later, Dan walked into the office, violin in hand. "Somebody's looking for Chat," he said.

44

I looked up from the keyboard. "Tell whoever it is to come to the office and talk to me. Chat's in school."

"There are three of them," Dan said.

"Well, then tell three of them to come to the office."

Dan nodded and left. A couple of minutes later, he returned. "They won't come to the office. You'll have to go to the apartment."

"Okay," I said, and continued typing on the keyboard. I didn't know who Chat's friends were, but I was anxious to complete my thoughts first. When I finished, I got up and went to the bathroom. I heard Dan's voice outside the bathroom door, "They want you to come NOW!" He sounded agitated.

I walked out wiping my hands on a towel and was confronted by a very irritated little man in baggy clothes who was yelling at me in Thai. He was talking so fast that I couldn't understand a thing he was saying.

"Poleet," Kachon explained quickly. "He wan' go in your parmen."

"The police?" A chill ran down my spine. "What do they want?"

Kachon watched as I accompanied the officer down the hall. "Stay in the office in case the phone rings," I told him.

Two more men were waiting in front of my apartment door. I fumbled for my keys. Before I could find the right one, an officer impatiently reached past me and turned the doorknob. The door swung open.

The three men immediately began a sweep of the place, tearing through everything. I was dumbfounded. One officer found a bottle of pills in the bedroom dresser. He grinned like the Cheshire Cat and said, "Ni arai? What is this?"

"Vitamins," I replied. He looked disappointed.

"What is this about?" I asked.

One of the other officers picked up a photo. "Who is this?" he demanded.

"It's Chat." I thought they knew him since the pretext of their visit was to find him. "What is this about?" I said again.

Another officer found a picture in Chat's desk. "Who are these boys?"

I shrugged. I had no idea. It was a group of Chat's school buddies dressed in their uniforms. The photo had been taken during one of his school outings.

At that point, Dan, appeared in the doorway, violin still in hand. "There are three more of them in David's apartment," he announced.

"Where is Chat?" an officer snapped.

"He's in school."

"Where is the school?"

"It's in Pratunam. Near the Indra Regent. Maybe there are some school papers in his desk that give the name."

At that, the officer opened the drawers in Chat's desk and pulled out an envelope. Inside, he found Chat's report card with the name of the school printed on it. "And Nu?" he asked.

"He's in school, too. His school is in Lardprao. I don't know the name of that one either." I continued to ask for an explanation and I continued to be ignored.

The officer searched Nu's desk and found a paper with the name and address of the school. Soon after, they joined their colleagues in David's apartment. I made sure that everything had been put back, then locked the door and followed the police to David's.

His door was wide open. An officer had dumped all of Dan's luggage onto the floor and was searching through the contents, while others were going through David's things. "Open that!" one of them demanded in English as he pointed to a cabinet.

"I left the key in the office," David said to the officer, then quickly motioned to me to follow him. David was in a panic. For the first time, it hit me that he might be in major trouble. He had been arrested in the United States years before and jumped bail, something on which I never got the full story. He had been living in various countries in Europe and Asia, petrified to return to America because of the terrible beating he suffered in jail. He said he was worried the Thai police might report his whereabouts. The little man in baggy clothes followed us back to the office, but because he didn't speak English he couldn't understand what we had said.

I returned with David to his apartment. The officer had finished searching Dan's luggage and was replacing the contents. David unlocked the cabinet and the police removed his personal records, some photos he had taken at his home in Indonesia, and a collection of magazine clippings he had been saving.

During the search, a boy named Thep appeared at the door. Thep had lived in Mark's home for a short time in late 1987, but preferred the freedom of being on his own even if it meant being in the streets — so, in early 1988 he left. He had struck up a friendship with David and, when he wasn't running around the city with his friends, he stayed in David's apartment. David had once attempted to get him into school, but Thep was too much of a free spirit.

Thep had decided to take the bus to Trat to visit his father and had come to ask David for money for the trip. "You'll have to come to the station with us," the English-speaking officer said to Thep and to Dan, David, and me. "We want to ask you some questions."

The elevator brought us to the lobby entrance where two police pickup trucks were parked. I put my hand on the shoulder of one of the officers and asked his name. I wasn't really too concerned for myself. I hadn't done anything wrong. I was more concerned about David's problems with U.S. authorities.

The four of us climbed into the back of one of the pickups and rode to Din Daeng Police Station. There, we were directed up a flight of stairs to the second floor and into an air-conditioned office.

Soon after our arrival, two officers left the station with the names and addresses of the boys' schools in hand. Three others took Thep into an interrogation room adjacent to the office. After a few minutes, one of the men returned and went to a filing cabinet behind two desks.

He removed a long black truncheon, which looked like a cattle prod, unscrewed a cap on the bottom, pulled out a number of batteries, checked their potency on a battery meter, replaced them, then returned with it to the interrogation room.

"I hope that isn't what I think it is!" David exclaimed.

My head was spinning. I wasn't quite sure what he meant. I was dumbfounded by this whole thing. Earlier, one officer had told me that the Matichon newspaper article was the reason they wanted to ask us questions. But if our arrest was a result of the story, what had Chat and Nu to do with it? Where was the boy who had been mentioned in it? He would surely tell the officers that the article hadn't been about us.

Inside the interrogation room, the police asked Thep if he and David had ever been sexually involved. When he answered that they had not, one officer left the room to retrieve the electric prod. He returned and ordered Thep to remove his clothes. The man then poked the truncheon into Thep's genitals, sending an electric current into his body. After the first shock, Thep was asked again if he and David had ever engaged in sex. He replied that maybe they had done something once when they first met, but not since. That was enough for the officers. They told Thep to put on his clothes and wait until later to sign a statement.

Soon after, Chat and then Nu were ushered into the office and ordered to be seated. I hugged them both and wished I had a father's wisdom to comfort them. I did not, and in my inept search for the proper words, sat in helplessness and said nothing.

When Thep emerged from the interrogation room, his normally cheerful demeanor had turned bleak. Using one of the few Thai expressions that he knew, David asked Thep if he was okay. Thep nodded his head, but we were not reassured.

The police then took Chat into the same room. He was asked if I had sexually assaulted him. When he told the police that I hadn't, they ordered him to remove his clothes and they stuck the cattle prod

48

between his legs. He was so intimidated that he agreed to sign whatever they wanted. "I'll deny it later," he thought to himself.

The police officers who had brought the two boys from their schools joined their colleagues in the interrogation room. By the time Nu went in, there were five of them in there. He was asked if I had assaulted him sexually. He said I had done nothing to him and that I was like a father to him. The officers pulled off his clothes and shocked him with the prod. He still denied that anything sexual had happened between us, so they shocked him again and told him they would continue to do so until he died unless he agreed to sign a statement saying that I had masturbated him. When his resistance broke down, they ordered him to get dressed and join us out on the bench. He had received two very painful electric shocks. He didn't understand why the police were doing this. He had done nothing. When he emerged, his eyes were red and swollen. I asked him what had happened inside the room, but he refused to answer.

When the senior officer, Lieutenant Suthep Chanasithi, returned to his desk, he looked at Dan and said, "Why did you come to Thailand? How long do you plan to stay?" Dan replied that he was visiting Thailand for a few weeks and that, as soon as he finished his performance with the Bangkok Symphony, he would be leaving. The officer returned his passport and told him that he was free to go.

Kenji had arrived while Chat and Nu were being interrogated. He was too shy to ask Chanasithi what was going on and, instead, thought that Dan should tell Kachon to come to the station. Dan promised to do that and suggested that it might be better if he moved to a hotel for the remainder of his visit. He was visibly shaken.

I finally turned to Chanasithi. "You said that you brought us here to ask us questions," I protested. "We've now been here for nearly three hours and you've ignored us. I have work to do in the office. If you need me, I'll be there." I got up and started to leave.

"You cannot go," he said stonefaced. "As a matter of fact, you should call your embassy and probably get yourself a lawyer."

49

"I intend to!" I cried indignantly. "Are we being arrested? If so, what is the charge?"

"Wait for the colonel. He will decide. You can wait outside if you want."

"When will the colonel arrive?" I said, flustered.

"Later."

"When?" Later in Thailand could mean anything.

He shrugged. "Before midnight. Relax. Are you hungry?" he suddenly asked. "I'm sending for dinner. Tell me if you want something."

I shook my head. How could I possibly eat?

"I don't like the looks of this," David said in a morose and faintly desperate tone.

I asked Chanasithi if I could use the pay phone. He told a uniformed officer to take me downstairs and stay with me while I made my call. I phoned Mark Morgan, told him that David and I had been arrested, and asked if he could recommend a criminal lawyer. The only Thai lawyers I had ever dealt with had been corporate attorneys. Mark said he didn't know any but would try to find one.

When I returned upstairs, David, Kenji, Thep, Chat, and Nu were outside Chanasithi's office sitting on a bench. I silently joined them. From the second story, we stared down at a courtyard. The traffic on the street was at its usual rush hour standstill, but we paid little notice. We were all lost in our private confusions and bewilderments. Why was this happening?

A couple of the officers who had interrogated Thep, Chat and Nu appeared and ordered the boys to go with them. David, Kenji and I watched helplessly as they were taken from us, put in the back of a police truck, and driven away.

David repeated the obvious. "I don't like the looks of this," he said once more.

Kachon arrived and talked to Lieutenant Chanasithi. He came out of the office a few minutes later. "The poleet say you haf to wai' for the colonel. He cannot do anytheen," he reported. "I don'no why."

Food arrived. Chanasithi had bought dinner for David and me in spite of our refusals. Kenji and Kachon ate ours, but none of us had much to say. Finally, Kachon decided he could do nothing and went home. Kenji said he'd remain for moral support.

At about 9 PM, the police truck pulled into the courtyard and the boys jumped out. They seemed to be in much better spirits, actually laughing and joking. They came up the stairs and joined us.

"Bai nai ma? Where did you go?" I asked.

"Bai rongphayaban. To a hospital," Chat answered. "The doctor looked all over our bodies and in our butt."

"What?" I laughed.

The boys all laughed too. This had become comically absurd.

"Keystone cops," said David.

That description struck me and I started to laugh again. Just then, Chanasithi appeared and ushered us downstairs to the office where we had spent so much time two days earlier trying to get fingerprinted. One of the officers who had taken our report looked startled when we entered. "Is there something else?" he asked fitfully, thinking we were there to give him still more paperwork.

"We're not here because of the theft," I said. David, Kenji and I dropped down on a bench while the boys were ordered to sit before a couple of uniformed officers who were pecking away on antiquated typewriters. Chanasithi handed a file to another officer with a three-star rank, a sergeant I presumed.

A policeman came out of a small radio room into the reception area. "Steve Raymond, telephone," he announced in English. I followed him back to the room and picked up the receiver.

"Hello. This is the duty officer at the United States Embassy," the voice on the line said. "Mark Morgan called and asked that I contact you to see if there's anything I can do."

"Oh wonderful!" I said to the officer. "Did he call the newspaper too?"

I had incorrectly assumed that Mark would call his Thai friends for help. Because of David's precarious situation, I had not thought to involve the Embassy.

"I haven't done anything. This is all a misunderstanding. Whatever the charge, I'm not guilty," I said excitedly. I was agitated and a bit angry at Mark. But from the conversation, I assumed the Embassy was still not aware of David's involvement. When I finally calmed down, the duty officer told me that he'd send para-consul Pat Hansford to visit the next day in case I was still in custody. "That would be fine." I said and hung up the phone.

I returned to the reception area. The three-star official who had been given our file was complaining to the others who were prepping statements from the boys. "What is this?" he boomed. "There's nothing in this file except a newspaper article from Matichon and some notes." He then sent someone upstairs to get the lieutenant to explain what they were supposed to do. Chanasithi came down and told him that the boys would simply repeat what they had said in the interrogation room. He eyed them and said, "As soon as you have given your statements, you can go home."

Chat didn't have his residence papers with him to prove that he was legally a resident in my apartment. He was told to go back to the condominium and get them. The three-star officer began to take a statement from Thep. He looked more and more irritated as the conversation progressed. We could not hear what Thep was saying, but, whatever it was, it did not please the officer. He suddenly burst forth into an orgy of complaint. Using a few words that Kenji did not care to translate, he asked someone to go upstairs and get the lieutenant again.

When Chanasithi came down for the second time, the three-star official asked, "What is this whole thing about? This boy says nothing has happened and he doesn't have any statement to make." Thep was refusing to repeat what he had been forced to say under duress. A second officer gave up trying to extract a statement from Nu as well, so Chanasithi waited for Chat and took all three boys upstairs again.

Just before midnight, they were brought down to the reception area. Soon after their return, the pompous roundfaced police official whom we had seen when we reported the office theft — the one to whom everyone had stood and bowed while we had sat dumbly in our seats — marched across the courtyard toward the entry. "The colonel!" an officer exclaimed.

As on the previous day, the man carried himself perfectly erect, with head held high in a sort of regal arrogance. Again everyone in the station leapt to their feet and bowed as he entered. What luck that our fate would land in the hands of Colonel Khongdej Choosri!

He sat down at a desk near the radio room. On it was a log book, which he perused for a few minutes.

"Tell him that I want to talk to him, Kenji," I begged.

"Wait," Kenji said.

Just then, the colonel turned to Chat and asked him to come closer and stand before him. Chat did as he asked.

"Why isn't Chat waiing him?" I whispered to David.

"You can't see Chat's face," he said. "He's doing all he can just to stand there without crying and falling completely apart."

When the colonel was finished talking to Chat and after what seemed like an interminable period of time, he turned to me and indicated that I could talk to him. I walked up to the desk, waied him, and sat down. "Are we under arrest?" I asked.

He nodded.

"Why?" I blurted. "Is it concerning Chat and Nu? I love those boys. I would certainly do nothing to hurt them."

He looked at me with anger in his eyes and said in perfect English, "What you do is wrong!"

I was agape. "What I do is wrong?" I couldn't believe what I'd heard. What I do is wrong? What the hell was he talking about? I definitely wanted to see a lawyer.

The colonel rose to his feet, looked at me with utter contempt, and walked out. Moments later, David and I were taken to a row of grungy-looking cells that I had glimpsed on my previous visit. The boys were ordered back upstairs by the policeman who had tortured them earlier. "What you do is wrong." That comment kept ringing in my ears.

David suddenly turned to me. "Talk to them," he pleaded. "Don't let them put us in the cells with the other prisoners." He was white with fear.

"I looked at him quizzically. "What's the matter with being with other prisoners?"

"You don't understand," he cried. "You just don't understand. It's dangerous! Kenji, will you stay? They might beat us!" David's fear was palpable. In a U.S. prison, guards tossed him into a crowd of hardened criminals who set upon him like animals. They kicked out almost all of his teeth and he had to be hospitalized for more than a week. Now he was petrified it would happen in Thailand.

I asked the deputy if we could take the empty cell and he allowed us that much. With startling quickness, the iron door closed behind us with a metallic clang, followed by the hollow sound of the key turning in the lock and the deputy's footsteps retreating into an office. Suddenly I was gripped by a feeling of panic. The reality of it finally hit me. *I WAS IN JAIL!* The tiny six foot by six foot cell was disgustingly filthy. Cockroaches scampered in and out of cracks and up the graffitied walls. The squat toilet and adjacent faucet were black with years of grime and dried excrement. An oily film of blackish brown dirt clung to everything.

There was nowhere to sleep but on the floor. Kachon had brought me a pillow but a guard jerked it away. "You're in jail. This is no hotel," the officer scowled.

Justice Perverted, Virtue Condemned

David and I gingerly laid down to try to sleep, but sleep was impossible. We rolled up extra shirts which Kachon had also brought and placed our heads atop them. The mosquitoes were out in force and the noise of the passing traffic outside Din Daeng was deafening. Trailer trucks, constantly downshifting as they exited from the expressway, created noises so loud that my weary eyes popped open, expecting the things to come crashing through a wall on top of me.

We tossed back and forth on the hard floor all night long, hoping for quick daylight so that we could arrange for bail and get out of this hell-hole.

March 2, 1989

The light of day filtered through the brown smoke that seemed to permanently engulf Din Daeng Police Station. At 6 AM, there was a change of shifts and every officer coming in for day work gawked at us, as if the sight of imprisoned farangs was a spectacle.

Soon after, visitors arriving with food for the other prisoners would giggle when they saw us and alert their friends that two farangs were being held. I began to feel like an animal in a zoo.

All I could think of was getting out. Bail had been set at 100,000 baht ($4,000) apiece. I didn't have that much cash at the office, but Mark offered to post it, so that I could get to a bank, reimburse him and withdraw another 100,000 for David.

It seemed like an eternity before I saw any familiar faces. Finally, at 8 AM, Kachon arrived with breakfast — rice and meat in a plastic bag. My stomach had not settled sufficiently for hunger to set in. I looked at the food and put it down. "Water, Kachon, we're thirsty," I implored.

He disappeared, then quickly returned with two bottles of water which he handed us through the cell bars. We gulped them down as if we had been in the Sahara Desert.

I was grateful for Kachon's presence. He added a sense of familiarity that was reassuring. The other visitors weren't nearly as amused by our incarceration with a Thai man at the cell talking to us. "Kenji go to Mark for money," Kachon said. "He gonna come here welly soon."

Time dragged on. Besides wanting to get as far away from this place as I could, I had a nagging fear that someone from the travel industry would see me, or someone from the news media would show up, and that would be the end of my business. But I was certain too, that the police would soon discover their mistake and release us. They had to!

I was upset that the boys were still upstairs and asked Kachon to check on them. "Chat and Nu sleep upstai' in the fooh," Kachon reported back. "The poleet say they mus' stay here."

"But they have school today. Don't the police care if they miss their classes?"

Kachon shrugged.

"They have to get ready for their final exams," I said angrily. "If they don't take their tests, they'll have to repeat their classes next term. Would you go get Nu's father and Chat's sister to see if they can get the boys out of here?"

"Okay, when Kenji come," Kachon said.

We waited. Every minute seemed like an eternity... 9 AM... 10 AM... Kenji had not arrived. "What is keeping him?" I demanded, as if either David or Kachon could answer. I was getting more and more anxious. At 10:30 he finally appeared, waved and went to the captain's office, an envelope containing my bail money in hand. A couple of minutes later, he returned with an officer who fumbled with a ring of rusty keys, found the one he wanted and slid it in the lock. The sound of freedom, I thought, metal scraping against metal. I grabbed the shirt I had rolled up to use as a pillow and started to walk out. The officer stopped me and pointed to David. "You," he said.

David looked as bewildered as I did. He pointed to himself, questioning the man's intention. The officer nodded. David shrugged, grabbed his things and stepped out of the cell. Kenji and Kachon followed David and the officer into the reception area.

Minutes dragged on. An hour passed, then two. They were still in the reception room. Tension and anxiety surged through me — I was a wreck. What was happening? Why didn't Kenji just pay the bail and let me out so that I could go to the bank? I was exhausted from worry and lack of sleep and felt like I might get sick. The courtyard was jammed with people filing reports or making claims. The noise of the traffic, the exhaust fumes, the clacking of the old police typewriters, all combined to stretch my nerves to the point of snapping.

Finally, Kachon reappeared. "What's going on?" I asked anxiously.

"Poleet ask some question to Dawit."

"Good," I said. "Finally they got around to asking some questions. Now they'll realize that they made a mistake and that we had nothing to do with that story in Matichon. What's taking so long? You've been in there for two hours."

"Poleet has to ask Dawit too many question," Kachon said, "I haf to speak in engrit to Dawit and to poleet in Thai. On every question, he haf to type an he type welly slow, an after finit he gonna ask you some question too."

"Well, it looks like I'm not going to make it to the bank today," I moaned.

A few minutes later, David reappeared, accompanied by the officer with the keys. He was ordered back into the cell and I was ordered out and taken into the air-conditioned reception area where I was seated in front of another uniformed officer. He began asking questions and, although I understood some of it, Kenji translated everything for me, then translated my replies into Thai for the officer.

The policeman was indeed slow, hunting through a forest of keys on the typewriter before pecking one with a finger. "How long have you known Chat and Nu? How long have they lived with you? Do you give them money? How long have you lived in Thailand? What business do you work for?" It was laborious.

After about an hour, the officer stopped typing, looked at me and said, "This is not the same as the story in the newspaper." Kachon then explained to him that the newspaper story had nothing to do with us. "Khun Sateef khon dee mak. Steve is a very good man," he said over and over in Thai. The officer was sympathetic. He seemed to realize that a mistake had been made. For the first time, I felt that we were getting that message across.

"Will this be in the newspapers?" I asked timidly.

"Give the reporters a false name," he advised.

"What??!!" I screeched. I was frantic. I looked around. What reporters? I thought I would be getting out on bail!

Just then, a plainclothes officer escorted David in again. "Come with us," the man said to me. The two of us were quickly taken to a Toyota police car in the parking lot. "Get in the back!" he barked in English.

"Kachon, get in!" I cried. "Come with us!"

"He can't go!" the officer said flatly.

I protested. "But the policeman with the three stars said that he could go with us!" The officer looked at me sharply, then relented. But, in any event, Kachon's presence would very soon become irrelevant. We were being taken to a police press conference where "evidence" of an international conspiracy would be shown to legions of media people.

The press conference that followed was a ludicrous affair to begin with but grew increasingly Kafkaesque until it peaked with an extraordinary story that Colonel Choosri and General Krutchaiyan glossed over — an officer had shot and killed a top government official! The Deputy Director of the Tourism Authority of Thailand had been gunned down by a policeman on a busy Bangkok street. The officer himself had then been shot and killed by a colleague.

Justice Perverted, Virtue Condemned

The press conference had initially been called to discuss the shooting, but the general — no doubt mindful of the loss of face the department would suffer if it were sensationalized in the press — controlled the attention of the media by only briefly mentioning it and spending a considerable amount of energy boasting about the department's diligence in cracking the "international sex ring". I didn't stand a chance.

David and I were paraded back to the police car. I looked around for a bridge. I wanted to jump — or bolt from my captors and leap into onrushing traffic, commit suicide. My dreams, my career, my business, my reputation, my freedom, gone! All I could feel was misery. It didn't matter that I had not done what General Krutchaiyan accused me of doing. The media perceived him as an authority on the matter — and what is truth divorced from perception? In one agonizing day, my euphoric life in Thailand had been extinguished.

When we arrived back at Din Daeng Police Station, I was so overwhelmed that I rushed with a dizzying energy from one cop to the next, trying to find the one who had told me to "give the reporters a false name". But in my state of mind, all the officers looked the same. I grabbed the arm of one and blubbered frantically, "They wouldn't let me!" He looked at me as if I were crazy. At that moment, I was.

David and I were thrown back in our cell. Suddenly I hugged him and said, "It's all over." The arrest and incarceration were shocks, but the press conference was devastating.

Moments later, an officer opened the cell and called me out. A young lawyer from Siam Legal Aid had arrived. It was the firm that the Embassy staff had recommended to Kenji. The lawyer had taken the envelope with the bail money and paid my bail. I was fingerprinted, and — just like that — I was released. Though the police had confiscated my passport, I would get it another time. I couldn't get out of there fast enough.

I returned to my office, but it wasn't the same. Something fundamental had changed forever. Its sanctity had been violated. Yet my spirits began to lift — perhaps as a reaction to my release. I picked up the phone and called the American Embassy.

"Where did you go?" para-consul Pat Hansford asked. "I was at Din Daeng Police Station."

"Why didn't you wait for us?" I responded, not realizing that she couldn't speak Thai and therefore was unable to learn either where we had been taken or when we would be returned. I told her about the "press conference," hoping for a little compassion. Instead, she admonished me for not being at the station when she arrived, as if I had made the decision to attend the "press conference" on my own and had broken a pre-arranged appointment with her.

After a shower and shave, I actually went back to the police station. It wasn't for love of the place, I assure you, but because David was petrified of being left alone. Kachon and Kenji had been joined there by Marcus, an 18-year-old American who had done volunteer work at Mark's children's shelter. The four of us agreed to take shifts throughout the night to make sure nothing happened to David.

I was finally beginning to reunite with my sanity. The enormity of what had occurred had not fully sunk in. As evening arrived and the daytime heat waned, Marcus and I walked across the alley from the police station to an outdoor restaurant for dinner. As we each sipped a beer, I glanced up at the second floor of the station. I was still worried about the boys. They would be kept locked up until they agreed to sign statements implicating me for sexual abuse, the officers had told them. Kenji, meanwhile, had contacted Nu's father. I planned to catch a bus to Ubon on Saturday to bring Chat's mother down to Bangkok. I hoped the parents would be able to pressure the police into releasing their sons.

"You're taking this much better than Cummings did," Marcus said.

Marcus had come to Thailand in early 1988 with John Cummings, a man I had met one winter afternoon in 1969 on the Sonoma State

University campus. I was organizing a day trip to the mountains for a group of underprivileged girls and boys who had never seen snow, and he volunteered to drive a car.

During the civil rights movement of the '60s, I created an all-volunteer organization in a minority community to help black and Latino youth. In addition to running trips to the snow, my South Park Youth Organization found jobs for young people who had dropped out of school, taught skills like cooking and sewing, and operated a summer camp program.

I had actually hoped to associate it with the United Way, which would have assured its continuing existence. But, one evening, Cummings informed me that he had heard the United Way wasn't interested in the South Park Youth Organization because "Steve Raymond is a queer."

I was devastated. Although I had confessed my sexual preference to my mother years before, I wasn't aware that anyone else knew. With the exception of one discreet relationship three years earlier, I had not been sexually active. How did they know?

Cummings proceeded to tell me that he, too, was gay. And I thought I had found someone to whom I could divulge my deep secrets. In retrospect, it's doubtful the United Way directors had an opinion about my sexuality. But Cummings convinced me they did and, consequently, I never approached them.

In college, he and I became platonic friends. We would occasionally go camping or to movies together, but for day-to-day socializing, I had a different group of friends with whom I could discuss politics and philosophy. Over the years, we drifted apart. Our commonality was overshadowed by greater differences. I majored in psychology, he studied law. I graduated in four years — it took him, literally, 20. I was one of those anti-war demonstrators from the lower middleclass the insipid Spiro Agnew called "radiclibs" — Cummings was conservative and from a wealthy family. I wanted my own business. He never worked — and, although he claimed he never got money from his parents, I don't know how else he could have survived. Far more important than these differences, however, was a basic conflict of ideals. Cummings, who never accepted his own homosexuality, became an Evangelist and thrived in an Evangelical Christian atmosphere, eventually marrying and outwardly denigrating gay people. I moved to San Francisco and became a politically active member of the gay community.

Yet Cummings continued to involve himself in my affairs. A couple of years after graduating from Sonoma State, I hiked for several months through the Sierra Madre Mountains in Mexico and became fascinated by and lived with the Tarahumara Indians. I later returned to Santa Rosa anxious to raise money to help these people.

Using a concept borrowed from the "March of Dimes", I walked 1,800 miles from Santa Rosa to Guachochic, Mexico and solicited contributions for each mile. Cummings offered to do publicity and borrowed several expensive cameras. I welcomed the gesture because I thought the publicity would encourage donations. But along the way, his homemade pannier was melted by the exhaust pipes on his motorcycle and the expensive cameras scattered along a Mexican highway. He insisted I pay for half the loss and hounded me for weeks about giving him the money.

Then, after spending four months walking to Guachochic, I learned that, because of Cummings, the $5,000.00 in pledges I had raised was about to be turned over to an Evangelical Christian Missionary who intended to convert the Tarahumaras. With considerable effort, I managed to divert the pledged donations to a free clinic and school in Tijuana. But I was so angry with Cummings for his deceit and his demands for money that I severed my acquaintanceship with him. The two of us did not speak again for many years.

In 1977, a colleague and I were just starting Tour Service Unlimited when Cummings reappeared asking if he could purchase stock. My partner, however, had a discerning eye and wanted nothing to do with him.

At that time in his 30's, Cummings, who had always been an extremely large man, had already become overweight. He had one brown and one blue eye, seldom wore clothes that fit properly or were ironed, and generally had an unkempt appearance. In college, he had been nicknamed "J. Wakefield Snake" and "Cummings, Con and Corrupt" because he was always plotting cons and scams. He had a telephone "black box" which enabled him to make free long distance phone calls. He became a mail order bishop in the Universal Life Church so that he could "ordain" ministers and hold wedding ceremonies for quick bucks.

Some of the things he bragged about actually turned my stomach. He once boasted that he had conspired with two employees of a San Francisco backpacking store to steal the owner's merchandise while he and the owner — a disabled veteran — were having dinner. He then opened his own backpacking store, but sold it when he failed to show a profit.

After my partner sold his half of Tour Service Unlimited to me, Cummings continued to press to buy shares. At one point, in need of additional working capital and against my better judgment, I agreed. Soon after, I landed a large account with the potential of bringing hundreds of tourists a week through San Francisco. "I'll be able to double your investment in a year," I crowed. When I was unable to make good on my boast, Cummings sold his shares for what he paid for them and insisted I owed him the dividend.

In February 1988, Cummings and his wife arrived in Thailand, accompanied by Marcus and another couple from Sacramento. The two couples continued on to Nepal and India to visit Christian missions, while Marcus remained in Bangkok and joined a Thai rock band. Meanwhile, I received a phone call from Cummings' sister in California. "It's urgent," she explained. "If John comes back to Thailand have him call me."

When they returned from Nepal, Cummings contacted his sister and, after their conversation, went into a prolonged state of depression and anxiety. He refused to explain himself, but asked if he could stay with Chat and me. (Nu was living at the Bangkok Children's Shelter at the time.) His wife and their traveling companions, meanwhile, returned to Sacramento.

After imposing on me for a month, I asked him to leave. He became irate, then contacted an Evangelical Christian colleague in the Reagan White House who put him in touch with a "born-again" at the United States Embassy. The next day he packed his clothes and moved out, refusing to say where he was going.

"You told me that I could stay with you when I came to Bangkok," he complained bitterly.

"A month is a stay," I replied. "More than that becomes a *live*. I didn't tell you that you could LIVE here."

Four weeks later, I ran into Marcus and asked if Cummings was still in the country. Only a few days passed before the two of them knocked on the door of the office. Standing before me was a man I hardly recognized. He had lost 50 pounds, was pallid, sickly-looking, and sweated profusely. His eyes had taken on the appearance of a dead man. As he sat on a chair in the office, he kept looking around, claiming that he couldn't remember anything.

"I would think that if you are ill," I said, "it would be better to let people know where you're living."

"No, it's better this way," he replied. Then he stood up, unsteadily, and grabbed Marcus for support. He looked like an old man.

I followed them out to Victory Monument and bid them goodbye. I felt such pity for him that I couldn't bring myself to mention the 10,000 baht ($400) worth of long-distance calls he had run up on my phone.

As he walked away, he turned and said, "Some day the two of us ought to pay each other back what we owe each other." I didn't quite understand what he meant.

A month or so later, Cummings dropped by the children's shelter looking for Mark Morgan. Mark wasn't in, but Cummings asked the volunteers to call all of the kids together. Though the children didn't know him, he sat down in front of them and started crying.

The workers at the shelter said he carried on for half an hour. Everyone was embarrassed, but they didn't know what to say. Finally, he stood up, asked all the kids to let him hug them, then left. No one had heard from him since.

"Those last months before he left Thailand," Marcus said, "I had to play wet nurse to him. He would just sit or lie on the bed. He never went out. He had chills and fever, but the medicine didn't seem to help him. I never want to go through that again."

Marcus and I paid the bill and went back to the jail to check on David. Kenji and Kachon wandered in at the same time. "You made the top story on all the television stations," Kenji reported. "It was not good. It was real bad as a matter of fact."

As he fed me the details, Nu's father, brothers and sister arrived. Kachon took them upstairs where Nu was being held and the rest of us worked out shifts to stay with David throughout the night.

At midnight, I returned to an empty apartment.

Four

More Trouble in Paradise

*"Tis slander; whose edge is sharper than the
sword; whose tongue outvenoms all the
worms of Nile, whose breath rides on the
posting winds, and doth belie all corners of
the world: Kings, Queens and States,
Maids, Matrons, nay the secrets of the grave
this viperous slander enters."*
— Shakespeare *Cymbeline*

March 3, 1989

I woke up in a sweat. It was still dark outside. I couldn't get the
nightmare of the press conference out of my head and dreaded
what the newspapers would say.

Exhausted but unable to fall back to sleep, I took a shower just to
kill time. I was agitated, restless. My heart raced like a bird's and my
stomach churned. At last the dawn sky began to light the city and
colors reappeared. I left the apartment and walked to the newsstand
next to Robinson's, frightened of what I would see. I stood there
gawking. My throat tightened, yet I also felt a masochistic titillation.
There I was — or rather, there was a horribly sad version of what I
was — sprawled across the pages of most of the morning editions.
The exception was Thai Rath. The country's largest newspaper had
thankfully decided not to report the story. However, the article in the
English-language Nation with an accompanying photo from the press
conference covered most of the front page.[2] The other English-
language paper, the Bangkok Post, ran a smaller picture and report on

page three.[3] The newspaper that had fueled this entire ignominy, Matichon, ran an inside column.

Because I couldn't read the stories in the Thai-language newspapers, I turned to the one in The Nation. I couldn't believe my eyes! It was a piece of gutter journalism. As I had barely understood what General Krutchaiyan and Colonel Choosri had said at the press conference, I didn't know until this moment the extent of the defamation. Here I learned exactly what the press release had said — that I was accused of running a sex tour ring and that Mark Morgan's shelter was a front for child prostitution. As I buried myself in the entire unbelievable story, I actually felt a sense of relief. No one would believe this, I thought. It was just too absurd. This was something from a fourth-rate movie.

I went back to the apartment and called Mark Morgan. "Nobody's going to believe this shit," I said to him. "It's so utterly ridiculous. They call your home `Mark Morgan, Incorporated' instead of the Bangkok Children's Shelter. The simplest details aren't even accurate."

"Where did the police get my name?" Mark asked.

"I don't know. I certainly never brought you up and Chat or Nu would have no reason to mention you. David told the investigating officer that he renewed his visa so that he could help with the Bangkok Children's Shelter, but I don't even know if he mentioned your name."

"Why did he say that?"

"Because it's the truth — that's what he told the Thai Embassy in Singapore. He was doing your books and helping with your mailings," I said. Mark groaned.

"Why don't we call our own press conference and tell the truth," I suggested.

"That sounds like a good idea, but I should talk it over with Khun Thammarat. I'll call you back."

Thammarat Narksuriya, a former television celebrity who had joined the Phalang Dharma Party and had gone into politics, was on the board of directors of the children's home. Mark relied on him to help set up the foundation so that everything would be legal.

I went to the office and left the newspapers on Kachon's desk, then hurried to Din Daeng Station. I told David that I had made an appointment with Khun Puttri at Siam Legal Aid and would pick up bail money for him on the way.

"Hurry!" he implored. He was sounding increasingly desperate.

My bank balance would not cover his bail and so I tried to borrow the rest on my credit card. But the bank would not let me make the transaction without my passport and my passport had been confiscated by the police. I went back to the station, explained to an officer why I needed my passport, and was assigned a chaperon to accompany me back to the bank. Such an odd assignment and waste of an officer's time, I thought. After all my years in Thailand, I still didn't understand that money was the only thing that really motivated the police.[4]

When we entered the bank, the American manager saw me and beckoned me into his office. "What's this all about?" he asked.

"It's all a lie!" I exclaimed. "I think the story was created by a competitor, or maybe Tone, the manager I fired in 1987. Last year, someone tried to sabotage my residence visa by telling immigration that I shipped women overseas for sex. The renewal was held up until my lawyer schmoozed the immigration officials. Now this."

"They should make up their minds. Is it women or is it children?" he joked. My cash advance was approved.

When we left the bank, I paid a taxi driver to take the chaperon back to the police station, then continued to Khun Puttri's office. Siam Legal Aid was on the second floor of a building in a Silom soi. Inside, it looked like the office of a relatively-affluent law firm, not ostentatious but substantial. The receptionist ushered me into Puttri's office. A good-looking man in his early 40's rose to shake my hand.

As soon as he spoke, I felt comfortable. Not only was his English impeccable, but his manner indicated that he was used to dealing with farangs.

I explained what had happened and told him that I would be returning to the police station to pay David Groat' bail. "Come back at 4 PM with David," Puttri instructed, "and I'll arrange a meeting with the director of the firm."

When the taxi dropped me back at the station, David was holding court with an entourage of visitors — Kenji, Kachon, Marcus, my part-time company driver Vic, and three Thai women, Lu, Al and Joi, freelance tour escorts who worked part-time for my company. "The police were real surprised when the ladies came to visit," David said with a twinkle in his eye. "I guess they believe their own bullshit and don't think we have any female friends."

Again, the absurdity of the whole thing hit me and I started to laugh.

Then he suddenly turned grim. "The police have taken Chat and Nu someplace, but Thep is still here," David said. "He came to the cell a couple of hours ago in tears and told me that he couldn't hold out much longer. I think the police are beating him now." He was close to shaking. I knew that he cared a lot for that feisty street kid.

I went into the Captain's office and posted David's bail.

"Let's get out of here!" he said when the cell door finally swung open.

Vic was waiting outside to return us to the office. David, Kenji, Kachon, the escorts and I all squeezed into his Toyota Crown and drove back to Victory Monument. At the condominium David went with us to the office for a cup of coffee, then retreated to his apartment to wash his rancid-smelling body.

I was still physically and emotionally drained, but I decided that I had to take care of what business I could before our appointment with the lawyer. I poured a large cup of caffeine, then started making phone calls.

My first was to the Embassy. When para-consul Pat Hansford picked up the phone, she said, "Why didn't you tell me there were two of you?"

"When I talked to you last, I said *we* had been arrested," I replied feebly, knowing that I had intentionally not mentioned David Groat by name. Again, she was brusque and accusing.

Then I called some of my colleagues in the industry to gauge their reactions to the news stories. I tried to create the impression that all was business as usual. "Sandy isn't in," his receptionist said when I called to apologize for not getting the S.I.T.E. newsletter to him on time. I had a feeling he was "in", but wouldn't talk.

Next I called Khun Sawalee at T.I.C.A. to suggest airline participation in our S.I.T.E. contest. "The chapter has the money to pay the air fare," she stated flatly, inferring there was no need. Cold as a fish, I thought as I hung up. Finally, I called my biggest competitor, Sumate Sudasna Ayudhaya, to ask him to take over my future programs. I didn't know how fast the stories would travel, but I didn't want my clients to suffer and I knew Sumate would do a good job with the programs.

"I'll commission you on anything that comes through," he said.

"Thank you, Sumate, I'm sure I can use the money at this point."

At 3 PM I woke David and the two of us caught the #77 bus to make our four o'clock appointment with Khun Puttri. We were directed into a board room with a large teak table. Puttri was joined by his partner, a secretary to take notes, and the young lawyer who had instituted my bail proceedings at Din Daeng Station.

As I told my story, Puttri turned to his partner and said, "It's not at all like the other case." The firm was currently handling the case of a man arrested for taking sexually-explicit pictures of young children in the Rose Hotel the year before. I wondered if those pictures were the ones the police had used to implicate me at the kangaroo court press conference.

"What about all the newspaper and television stories?" I asked.

"Oh that's nothing," Puttri said assuredly. "The police here always make up big stories for the papers, especially when it involves foreigners. Don't worry about that. It won't be the first time the press has been used to ruin somebody's reputation. It doesn't mean anything in court."

Maybe not, I thought. But in the business world, it meant that I was finished. I was infuriated but managed to control myself.

"The police may want to search your office," Puttri continued. "They've alleged that you ran a sex tour business, so they'll need to get evidence."

"They can't take my current files!" I protested. "I still have groups scheduled to come in."

"You'd better make copies of the important papers," he said.

The rest of the meeting was devoted to strategy. I asked them to get the boys out of jail. And we agreed to meet again with their parents. I was to spend the weekend going to Ubon to pick up Chat's mother.

As I got up to leave, I asked Puttri if we could go home. "Will the police come back?" I wanted to know.

"Don't worry about that," he said. "Once you're out on bail, they will leave you alone. You can go home and relax."

* * *

March 4, 1989

"Thammarat doesn't think it's a good idea to call a press conference."

I was wiping the sleep from my eyes. The jarring ring of the phone had awakened me from a sound sleep of more than 12 hours. "Instead, we decided to go around to the newspapers and give them our side of the story." Mark went on, "We went to three or four papers yesterday. We picked those that Thammarat has a good relationship with. The Nation reporter even said he was interested in doing a favorable story about the shelter similar to the one the Bangkok Post ran last year. I think this is the best way to go about it. Where would we hold a press conference anyway?"

"We could rent a meeting room at the Dusit Thani for Christ's sake!" I felt that Mark was taking the easiest way out, which, in my mind, wasn't necessarily the best way. I wanted to put the bastards in the police department on the defensive, let them try and prove any of what they claimed to be true while the media was watching. "I'm going to go check the newspapers and see if they printed what you told them," I said. "I'll let you know if there's anything."

I threw on my clothes and headed to the newsstand. When I returned I called Mark back, seething. "What are you doing to us?" I screamed. "This article[5] says that you are claiming to have nothing to do with me and David. Instead of denying the lies and telling the truth, Goddammit, you're trying to save your own skin and you're hanging the two of us out on the line!!"

"That's not what I told them," he replied feebly. "They misquoted me."

I was livid! I had been publicly vilified and Mark was attempting to cut his losses. When I hung up, I sat for a moment trying to compose myself. This must have been Thammarat's idea. That's why he didn't want to hold a press conference. He wanted to deny any association with me.

I got up and went to Groat's apartment. He agreed we were being thrown to the wolves and our "friend" Mark was deserting us. "He's a schmuck," David said matter-of-factly.

After lunch, I went to find Chat's sister, Rekha. In the soi, I ran into Nu's father. "The police won't tell me where the boys have been sent," he complained to me in Thai. "First they said that they were at a children's home in Bangkok. I went there and couldn't find them. Now they say the boys are at the children's prison in Pakred. I'm going there now."

"If you find them, let me know where they are," I said as he and his two youngest children went off to catch a bus.

I hurried to Rekha's shack and found her and her stepfather preparing food for the day's sales at Victory Monument. "My lawyer wants to meet with your mother and Nu's parents on Monday," I explained. "Would you go to Ubon with me to get your mother?"

"No. I can't leave. I have to sell food." She then turned to her stepfather and asked him to go.

"I'll pay for the ticket," I said. He agreed immediately. He seemed to like the idea of getting out of Bangkok and going home. "I'll go buy two tickets and meet you back here at 7 PM," I said. "There's an 8:30 bus."

When I walked out to catch the city bus to the terminal, I felt lonelier than I had ever felt in my life. I was still in shock. Everything seemed so unreal. I wanted to find someone to ride with me to Northern Station. It wasn't that far away, possibly a half hour, but I didn't want to go alone. I wandered out to the food stands to find a friend. Any friend would do. I just wanted someone to talk to. Just across the canal, I ran into Ot. He was sitting on a bench talking to his pals.

Everyone knew what had happened, but it was of no consequence to them. They didn't even bring up the subject of my arrest or the story in the papers.

Ot agreed to accompany me to the terminal. The weekend market at Chatuchak Park had brought every vehicle to a standstill and the traffic bothered me more than usual. I couldn't talk to Ot on the bus, but his presence was comforting.

I bought only a ticket for Chat's stepfather and a second one for his mother. I had decided that I was not in the right frame of mind to handle a 16-hour bus ride to Ubon.

When we returned, I thanked Ot and went to David's for a gin-and-tonic. He had dinner prepared, so we sat and commiserated.

At 7 PM, I asked if he wanted to go to Northern Station with me. "I'm too much of a wreck," he said. "I don't feel like going anywhere. Lock the padlock on the door so that no one will know I'm home. Come back here when you get back. I don't want to be alone."

Tickets in hand, I walked downstairs and headed toward the soi. A voice behind me called out "David!" It was repeated. When I paid no attention, the same voice called "Steve?" I looked behind me. The building's security guard was standing next to a uniformed policeman. Both seemed cheerful. "Well," I thought. "They've discovered they made a mistake and they're coming to tell me everything has been cleared up."

Instead, the officer politely asked in Thai that I go with him to the station. I couldn't handle this. I broke into a howl of despair. I looked at one of the tenants who was leaving the parking area and shrieked, "Eeeyaaargh! Chee wit mot!!... My life is finished!!"

She looked at me like I was nuts and walked on.

I turned and threw myself in the direction of Rekha's shack. The officer grew frustrated, then followed me. I cried that I had to give bus tickets to somebody, that I'd be back. He kept walking behind me and glanced toward the monument, as if he were looking for someone. "Okay," he said.

At Rekha's shanty, another officer — this one in plainclothes — was standing inside questioning her. I handed the stepfather the ticket and told them that I was being re-arrested. They looked at me stoically. Then I returned with the policeman to the condominium.

When we arrived at the guard's gate, there were two others in uniform waiting. "Where is David?" one of them asked.

"I don't know," I said.

"When did you see him last?"

"This afternoon. I ate lunch with him."

"You know where he is! Tell us!"

"I told you, I haven't seen him since this afternoon."

"Get in the truck!"

I climbed into the front seat of the police pickup. An officer sat on each side of me. On the way to Din Daeng, one of them pulled a vial of white powder from his pocket and said, "You were selling this, weren't you?"

"What is that?"

"You know," he growled. "It's heroin. The FBI wants you. You were in Thailand selling this."

In a moment I was going to lose it. I wanted to scream and shout and kick and I was helpless. I had to struggle to hang on to my wits, to keep my emotions in check, but I didn't feel like I was doing it very successfully.

"Why are you doing this?" I cried.

I tried to think like a Buddhist and wondered what sins I had committed that could have brought this on, what awful deeds were overtaking me? I vowed that, if I ever again had the chance, I would devote the rest of my life to improving mankind. I would be humble, gentle and kind. I would do nothing to create bad karma.

When the cell door thundered shut behind me, I sank to the floor of the wretched-looking cell and began to daydream about snatches of my life. My head was pulsing feverishly. "It had been a good life," I thought. And maybe I was going mad.

"God, I hope David got away." The thought that just perhaps he did made me happy and hopeful. The walls seemed to close in on me.

The hours dragged on. With each passing minute, I became more and more optimistic about his flight. It was a perverse pleasure, but it *was* pleasure. Then, just before midnight, the door of the cell flew open. I looked up. David shuffled in and I stood up. His clothes were torn and filthy. I thought they were covered with mud, until I saw bandages. "Oh my God, they beat you," I exclaimed.

"No." He looked at me. His eyes were swollen with tears. He started to sob and blubbered, "I tried to kill myself."

I grabbed him and held him close. For several minutes the two of us just stood there in the center of the cell holding each other in an embrace. Neither of us could speak.

After what seemed like an eternity, he said quietly, "After you left, the police pounded on the door. I was so paranoid that I thought it was a neighborhood lynch mob coming after me. The banging stopped, then started again a few minutes later. I took a knife and slit my wrists. The apartment is a mess! Then I thought about Thep. If I killed myself, he would live the rest of his life feeling guilty. He would think he was the cause. I covered my bleeding arms with a towel and called the Embassy. They called the police who broke down the door and rushed me to the hospital. I've got a lot of stitches in this arm. It hurts like hell, but they gave me something to ease the pain."

* * *

"Imprisoned! Oh irreparable misery! Handed over to evil spirits and judging, unfeeling mankind!"
— Goethe *Faust*

March 5, 1989

The mosquitoes were voracious. We no longer had the luxury of extra shirts and pants to use as pillows. We laid our heads on the wooden floor, stared at the ceiling and tried to close our eyes.

In the middle of the night, while attempting to sleep, I touched my face and felt something crawling on my cheek. I leapt up, shuddering involuntarily, arms flailing, and flicked away a monstrous cockroach. It was hours before I could lie down again. I began pacing the floor like a caged animal. Back and forth, back and forth. The rhythm seemed to calm me. It only irritated David, but he just lay silently nursing his self-inflicted wounds.

I tried to logically determine who might be responsible for attempting to wreck my life. Puttri said the police often made up stories, but they had to get their information from somewhere. It couldn't have been just the Matichon newspaper story. Ulit, the house father whom Mark had fired, had a motive for implicating his ex-boss but would have had nothing against me. Besides, he knew the proper name of the home was the "Bangkok Children's Shelter", not "Mark Morgan Incorporated", as it had appeared in the press. Conversely, a nasty competitor might have had motives for implicating me but certainly none for hurting the shelter. The common denominator was missing.

Mid-afternoon, Kenji's smiling face mercifully appeared at the bars. "What happened?"

"I don't know!" I cried. "The police claim the FBI asked them to re-arrest us. They told me I was wanted for selling heroin."

David knew why he had been re-arrested. The FBI had asked the Thais to hold him because of his warrant in the United States. But I had no idea why I had been picked up. The allegation that I had been selling heroin was as ridiculous as all the others.

"Call the Embassy," I howled at Kenji. "I want to know what this is all about. Tell them to send someone over to explain why the U.S. government is asking the Thais to hold me. I'm not wanted in the States. Then call Puttri as soon as his office opens tomorrow and ask him to come down to see if he can get us out."

Kenji slipped plastic bags of food and water through the bars and left. I looked at my surroundings and felt sickened by it. I caught David doing the same thing. We glanced at each other, then in unison said, "Might as well", and went to work cleaning it up. The duty officers looked at us with amazement. They had never seen prisoners voluntarily scrubbing a cell.

Later that evening, Colonel Choosri arrived for his daily station check. He spotted the two of us and walked over. Smiling gleefully, he said with a sanctimonious air of contempt, "So the FBI wants you." He turned and started to walk away, chuckling to himself. I blurted out, "They don't want me, they want him!" gesturing at David. Choosri then started laughing louder.

I was furious with myself. I had allowed this egotistical, arrogant policeman to anger me so much that I had become base and self-serving. I turned on a friend who desperately needed compassion and kindness. A revulsion swept over me and I slid down next to David and tried to assuage the pain of betrayal by talking about how much I disliked Colonel Choosri.

David said nothing. His silence was chastising and covered me with a sense of deep shame.

March 6, 1989

After scrubbing years of accumulated excrement from the toilet, I felt a little more human. Only the mosquitoes kept me awake now, but because of David's attempt to kill himself, the police refused us bug spray. Evidently, they thought he might try to swallow it.

Kenji arrived just after 8 AM and brought a stack of newspapers. "It's not good!" he exclaimed as he shoved them through the bars. I asked if he had called my lawyer or the Embassy. He hadn't. He said it was too early to get anyone in. I was aware of Kenji's shyness and aversion to any kind of confrontation, but I couldn't help feeling impatient.

The Nation was continuing its sensationalist attacks. The photograph of me and David at the police press conference was rerun, this time blanketing the cover of the features section, accusing us of being the type of foreigners who bring AIDS into the "Land of Smiles".[6]

Kachon arrived with breakfast, but the newspapers had again destroyed my appetite. I asked for a pen and note paper and wrote detailed instructions for Kenji, Kachon and the escorts, Lu, Al and Joi. A representative from the incentive house was due at the airport in three days. Glaxo Pharmaceutical was due two days after that. Chat and Nu were still being held. I was desperate.

"You're in charge now, Kenji," I said. I had been training him for over a year and he had always followed instructions well, but I worried about the client's perception of his abilities. He was still very young — just in his early 20's.

After they left, the day dragged on endlessly. I kept hoping to see Pat Hansford. Finally, at 6 PM, an American named Ron Fry arrived. "I'm here from the Embassy. Pat Hansford was busy and couldn't make it. I'm filling in."

"Why has the FBI asked for my arrest?" I demanded.

"I don't know anything about that. I don't work in the consular section. I'm only doing this as a favor." Then he told me how lucky I was to have been arrested in Thailand. "The system here is similar to ours. A lot of other countries are much worse."

He pulled some papers from his briefcase. "These are Privacy Act waivers. I've been asked to have you sign them. It authorizes us to release any information we have on you." I took the papers and signed them. So did David. Because I had nothing to hide and believed that my problems were simply a mistake, I checked every blank, authorizing the Embassy to give any information they had about me to anybody who asked, including the Thai police. If I couldn't trust the Embassy, I reasoned, who could I trust? I was sure their actions would be to our benefit. I was incredibly naive.

"Will you call my mother?" I asked.

"Sure, if you want," he replied.

Kenji, Kachon and Puttri's young assistant from Siam Legal Aid arrived while we were signing the waivers. Fry tucked them into his briefcase and departed.

"Thai law says the police can keep you here for seven days," the lawyer explained. "Then they have to transfer you to a regular prison."

I didn't want to hear that. "Get the elusive Pat Hansford on the phone!" I demanded. "Tell her that I want her to explain the Embassy's actions to me."

The lawyer nodded and left. Kenji and Kachon went with him. I settled down for another night of fighting mosquitoes.

Five

Bangkok Special Prison

March 7, 1989

"**Y**ou made the papers again," Kenji announced when he arrived at 7:30 with our breakfasts.

Incredulously I gazed at the two English-language newspapers. This time, the front page of the Bangkok Post heralded our re-arrest, stating that I had been taken in at the request of American authorities — however, because of the Privacy Act, Embassy officials were not able to divulge the reason.[7] The Nation, meanwhile, repeated the allegations made by the police at the press conference.[8]

"Tone called," Kenji said, referring to my former office manager whom I had fired. "He told me that he read the story in the newspaper, then he started laughing."

"Is he responsible for this?" I cried. I had always suspected Tone of calling immigration in an attempt to have my work permit rejected.

But Kenji looked dubious. This kind of deviousness was beyond Tone's capabilities, he felt. Nevertheless, I kept thinking I could clarify everything if there was but one investigative journalist willing to listen to my side of the story.

Soon after Kenji and Kachon left, David and I were ordered to gather our things, handcuffed to four other prisoners, and packed into a police van.

We drove through Chinatown and entered a courtyard not far from Bangkok's Giant Swing, a towering eight-story device that a young Goliath would have loved; then ushered into a rambling old two-story

81

building where we sank into a row of wooden folding chairs that faced a wood stand.

After waiting for what seemed an eternity, a Thai judge in black robes entered from a side door accompanied by a woman carrying a stack of files. He seated himself behind the stand while the lady remained at arm's length, handing over the files one by one which he read silently.

As I observed this ritual, I crossed my legs. One of the guards rushed over and angrily motioned for me to uncross them. Apparently such action in a courtroom was a sign of disrespect.

The six of us were ordered to our feet and, as the judge called out names, I felt my wallet move in my back pocket. I reached behind me and grabbed a hand. The prisoner standing next to me was trying to lift my money. I couldn't believe the audacity of the man. I turned to him, "Tham arai?" I asked. "What are you doing?" The judge stopped and looked at me. "He just tried to steal my wallet," I blurted out.

A guard unlocked the chain that held me and David to the other prisoners, then pushed us to the judge's stand.

"Just sign here," the judge said as he shoved two documents at us.

"I'm not signing anything until I talk to my lawyer," David muttered.

The document was written in Thai. I had no idea what it said and it was obvious that the court felt no compunction to provide an interpreter. I refused to sign as well.

This flustered the judge. He ordered the secretary to go find someone who spoke English. A couple of minutes later, she returned, shrugged and said there was nobody available who could translate. After a second attempt to prod us to sign, the judge ordered the guard to take us away.

We were led through a back door, then a second door and into a hallway echoing with a hundred noisy conversations. To the left and right were cells crammed with prisoners in uniform brown short-sleeved shirts and pants.

We were put into one with about 50 Thai prisoners, who were sitting on a horribly filthy cement floor or were hanging on the bars like chimpanzees yelling to visitors behind screened windows. They, in turn, yelled back — each trying to be heard above the cacophony.

A squat toilet sat on a raised cement block at the rear with two yellow-streaked urinals. Behind them, an open sewer gave off the unbreathably disgusting odor of urine which, with the stench of 50 sweating bodies in densely-humid weather, was overwhelming.

"This isn't it?" I cried to David.

"I hope not," he said quietly. I could not imagine spending a few hours here, much less weeks or — perish the thought — months. Suddenly, through the bars of another cell, I spotted a western face and noticed that he and the others with him were in chains.

I called out. "Do you know how long we have to stay here?"

His eyes were wild, distant, as if he were not consciously there. "I've been in all the prisons," he said.

"Do they have beds in the prisons?" I asked with some measure of hope. Without realizing it at the moment, my question meant I was preparing myself to spend more than a day or two locked up.

"Sure," he said. Then he smirked and turned away.

I rushed back to where David was sitting. "The guy in the next cell said that we'll have beds," I exclaimed.

Just then, Kachon appeared at a screen and called to me. "Thank God!" I cried. "How long do we stay here?"

"You no lif here for long," he yelled back.

"Are they taking us someplace better than this?"

"Yes," he said. "They tay you to other jail. Is better than here."

The young lawyer from Puttri's office was standing behind Kachon. I asked about the forms that we had refused to sign. "It's nothing," he said. "Just a formality. You must sign them."

"If we sign them, does it mean that we are accepting incarceration?" David asked.

The long English word threw him. He looked bewildered for a minute, then said, "It doesn't mean anything. It just says that you will be remanded to the prison for 12 days. They have to remand you every 12 days until you're charged with a crime. You'll have to sign again in 12 days."

At that moment, a guard passed the forms through the bars and ordered us to sign them. The whole Thai system was very bewildering.

Kachon sent in some fried rice, wrapped in newspapers, along with a soft drink in a plastic bag. I was very grateful for his and Kenji's constant help, but wondered what happened to prisoners with no friends or family to bring them food.

A couple of hours later, the guard opened the cell door and called out, "Sateefen Lehmon". I followed him into the hallway, past the cell with the wild-eyed farang to a reception area. My lawyer asked me to sit down and said, "There is no warrant for you in America, so you can bail out. But because the U.S. Embassy requested your arrest, we must get a letter from the Embassy indicating that you are not wanted in America and that you can be released. I'll get in touch with them and ask for the letter. We should be able to get you out tomorrow."

"Tell the Embassy I want someone to come and explain why I was arrested," I again demanded.

When I returned to the cell, I was afraid to tell David the news. I didn't want him to feel any worse than he already felt. But it was hard to conceal my relief.

"What was that all about?" he asked.

"The lawyer," I replied.

"Why did he call you out and not me?"

I just shrugged.

A few minutes later, a guard came into the cell and sat down. He called each prisoner by name and, as we came forward, he took our fingerprints. His manner was gruff and demanding, unlike that of any Thai I had ever known. He ordered each prisoner to squat in a line.

Nothing was offered to remove the black ink from our hands, so everyone rubbed it onto the floor rather than wipe it on their clothes.

After squatting for half an hour, the cell door swung open and we were paraded, single file, down the hall and through a double entrance into the back door of an antiquated blue bus. Everyone scrambled for a seat, but most of us were forced to stand, crammed in so tight that we could hardly breathe.

Guards toting shotguns climbed aboard and the bus crawled away from the curb into city traffic, causing a very slight but welcome breeze. Fortunately, the ride was short — only a few blocks from the courthouse. We rode in through a gate and entered a parking lot surrounded by steep concrete walls, then backed through a second gate and jerked to a halt. We poured out of the bus into a single file march to a putrid green barracks-style building. Once inside, we were commanded to squat along the walls. I was in Bangkok Special Prison.

One of the guards made an announcement which I understood to be our bathing and eating schedule. We subsequently lined up behind two tables — one to surrender our cash, which was recorded on cardboard forms; the other to surrender valuables for which we were given receipts. We were stripped and searched for contraband, then forced to bend down and "spread our cheeks."

Once we had reclaimed our clothes and a bit of our dignity, we were marched out the back of the building, through a well-tended garden into a long rectangular-shaped cafeteria. "This is much better," David said.

After Din Daeng Police Station and the holding cell at the courthouse, it seemed almost pleasant. The cafeteria was lined with wooden tables and benches. On the tables were metal trays containing lumps of brown rice and limp overcooked vegetables. Things were definitely looking up. It didn't matter that the food was awful, what mattered was that it looked humane.

85

Still, I could barely nibble the dinner. Afterwards, we were assigned to a cell on the first floor of another two-story barracks-style building. When we were ordered to squat, one prisoner mumbled something inaudible. A large, burly man — enormous for a Thai — approached and viciously kicked him several times. Everyone cowered in fear. The point had been made — no further comments were forthcoming from inmates.

The large burly man stood at the center of the room and began telling us what to expect. Suddenly, he unleashed a fury of punches and kicks at another prisoner — seemingly unprovoked — and pummeled him into near unconsciousness. I didn't understand what had set him off, but when he finally let up, he walked to a corner away from everyone, sat down and looked me in the eye. Then he motioned for me and David to join him. Reluctantly, we complied.

"You're the two Americans who had sex with children," he said in excellent English. "I read about you in the newspaper. I knew you'd be coming through here."

I was practically shaking in fear, anticipating the worst. Instead he said, "My name is Joe. Would you like a cup of coffee?" Within minutes, he was speaking to us like we were old friends.

He talked about his American nickname, which many Thais give to themselves, and about his home and family. I soon learned that he was related to Suchada Yuvaboon, the owner of Bangkok's magnificent Rose Garden. When I told him I knew Khun Suchada, he became even friendlier. I asked when he would go home to sleep and he snarled, "I hate this fucking place. I've been here for years." I was momentarily confused, then I realized that he wasn't a guard at all but a prison trustee.

"Tomorrow you'll move to Building Three," he said. "There your status changes as far as the guards are concerned. You are no longer a prisoner. You become a customer. If you want food, messages to go out, favors done, things brought in, you must pay the guards. They'll treat you well in Building Three because they want your business.

86

Tomorrow, look for an Australian named Peter. He'll explain to you how things work. He's been here a couple of years."

Abruptly, Joe decided that he was sleepy and told us to go back to our spots on the floor.

"I feel much better now," David whispered.

In a peculiar way, I suppose I did too. For the first time since my re-arrest, I slept soundly.

March 8, 1989

I felt refreshed when I woke. The air was better, there were fewer mosquitoes and no semis rumbling outside keeping me up all night. We were roused at 6 AM by Joe barking orders like a drill sergeant. The cell door banged open. Everyone leapt to their feet and formed a long single line stretching from a toilet in the cell into the hallway and out to the courtyard where plastic buckets were filled from a holding tank, passed from prisoner to prisoner as in a fire brigade, and emptied into a water tank inside the cell. The building had no plumbing, so we had to bring the toilet water from outside.

Once the tank in the cell was filled, prisoners began mopping the wooden floor with damp rags. "At least it's clean," I thought gratefully.

Joe's booming commands continued to keep me on edge. I grabbed toothbrush, soap and towel, picked up my thongs and lined up with everyone else outside the building.

We stood before a large water tank resembling a feeding trough for horses, spaced ourselves equidistant from one another to our front, rear and sides, and stripped down and tied sarongs around our waists.

A guard blew a whistle, signaling us to fill a plastic bowl; a second whistle was the cue to pour water over ourselves; the third to lather up; and the fourth to rinse off. I didn't quite get the knack of the thing and was constantly out of synch, soaping when I was supposed to rinse. David thought my lack of coordination funny and laughed to himself when a guard yelled at me.

After the shower, we were allowed a few seconds for brushing teeth and dressing, and then forced to, once again, squat. A guard made me roll my long pants to my knees, which made the squat even more uncomfortable. Joe would later explain, "Only guards are allowed to wear long pants."

One of them began a discourse on the prison monetary system. We were allowed 40 baht worth of coupons each day. No cash. Any money that we had forfeited upon arrival was on our "card" and coupons were allocated each day until the money was gone. If we needed more money, someone on the outside would have to deposit it into our account.

We were allowed to wander for a short time to the garden courtyard, which was filled with other prisoners — hundreds of them — just standing around talking. I stopped and asked one where I could use the coupons. He pointed to a creaky structure with a corrugated aluminum roof and a wide entrance through which inmates were streaming in and out like worker ants.

I wandered inside and looked around. Dirty wooden counters lined the walls. Some of them held large steaming pots from which ladles of food were drawn and dumped into plastic bowls. I looked at it and instead bought a cold bottle of soy milk.

"I saw you come in last night and Joe told me to look for you." A tall lanky farang was speaking to me and David. "My name is Peter." His Australian accent was as strong as Kenji's.

"Your case was so highly publicized that you're bound to be sent to Building Two and put in chains. That's what happens to people with high profile cases. You sit inside all day long attached to the wall. It's not fun. You've got to pay a bribe or you'll probably be sent there tomorrow."

"How much?" David asked.

"Ask Joe," Peter replied. "He'll know."

We walked back to our building and asked Joe what it would take to remain out of chains, but I suggested the bribe cover only David because "I expect to be getting out on bail today."

He gave me a bemused look and said, "I'll check for you too."

Minutes later, Joe returned with news that it would cost 3000 baht ($120) each. "And, by the way," he added, "I haven't heard anything about your being released on bail."

At 8 AM, we were ordered to attention while the Thai National Anthem blared from a nearby loudspeaker. Then in a rundown building across from the commissary, each prisoner was called for an interview, inspected for tattoos and identifying marks, fingerprinted, and directed to squat on the cement floor and wait.

I was then taken with the others to Building Four for haircuts. Peter had told me to arrange something with the guards or I "would be shaved bald". Bald! How could I explain *that* to a client from Glaxo?! I pleaded with the guard but he would not acknowledge me. In desperation, I began slipping behind other prisoners in line, trying to forestall this next assault on my dignity. But all too quickly, there was no one left in front of me.

I was ordered to the chair and slunk down upon it, seizing a moment to first offer the barber some coupons in exchange for a more artfully-designed cut. Without wavering, he tore into my scalp with his razor and I tensed with each clump that fell to the ground.

It was over in a matter of moments. I felt the top of my head. He had spared only a few wretched whisps — as if he'd mowed a lawn and missed a blade of grass or two. I threw myself out of the chair, furious, and walked toward the gate.

Suddenly the barber's voice rang out. "Where are my coupons?"

I turned and fired a glare aimed like a rifle. "But I'm bald!" I shrieked.

"No you're not," he said, pointing to the cartoon-like strands that still clung to the top of my scalp. In a rage, I fumbled for a handful of coupons in my pocket and threw them at him.

From there, I moved to the medical compound and was given a cholera shot. I watched the doctor closely, fearing that the needles would be reused and AIDS would be the legacy of my short stay in Bangkok Special Prison. Mercifully, new needles were utilized for each shot, and I breathed easier. I would learn later, however, that doctors had only recently begun the procedure and that hundreds of prisoners, some of them farangs, had contracted the dread disease while being processed through.

At lunch time, we were released into the central compound once again where I anxiously looked for Peter. Although I found the idea of bribing guards reprehensible, I did not wish to repeat my experience with the barber and end up chained to a wall in my cell. Peter assured me that everything had been arranged.

Joe was in a foul mood that afternoon. He was like a time bomb, subject to sudden violent explosions. He began to savagely beat a retarded prisoner for not following his instructions. The rest of us, made keenly aware of our helplessness, could only watch in agonizing silence. Witnessing these beatings was difficult for me. I knew nothing I could do would dissuade him — and yet I felt like a coward for not trying. If his outbursts were intended to intimidate us, they had certainly fulfilled their purpose.

Building assignments were given out later in the day. David and I were sent to Building Three, as Joe had predicted, and scrutinized there by the assistant building chief. We crouched in front of his desk and bowed low.

"So you like to do indecent assault?" he said in Thai.

He didn't expect a reply, but I timidly countered that a big mistake had been made. He ignored me and went on with a lecture. Afterwards, I was assigned a room cell on the second floor and David one on the first.

A guard took me upstairs and unlocked a solid metal door with a barred window. I looked into a 15-foot cubicle and upon the forlorn faces of 10 Thais and one Pakistani. They were seated on pads against three of the walls with their shoes and thongs lined up along the fourth. In one corner was a raised platform containing a squat toilet.

To be on the safe side, I bowed to everyone as I entered. There was no space for me along the walls, so I was forced to lay down in the middle of the floor.

I tried to close my eyes, but suddenly I was aware of something strange and the feeling descended on me like a bad dream. "I am really in prison! The lawyer didn't bail me out and I am really in prison!" A wave of icy shivers sliced through my whole body. I trembled. I felt sick. The chills continued in sudden spasms. I sweated — I shook, one moment my head pounding hot, the next my body turning blue like ice. My thoughts were a blur. My thoughts turned to death. I thought that I just might die in this place.

One of the prisoners covered me with a blanket and motioned to my shoulder, pantomiming an injection. Then it hit me. Cholera was rushing through my system. They had shot too much cholera into my bloodstream.

My cellmate's act of kindness made me feel unalone. Gradually my thoughts of death became less frenzied, were stilled, became nothing, something less than nothing, until I only wondered when the lights would go out.

March 9, 1989

The lights never went out. We were awakened abruptly at 6 AM. The chills had subsided, but I was exhausted. I had been sick all night. The mosquitoes added to my misery. I kept thinking what it would be like to have malaria and cholera at the same time. My arm was in terrible pain and throbbed with every heartbeat.

The newest prisoners were expected to carry in buckets of water to flush the toilet but I was temporarily exempted because the Pakistani had just arrived two days earlier and had been assigned the job for a week. The way I felt, I was very grateful for the reprieve.

91

I had no sarong to wear for the outdoor "shower", but the Thai man who had covered me with his blanket during the night gave me one of his. He introduced himself as Napodol Na Ayudhaya, a very prestigious old Thai name. I wondered how someone from such a family could have wound up in here. He must have done something to an even more powerful member of society.

Napodol showed me how to tie the sarong in front so that it wouldn't unravel during my shower. "You'll need a bowl," he said. "You can use mine this time." It was not only a necessity for the twice-daily showers, but it doubled as a rice bowl.

After showering, a contingent of 80 or 90 prisoners lined up in front of a table to collect their daily supply of coupons. There I ran into David and we walked together to the central compound for breakfast. Two free meals a day were provided, but they were so bad that anyone who could afford it bought his own food. The food sold at the commissary was bad too — but it was certainly better than the free brown rice and fish heads.

After breakfast, I wandered around the central compound. Nine buildings surrounded the courtyard. Each area was called a *daeng*, which literally means "frontier" or "border". Prisoners from each daeng were allowed access to the central courtyard, but not to the other daengs. The courtyard held the dining hall, processing center, library, commissary, and, at the center, a raised platform where the guards sat.

"What are visiting hours here?" I asked Peter.

"Between 8:30 and 11:30, then between 1:00 and 2:30," he said. "You're allowed 15 minutes per visit."

I was desperate to learn what had happened to my bail and to the boys, to my demand for an explanation from the Embassy, and desperate to talk to Kenji about the Glaxo program. Even now I couldn't separate myself from my work. The incentive client was due to arrive today, and Glaxo two days later. "How do I get a message outside? Is there a phone I can use?" I asked.

Peter laughed. "A phone? You're joking! The government doesn't like prisoners communicating with the outside. Newspapers and radios are strictly prohibited."

"But how does one communicate with a lawyer?" I asked incredulously.

"You pay a guard to make a phone call for you."

"But how do you pay a guard if you're not allowed to have money inside?"

"You arrange with a guard to meet a friend of yours and bring it in. You have to pay him a percentage of the money he brings in. About 20 percent."

First the police fabricate a preposterous lie to imprison me, then they re-arrest me without charging me with a crime, and now I have to give them money so I can get a message to my lawyer. The whole system was a travesty. I paced up and down the courtyard, hoping to dispel some of my exasperation. An hour later, a message arrived for me to go to the welfare section.

"You have a visit," Peter said.

Outside the welfare building, I was ordered to squat in the hot sun until my number was called, then marched to another area and ordered to squat again. Most of the Thais didn't seem to mind squatting. Many of them had no chairs at home and squatting on their haunches was natural, but for a middle-aged American the position was very uncomfortable. My leg and back muscles were beginning to feel the strain.

Eventually, a bell rang. A group of prisoners came out of the visiting area and I and others were permitted inside. We sat on stools before a wire mesh screen. A few feet behind it was a second screen through which visitors squinted in an effort to locate those they had come to see. The distance between prisoner and visitor was considerable enough to necessitate yelling in order to be heard. Thus within seconds, one became engulfed in a barnyard of noises.

Kenji and Kachon suddenly appeared. "This is impossible!" I shouted. "How can I give you instructions for the Glaxo program? How can we communicate? Why wasn't I released on bail yesterday?"

Kenji, as usual, took my volley in stride and responded with an "I don't know." He had found out nothing from the Embassy or from my attorney. I was irritated, perhaps bordering on nasty.

Kachon held up a bag with toiletries, food and two cartons of cigarettes, which could be used as currency inside.

"What about the boys?" I cried.

They were at Pakred Children's Prison, I was told, but they were all right. For that much, I was thankful.

"I need shorts," I shouted over the din. "They make me roll up the legs of my pants."

Kachon nodded and promised to return later with shorts and the lawyer.

With my share of the cigarettes I hoped to barter for a mattress. So spoiled was I that I knew I'd never be able to sleep without something between me and the floor.

A prisoner in the next room cell had fashioned a mattress by sewing some old rags and blankets together. He showed it to me and said what I thought was "eight two" in Thai. "Eighty-two baht," I thought. "That's not bad!" I began to count out a combination of cigarettes and coupons.

"Mai chai," he said, shaking his head. "Paet song." And grabbed eight packs of cigarettes. Rather than admit my elementary knowledge of Thai had not been sufficient to understand the difference in tones between the words "song" (two) and "song" (pack), I smiled painfully and accepted the deal, while grumbling to myself that the lumpy thing shouldn't cost eight packs of cigarettes.

A few hours later, Kachon returned with Voratham, a legal assistant from my lawyer Puttri's office, and with the bribe to keep me and David out of chains — 6,000 baht which he presented to one of the guards as if it were a common business transaction. Kachon passed himself off as an interpreter and was therefore able to join us in the small lawyer's room which was marginally better than the regular visiting area. Here, there was only one screen separating visitors from prisoners.

"The Embassy refuses to write a letter," Voratham began. "We can't apply for bail until we receive a letter from the Embassy stating that there is no warrant for your arrest in America. We called (Consul General) Ed Wehrli, but he won't do it."

This was puzzling to me. "Why not?"

"I don't know," he said.

I fought to maintain my composure. "Why won't (para-consul) Pat Hansford come to visit?" I asked.

"She said she couldn't come because she's busy," he replied. "You'll have to get the letter from the Embassy yourself."

"How am I supposed to do that from in here?" I asked in disbelief.

"Write a letter," he suggested.

"But my business... I have to get out now!"

"Write a letter and I'll come to pick it up tomorrow. But the earliest we could get you out would be Monday."

I groaned. "The Glaxo program arrives on Sunday. They have flight arrivals all day long and that night we have a dinner cruise. What a disaster!" I felt powerless and at the mercy of the Embassy and the U.S. government. They were destroying any opportunity I might have to salvage what remained of my business, or rather, to go out of it with some honor.

"When you come back tomorrow, bring Kenji with you," I said. "I can at least give him instructions from in here. It's impossible at the visiting area."

Kachon and Voratham left. I went back to the room cell and started to detail everything that Kenji would need to know. `What will we tell the client?' I wondered, `We can't tell her I'm in jail.'

The other inmates returned at 5 PM and the guards locked the door. Many prisoners emptied their plastic bags of meat and rice, purchased during the day, into their bowls, then gathered in groups and ate. I sat on my lumpy mat and wrote feverishly — first, further instructions to my staff, and then, to the Consul General at the Embassy asking for a letter to the Thai authorities stating that there was no warrant for my arrest in the United States.

Afterwards, I got up and went from prisoner to prisoner, introducing myself and asking each person's name. I didn't need to tell them why I was here. The charge was posted on the wall, along with everyone else's. But in Buddhist Thailand a case of "anachan" (indecent assault, or translated more literally, "immorality") is a minor crime. In Christian America, however, the crime known as child molestation (bothering a child), is considered worse than murder when sex is involved. I related the details of my arrest, but they were all skeptical when I told them that I hadn't done anything.

"Nobody ever admits that he is guilty when he first arrives," one man said. "Later we always learn the truth."

Most of the prisoners in my quarter were older Thai men causing Peter to dub it "The Old Men's Room", the average age being around 50. These were not typical criminals, but rather members of Thailand's upper class. One man had once been an elected member of Parliament; another, was a former naval officer; a third named Phisan, ironically owned a travel business and was an official of C.A.T., the organization my staffers had called to get our telex line repaired.

At 8 o'clock, we stood for the singing of the King's Anthem which some Thais followed with a Buddhist chant. Then, everyone sat down, picked up a book to read, or went to sleep. I was exhausted and tried to sleep. But every time I closed my eyes, the memories of the past week or worries about my life, about Chat and Nu, about my business and the Glaxo program, would not allow me to cull the rest I craved so much.

I now believed that police officials Manas Krutchaiyan and Khongdej Choosri had created the entire story as a smokescreen to draw attention from the scandalous fatal shooting of a government official by a Thai policeman. I recalled Krutchaiyan displaying to his subordinate the photograph of a man in bed with a boy. "It's him, isn't it?" he had said. I also believed that the Embassy would soon realize that I had been bushwacked and would help me.

My mind raced from incident to incident, trying to understand, aching to understand, why the Embassy might be refusing me a letter. Why had U.S. officials requested my arrest? Why was somebody trying to ruin me?

March 10, 1989

After breakfast and the National Anthem, David, Peter and I spent the morning pacing back and forth in front of the building. Peter explained how the Thai legal system operates. He had been fighting a drug case for four years. The Thais do not believe in speedy trials. "Prunee", the Thai word meaning "sometime in the future... maybe" applies here too. Instead of contiguous court sessions, sessions are often held months apart. Many times witnesses or even lawyers do not appear and cases are constantly delayed, forcing prisoners to be incarcerated for years before a verdict is finally reached. There are two appeals courts and each may take additional years. If a prisoner is acquitted, the prosecutor has the right to appeal the acquittal, which means that a person may be tried three times for the same crime, something that is unthinkable in the United States. It is not inconceivable or even uncommon for a case to remain in the courts for years while the accused languishes behind bars and is ultimately found not guilty.

Defendants in Thailand are considered guilty until proven innocent. Because the police are appointed by the King, they are perceived as intrinsically moral and correct, and anyone they arrest as guilty. If a defendant pleads not guilty and is found guilty by the courts, his sentence is doubled. Most Thais plead guilty rather than take a chance on a system weighted against them.

Voratham from Siam Legal Aid arrived late in the morning with Kenji and Kachon.

"Did the incentive client get in?" I asked Kenji after dropping into a stool in front of the screen.

"She's okay. She asked where you were. I told her you were up country and couldn't get to the airport to pick her up."

I handed detailed instructions for Kenji through an opening in the screen when a guard spotted me, rushed over and cried, "Mai dai!" I looked at Voratham, my eyes pleading for assistance. "Why can't I give the notes to Kenji?"

The guard told the lawyer that everything must be read before it can be given to anyone, even my attorney. He snapped the papers out of my hand and walked off with them.

I was desperate. Kenji needed my notes to function effectively. There was enough pressure on him already. Minutes later, the guard returned and said he was unable to find anyone to screen the material. Voratham explained that one of the letters was an important one, from me to the Embassy. The guard took it to yet another officer who spoke a little English. Though I was positive he wasn't able to understand what I'd written, to admit that would have meant to lose face. He told the other guard it was okay, and it was passed to my lawyer. But Kenji was denied my notes.

"I'll mail this today," Voratham said.

"Mail it?!!" I almost screamed with exasperation. "Take it to the Embassy and get them to write a letter while you're waiting!" He looked at me as if I were crazy and said he would have a service deliver it.

I spent the next half-hour verbally giving Kenji the instructions that took most of the previous evening to delineate on paper. I had begun to resign myself to the probability that I would be imprisoned during the entire Glaxo conference. I left my visitors sensing I must be growing increasingly obnoxious to them. I couldn't help it. My release on bail seemed like an impossibility.

Though I wanted to say something appreciative, I was feeling hopeless and depressed.

In the afternoon, I wandered back to the courtyard where an undersized iron cage now sat boiling in the sun. It looked like the type of device in which a wild circus animal might be kept subdued. Inside it, a Thai prisoner curled up in the fetal position, unable to stretch out. Each time he did, the black iron bars scorched his skin. It was over 90 degrees in the shade — the cage had been placed so that it would receive the worst of the sun's blistering rays.

I couldn't believe my eyes. Thailand is a civilized country, I thought. How could human beings treat other human beings so inhumanely? When I approached the cage, hoping to offer some kind of help, if only a drink of water, a guard chased me away.

I hurried back to Building Three to tell David and Peter what I had just witnessed. "That's the tiger cage," Peter said. "The guy in the cage was probably caught selling cigarettes. The guards make money on cigarette sales and they get angry if someone skims off their profit."

I went up to my room feeling sick. Thailand, "Land of Smiles", "the real Magic Kingdom", my promised land filled with gentle, loving people was only the face, the image. The real Thailand was just as cruel and inhumane as anywhere else. And here I was, living in its bowels.

March 11, 1989

I had no visitors today, and most of the day was spent pacing back and forth in front of Building Three. Peter occasionally took my mind off my woes with his ramblings about life in "Mahachai", the name given by inmates to Bangkok Special Prison because it faced Mahachai Road.

"Our building was supposed to be for Thais only," Peter said. "Foreigners aren't supposed to be in this prison at all. There have been so many complaints from embassies about conditions here that foreigners are usually shipped out as soon as they receive their charge papers. Whenever the prison commander walks past, all foreigners are supposed to hide."

I gasped. "You mean, the commander doesn't know that there are foreigners here?" I asked incredulously.

"Oh, he knows we're here. It's just the way the Thais do things. If they don't see us, it's like we don't exist. It's part of the Thai attitude. It's all right for anything to happen, as long as it happens out of sight. That was why your case was such a big deal. It was in the newspaper. It was public. Sex with young people is not uncommon. Most Thais have sex at an early age."

"But I didn't create the publicity, the police did," I snapped.

"That doesn't matter. The police can do nothing wrong."

"But we didn't do anything..."

"Come off it!" Peter smiled deprecatingly.

I shot an angry glare at him. He knew instantly I was offended. "Anyway, that doesn't matter," he said. "You're guilty of being responsible for the publicity."

I felt a sudden fury surging through my blood. I was more tense now than when I'd started pacing. I went up to the room cell, seething over Peter's remarks, and stewed in a corner. My whole being was as taut as a violin string. Then I remembered that for a pack of cigarettes, I could get massaged for an hour.

I reached into my rolled-up mat. The cigarette carton was gone. Even the pair of Levis that I had rolled the cigarettes in had been taken. I looked around. Nobody else was there.

I went out into the hallway. "Someone has taken my cigarettes and Levis," I complained to the first person I saw.

"Tell the commander," he said sympathetically.

I continued downstairs and reported my loss to the guard on duty. He just shrugged and threw me an expression which conveyed extreme disinterest, even irritation.

I stomped outside and ran into David. "There are thieves in here," I growled, not realizing the absurdity of my statement.

"Hm, probably," he replied. "This *is* a prison, remember?"

Dejectedly I went back inside, maneuvered through the bodies on the stairway that were hypnotized by the image from Lumpini Stadium, and slunk back to my room. The depression was overwhelming. I laid down and closed my eyes, but I couldn't sleep. I felt so totally powerless. The Levis had been a Christmas present from a woman who was like family to me. They held sentimental value. But it wasn't losing a pair of jeans that upset me as much as a sense that I was losing everything, everything I had been working for "my business, my future, a country I loved, my freedom.

"Why?" I cried beating my fist into the floor. "Why?"

March 13, 1989

Following the National Anthem, several prisoners lined up to go on outside work crews. Most of them weren't work crews at all, but escapes for the wealthy and powerful Thai prisoners. One particularly well-to-do businessman strolled out the front gate every day with a work crew, climbed into a waiting limousine, then returned in the limousine each evening when the work crew was due. Others staggered back in the afternoon so drunk they had to be assisted by fellow prisoners. Yet another, who had been a professional golfer prior to his arrest, left the prison every day with his clubs, played golf all day, then returned in the late afternoon.

I sat glumly in front of Building Three watching the crews depart when a message came for me to report to welfare. I took a number, squatted in the skin-scalding sun for 15 minutes, and at last was called into the visiting area. My niece, Maureen, and her husband, Ken, were waiting on the other side of the second screen.

"Where have you been?" I asked. "Didn't you see my picture in the papers?"

"No," Maureen replied. "We haven't seen any newspapers at all. We found out you had been arrested when we called Kenji. We were at a bungalow in Koh Samui, just relaxing on the beach. How can we help you?"

"Go to the Embassy," I said. "And make them write a letter to get me out of here."

"We'll go there tomorrow. What else can we do?"

"Help Kenji with the Glaxo group." Then I remembered that they were on their honeymoon. "No, don't let this spoil your trip. Forget that."

"Have you told Grandma yet? Do you want me to call her?" Maureen asked.

"No, I don't want her to get worried when there's nothing she can do." I had asked Ron Fry, the Embassy officer who had gotten me to sign the privacy waiver, to call my mother. Kenji hadn't mentioned that she called, so I assumed she was waiting to hear from me. I had also assumed I'd be out on bail and able to do that.

When the bell sounded signaling the end of our visit, I reluctantly bid them farewell, but walked back to Building Three feeling relieved that someone from my family was in Thailand and soon would be helping.

That evening, I looked out through the bars of my window and saw a clear sky and felt the warm air. I knew that only a couple of miles away, the people from Glaxo were boarding a cruise on the Chao Phraya River. I watched the clock and reflected on what they were doing minute by minute. Now they were boarding. Now they were being serenaded by Dan's classical violin. How is the catering? Does the boat look all right? Now they're leaving the dock. Now they're serving dinner. Did Kenji buy enough wine? I was tortured with worry. I had spent so many years here and in San Francisco involved in the planning and meticulous execution of incentive programs that it was part of my soul. And part of my soul died a little that night.

After much tossing and turning, I fell asleep and dreamt that the cruise had been a disaster.

March 14, 1989

Ken went to the U.S. Embassy as soon as the consul office opened for the day. At first, an officer told him that the letter I had asked for would be written immediately. He waited. Nothing happened. As the hours dragged on, the staff in the consular office began to backtrack. They couldn't issue the letter. Someone else would have to write it. When lunchtime arrived, they were still talking in circles. Ken refused to leave.

After lunch, an officer came to the waiting room and told Ken that the staff was trying to figure out how to word the letter so that they couldn't be sued. Finally, mid-afternoon, Ken was given a letter signed by Ed Wehrli, Consul General. The letter stated that there had been no United States government or Embassy involvement in my arrest or incarceration in Thailand. It also stated that no warrant had been issued for my arrest in America. However, the letter continued, unofficially the Embassy had received word that state police in California wished to question me upon my return to the United States and that the Embassy "could not rule out the possibility that there may be a warrant issued for Mr. Raymond in the future."[9]

By the time the Embassy officials handed the letter to Ken, visiting hours were over. Expecting him to return, I had become frantic, pacing nervously all day. I had all my hopes set on being released immediately.

Fifteen hours later, across the ocean in San Francisco, a warrant was issued for my arrest. The warrant was based on an interview that Inspectors Tom Eisenman and Glenn Pamfiloff of the San Francisco Police Department had had with a 16-year-old boy whom I barely knew.

March 15, 1989

Ken arrived at the prison immediately after the National Anthem. The Embassy staff had given him a visitation letter which allowed his entry to the lawyer's room. He handed me the letter from Ed Wehrli and apologized for Maureen not accompanying him. "Is there anything else we can do for you? Is there anything you need?"

"Please go to Puttri's office with a copy of the letter and tell Puttri to get me out of here," I pleaded. "Tell him that I'm angry that he hasn't worked harder for my release. I'm stuck in here while my business is falling apart and it seems like he isn't doing anything."

"I'll go to his office today," Ken assured me. "Do you want us to stay in Bangkok to help?"

I looked at him and played the roll of martyr. "You don't have to stay," I said. "You're on your honeymoon." I didn't really mean it. I desperately wanted them to stay and give me support and help me get out, but I couldn't bring myself to say it. I had been so self-sufficient for 25 years, it probably bordered on arrogance. I was used to being the benefactor. I couldn't face up to the fact that my life had spun this far out of control. "You and Maureen go back to Koh Samui. And don't miss Phuket and Phang Nga, too." I was still the tour guide, showing off the country.

When Ken left and I understood that he and Maureen would return to the south, I wanted to rush after him and beg him not to go. Instead, I walked slowly back to my building and went upstairs to write a letter to Consul General Ed Wehrli.

It turned into a major dissertation. I tried to appeal to his business sense and even recalled how helpful he had been when David Wood had died in 1986. I tried to make the tone of the letter friendly, without conveying too much of the outrage that boiled inside me. I even offered to return to prison if that was what he wanted after I had taken care of the myriad details involved in the dissolution of my business.

I told Werhli the letter he had written would confuse the Thai authorities and that they would not understand his intent. I knew in my heart that his intent was quite clear. He wanted me to remain in prison. I didn't know why, but for the first time, I really understood that. My government, which steadfastly positioned itself as a champion of human rights around the world, was actively working to deny me the basic rights guaranteed to me by the Constitution. The United States government had asked a foreign government to arrest and imprison an American citizen *without due process;* its officials had then lied about requesting such an arrest; and finally had refused to state on what charges they had had him incarcerated.

I finished the letter and put down the pen. I had become so engrossed I hadn't realized day had turned to night. I looked through the bars. Out there where people were free, the Glaxo group was watching a fireworks display.

Six

Tweedle Dee & Tweedle Dum

"A human being's first duty is to think of himself until he has exhausted the subject, then he is in a condition to take up minor interests and think of other people."

— Mark Twain

March 16-31, 1989

No word came from the Embassy. Ed Wehrli ignored my letter. It began to weigh on me that I just might be in prison for a long time. I had always considered myself a humanitarian, supremely interested in the affairs of others. I had believed that Mark Twain's words were simply the satirical quip of a cynic. But now I understood the genius of what he wrote, as well as the folly of my own idealism.

That my willingness to help others was something I practiced only after my own needs had been addressed was one of the most disturbing discoveries of my imprisonment. I found myself so spiritually empty I had nary a thought for the rest of humanity. Only on occasion did I worry about Chat and Nu. I could only muster the energy to care about my own predicament and this sad realization demoralized me all the more.

I began to have peculiar thoughts — because I was gay, it was necessary for me, in this heterosexual world, to forego my desire to help underprivileged children. Because of my sexual preference, I should not offer Chat and Nu a home. If I were a heterosexual, I wondered, wouldn't I be condemned for giving an education and a place to live to disadvantaged girls? Or was there a double standard and a separate set of rules for homosexual men and women? Since I was defined by society solely on the basis of my orientation, I could not also be a caring human being.

The Glaxo program turned out to be a disaster. All the materials needed for their conference had been left at the airport. And while Kenji and Kachon were out tending to details, no one was in the office to take calls. Each time the airport telephoned to inform us of the whereabouts of the Glaxo materials, they got no answer. The stuff sat there until the program ended.

Soon after Glaxo left, some wealthy clients of a client arrived from New York. Although they weren't on an incentive program, I had promised the people at Travelco that I would personally look after them. Travelco had been one of my first clients in San Francisco and I felt a particular obligation to take care of their VIP's. The guests were staying at the Oriental Hotel; then they were to travel to Chiang Mai.

Meanwhile, my lawyer received a copy of the letter that Ken had gotten from the Embassy but Puttri's intransigence and lack of obvious resolve distressed me further. Peter had been talking about his lawyer and I wondered if I should make a change. "Sombattsiri is a crook," he warned, "but in Thailand, you cannot win unless you have a crook as a lawyer. Puttri is one of the only honest lawyers in the country."

"But I *want* an honest lawyer," I argued.

"The next time you see him," Peter said, "ask him how many cases he's won. My lawyer is a snake, but he wins almost every case. You've got to pay off the prosecutor and the judge or you'll lose."

A few days later, Kenji came to report to me that the wealthy guests from New York had refused to pay part of their bill at the Oriental and had booked an earlier flight to Chiang Mai without informing my girls, Lu or Al, apparently to avoid the obligation to them of a large gratuity.

"That does it!" I howled at Kenji. "Go to Siam Legal Aid and tell them that if they don't apply for bail, I'll find another lawyer."

That afternoon, David and I were called to the lawyer's room. Kachon was standing there with two men, one of whom I had met a couple of years earlier in the soi. "He's the lawyer. He say he can hel," Kachon said. "He say here is Thailand. Is not belong to 'merican govermen'. Don' worry. He say he can get you out from the jail. No pobrem, reely! You don' haf to worry abou' 'merican govermen'. Is not contron by 'merican."

As angry as I was with Siam Legal Aid's intransigence, I wasn't quite ready to drop Putrri. I didn't really know what to do. Was Peter right? Did I really need a crooked lawyer? Siam Legal Aid had promised to apply for bail if only the Embassy would give them another letter. But the Embassy had recommended Puttri and maybe they did so because he would do only what they wanted.

"Why don't we ask them to get the boys out of jail," David said. "If they can do that, then we can hire them to get us out."

I turned to Kachon. "Ask them how much it would cost to get Chat, Nu and Thep out of jail?"

Kachon spoke to the lawyers, then said to me, "He haf to ask his boss how much he gonna charge. He come back tomorrow tell you how much."

The next day, the three of them returned. "Sicty tousan baht ($2,400)," Kachon reported.

My heart sank. "Sixty thousand baht!" I cried. "That's outrageous!"

"Becaw the lawyer haf to pay some money to poleet an welfare," Kachon replied.

I didn't know what to do. "I'll think about it and let you know." I got up and left.

David followed me out of the lawyer's room and turned on me with fire in his eyes. "Why didn't you tell them to do it?" he snarled. "We need to get the boys out of jail!"

I agreed. But this was outrageous! Chat, Nu and Thep had done nothing. They were victims, not criminals. Why should we have to pay anything? "Sixty thousand baht..."

Later that afternoon, Kenji came for a visit. "Pay Kachon's soi lawyers to get the boys out," I instructed him.

The lawyers returned with Kachon the next day. "The boys cannot go out becaw welfare he don' tay the money," Kachon reported.

"Get Chat's sister and Nu's mother and tell them to sue the police to force them to release the boys. Tell the lawyers to use the money for that."

"Okay, no pobrem," Kachon responded.

"Sue them for torturing the boys, too!" I added.

"Okay, okay," he said and turned to go. I wasn't sure if he could do what I asked. Still his two lawyers seemed to genuinely care. I hadn't seen Puttri in two weeks and when Voratham came in, all he did was tell me he couldn't apply for bail without a new letter from the Embassy. Yet these two were saying the U.S. couldn't keep me in a Thai prison.

On the morning of March 31st, David and I were called into the lawyer's room once again. As we were taking our seats in front of the screen, Voratham rushed in on the other side. "Bad news," he reported. "A warrant has been issued for your arrest in America. Here is the number of the penal code and the name of the San Francisco District Attorney that you must contact if you have any questions. He held a paper up to the screen. It read 288 (A) and the name Peter Cling. "You have been charged with oral copulation of an 11-year-old boy."

It took me a minute to realize what the man had just said. At first, I thought he meant that a warrant had been issued for David. When I realized it was meant for me, I was so totally stunned I didn't know what to say. Finally I looked up at him and said, "Get hold of Kenji and bring him back with you as soon as possible. Bring all of the records that you have on my case and the case file, as well as the 200,000 baht ($8,000) bail money that you are holding."

He understood that he was being fired and he started to apologize, but I didn't want to talk to him any more. I didn't want to talk to anybody. I stood up and walked out of the room. By the time I arrived at Building Three, I was in tears. I couldn't face anyone. I started to pace back and forth in front of the building. I couldn't focus on anything. I must have acted as if I had gone insane because at once David told me sharply to pull myself together "or they'll think you've lost it and send you to the nut hospital."

How could there be a warrant for my arrest in America? Except for a short visit for a stockholders meeting and to see my mother in October 1988, I hadn't been there for almost two years. What 11-year-old boy had said that I had given him a blow job? Eleven years old, my God! Who did I even know that was 11 years old? How could I find out what this was all about? I was prohibited from communicating with the outside world.

In the meantime, the news media in America, Japan, Europe and Australia repeated the lies and accusations against me as if my guilt were a foregone conclusion. I still could not understand why there wasn't a single journalist — not one reporter from anywhere — interested in what I had to say about the story. The most disappointing account of all appeared in an Asian travel industry magazine written by Imtiaz Muqbil. The story carried the headline "S.I.T.E. Chief Arrested."

Kenji brought a copy to the lawyer's room and handed it to me through the bars when the guard wasn't watching. The article sealed the coffin on my career. Its very existence meant that anybody in the travel industry who may have possibly missed stories in the mass media would certainly get a chance to read about it in the travel press.

Muqbil's story was as misinformed as those appearing in the Thai newspapers, but he carried the untruths even further. He incorrectly stated that I must have known about the impending arrest ahead of time because I had called a competitor and asked him to take over my accounts. Sumate had evidently told Muqbil that I had called, but Muqbil assumed the call had been made *before* my arrest. He obfuscated the issue entirely and appealed to homophobia by reporting that some of my colleagues in the travel industry believed me to be gay. This, of course, had absolutely nothing to do with the issue of my arrest. Nor did his disparagement of Mark Morgan's efforts to raise money for the children's shelter at travel industry functions. The tone of the entire article was vicious. It was more hurtful than the stories in the mass media because it had been written by a colleague, someone I had known for the past couple of years. And he hadn't bothered to hear my side of it either.

I resolved that, if no one else would print the truth, I would. That night, I began to write this book.

April 1-15, 1989

I was called to the lawyer's room which was so crowded with inmates and their attorneys that I couldn't find a seat. Kachon and Kenji appeared with the two soi lawyers whom I had begun to think of as the Thai Tweedle Dee and Tweedle Dum. With the 60,000 baht I had authorized, they were to have obtained releases for Chat, Nu and Thep. They looked dejected. They had come to report that they had failed once more in their attempts to free the boys.

"A warrant has been issued for my arrest in America," I said to Kenji. "How much would these guys charge to take our case?"

Kenji turned to them and asked in Thai. "Three hundred thousand baht," they responded, "to make everything as if nothing happened."

"Three hundred thousand baht is exorbitant!" I objected. "I don't have 300,000 baht."

"They said that they need that much to pay off the police, the prosecutor and the judge," Kenji explained.

I said, "Get me out and I'll borrow the money."

111

They agreed to apply for bail when my next "review date" came up.

As the lawyer from Siam Legal Aid had once explained, my "review date" would come up every 12 days. Then I would go through a meaningless ritual of being ordered to appear in a plaza, where I would have to squat in the hot sun, and await the appearance of a judge who would call out my name and order that I remain incarcerated for another 12 days. They could do this seven times for a period of 84 days before they were required to charge me with a crime.

Like all court functions in Thailand, these "small court" proceedings were held in Thai. When foreigners attended, an Indian man translated what the judge said and asked if there were any questions. Anytime a prisoner actually had the nerve to ask one, he would either be dismissed out of hand or be told that the question would have to be decided by a higher court.

One afternoon as I walked past the welfare building, the vice commander of the prison spotted me. He asked what I was doing. When I told him that I was trying to get some exercise, he beckoned me to follow him. We crossed the main courtyard, walked past the dining hall and entered a door marked "Daeng Six". To the left was a guard post and, beyond it, hundreds of Thai prisoners. Some were manufacturing paper bags, while others were scraping what seemed to be some type of animal hide.

The guards rose to attention when the vice commander entered. He ignored them and continued through the factory. Outside the building, police buses and private cars were being worked on by dozens of prisoner-mechanics. We turned a corner, walked through a barber shop, and into an office.

The vice commander offered me a chair and a cup of tea. I was unprepared for such deferential treatment from a prison official and couldn't imagine what he wanted. Then he said, "Will you teach me

English?" I was flabbergasted. But eager to do something I could feel good about, I readily accepted.

He began to talk to me and asked me to correct his grammar if it was not proper. He told me about his family and his home on the outskirts of Bangkok, and complained about his financial position. I kept thinking he was going to ask for money. I corrected his English and he seemed quite appreciative.

The following day at an appointed time, I returned. This time, the vice commander wanted only to learn the proper names and slang terms for a woman's anatomy. He asked for suggestions on how to go about picking up an American blonde and showed no perception of the sensibilities of a western woman, assuming they were all available for a price.

The rest of the sessions were similarly focused and I felt increasingly uncomfortable with them. However, the ability to wander in and out of another building at will gave me a certain amount of respect from the other prisoners and guards. "I've been in this place for over two years," Peter marveled, "and I've never been allowed into Daeng Six."

In the evening, I studied Thai with Phisan, the man in my room who had worked for C.A.T. and owned the travel company. A rather kind gentle person, he had been sentenced to a year in prison for having accidentally run over a drunk who wandered into the path of his car. It was his bad fortune that the drunk happened to be a general in the Thai army.

The studying and the teaching gave me something real to hang onto — it gave my existence a purpose, for which I previously had no conscious appreciation. When I wasn't studying Thai or writing the notes that would become the basis of this book, I was teaching American songs to other prisoners in the room. Our favorites were "I Wanna Go Home" and "Please Release Me".

Miraculously, the prison held a small library where I found "The Complete Works of William Shakespeare" which I ravenously

113

devoured. *Macbeth* had been my favorite play in high school, but I soon discovered the genius of *Hamlet* while *The Merchant of Venice* showed me that even a genius could be a bigot.

The soi lawyers usually visited with Kenji or Kachon who often came to discuss the upcoming National Travelers Life Insurance incentive program. The new legal team seemed to demonstrate they were genuinely interested in my welfare, something Siam Legal Aid hadn't done.

"Glenda Broderick said that some of her friends told her not to work with us," Kenji reported when everything was ready for National Travelers Life. "But she doesn't believe the stories in the newspaper and sent the money anyway."

I had known Glenda since the 70's when we had worked together at the same tour company in San Francisco. Her unwillingness to swallow the now-common belief that I was a heinous criminal made me wonder if others who knew me well might not have the same reaction. I even allowed myself a fleeting fantasy that, just maybe, I could save my career.

On the evening of April 11, a guard came to the door and told me that I was to report to the courthouse the following morning for a hearing on my bail.

After breakfast, I donned a brown shirt and brown shorts, the "uniform" for court appearances, and went to an area behind the receiving building to stand in line for chains. Shackles were fashioned from steel plates bent around one's ankles by an operator using an enormous crude vise.

I carried the chain itself high enough so that I wouldn't drag it behind me like a dog on a leash. I was herded onto a bus with barred windows, and packed so tightly with other prisoners that my breathing was impeded. The door slammed shut on us like an oven and, in seconds, we were drowning in sweat and the smell of body odor. We lurched forward as the coach began the drive in stop-and-go traffic to the courthouse.

There, we were pushed into a holding cell as putrid and foul-smelling as the one in which I had awaited my transfer to Mahachai. By 1 o'clock, almost everyone had been called to court. Of 80 prisoners, only three were left with me in the holding cell.

A couple more hours passed before a guard finally called my name. I stood up with anticipation, gathered my chains and started down the hall. Because a prisoner had once thrown his shoes at a judge, I was accompanied out of the building in bare feet, across a parking lot, and up the stairs to the second floor. Kachon and one of the soi lawyers were waiting outside a door. The courtroom was filled with desks and, at the rear, the judge — a middleaged Thai man with glasses — sat behind a cluttered one. He motioned me to a seat facing his desk.

"Is your name Steef Raymond, Steephen Raymond, Steephen Douglas Raymond, or Steephen Douglas?" he asked. As Thais only have two names, he was evidently puzzled by my middle name. I proceeded to explain.

After 15 a minute discourse, he still appeared confused and called in my lawyer who began to speak in animated yet reverential tones. He talked so rapidly I couldn't understand a thing, then pulled Consul General Ed Wehrli's letter from my file and repeatedly pointed to it. Finally, the judge turned to me and asked that I sign some papers. I did so.

That night, I couldn't sleep. I hoped to be called for release in the evening, but no one came.

The next day was the Thai New Year, one of the biggest of their holidays. While most of the country was celebrating and National Travelers Life Insurance Company was arriving at the airport, I sat in a cell full of self-pity.

Two days later, on Friday evening, the guards finally summoned me to be bailed. My spirits soared. I gathered my clothes, gave away the rest of my possessions, bid everyone farewell, and went to the reception center.

There I watched other inmates getting processed out. I had no idea why I was being kept — until I was called to sign for my wallet and watch. "FBI want you," the officer said. "You go 'merica." He started to laugh. My heart sank like a stone.

"They won't even let me try to prove my innocence," I thought bitterly. "They accuse me, then take me away and leave the issue unresolved so that the world believes their lies. The bastards!"

I was led through the gates to the prison parking area and ordered into a police pickup. One of my lawyers was waiting for me. When he saw the police escort, he ran up to ask what they were doing. A guard said something to him and climbed in behind me. "Follow us," I yelled.

The pickup drove out of the parking lot, circled the block, and stopped at a police station adjacent to the prison. The guards jumped out, and quickly moved me inside to a cell.

Hundreds of bugs and cockroaches scuttled across the wooden floor and through the cracks in the walls. Seven prisoners sat among them, talking and eating.

My lawyer appeared immediately after they locked me in. He began to argue with the officers who had brought me from the prison. "Din Daeng wants him," I heard one of the men say. The lawyer didn't quite know how to respond, but he promised to return in the morning.

Sometime later, I asked a guard for a drink of water. He told me it would cost. I offered 10 baht. He snapped up the bill, sneered, and threw it back at me. I pleaded with him to take more, but he ignored me. I retreated to a corner and put my head in my hands.

A transvestite in the cell offered some Mekhong whiskey. I thanked him but declined, and instead reached into my bag for a note pad. I spent the night writing letters to the papers suggesting that authorities were trying to cover up the truth by sending me back to America. Then, I sat facing the wall to hide my eyes, and cried myself to sleep from sheer frustration and anger.

In the morning, two officers pulled me from my sleep, handcuffed my hands behind my back, and threw me on the back of a motorcycle. As we raced around corners, I pictured myself getting thrown from the cycle and, with my hands cuffed behind my back, landing on my head.

I arrived shaken but safe at Din Daeng. Inside the station, the officers greeted me with uncharacteristic friendliness. I couldn't understand this change in attitude. One of them, the man who had taken my statement on the morning following my arrest six weeks before, actually offered to buy my lunch. Like an old pal, he gestured for me to join him at the outdoor restaurant adjacent to the station. I meekly followed him and the others to a table.

I was very suspicious. At first I even wondered if they had poisoned my food, a fear allayed only after I saw them eating from the same serving bowls. During the meal, the officers kept glancing at their watches and looking to the driveway, as if they were waiting for someone to arrive. Midway through lunch, a few more police drove up, spotted us, and came to our table.

"How much did you pay?" a commanding officer asked.

"What?" I didn't understand his question. He looked irritated. I recognized him, but couldn't be sure if he was the one who had tortured the boys.

"The lawyers," he growled. "How much do the lawyers want? How much is the bail? How much do you still need to pay?"

"Ask the lawyers," I said.

My reply was not what he was looking for, but I wasn't quite sure what he wanted. He suddenly stomped off. Another turned to the man who had bought my lunch and said, "He needs to get out so that he can get more money from his bank."

The second officer nodded, then stood up and asked me to follow him. We went into the air-conditioned office where he handed me a form written in Thai. "Sign this and you're free to go," he said. "Don't forget you have court next Friday."

I didn't understand what he meant, "You're free to go." I grabbed the pen and scribbled my name. My head was suddenly swimming. I didn't know what the hell was going on and I didn't care. "You're free to go." I burst out of the station and into the street.

"Do you want a taxi?" an officer called out.

"No," I replied. "I just want to walk down the street."

The smells, the sounds, the feel of freedom had never been so exhilirating. I was free and it was *wonderful* to be free! I tossed the notes I had written to the newspapers the night before into the first trash container I passed. And inhaled the air, deeply.

Seven

A Glimpse of Freedom

"Freedom is the oxygen of the soul!"
— Andrei Sakharov

April 15, 1989 to May 4, 1989

I went immediately to my apartment. After looking around to make sure that everything was in place, I tried the office hoping to find Kenji or Kachon. No one was there. I headed for the apartment on the sixth floor that Bob had occupied, making a mental note on the way to inquire about his missing money. Since the theft, Bob had left Thailand and Kenji had moved in. I knocked. The door opened and Kenji stood there. I fell upon him and burst into tears. Some of his friends were visiting and my display of emotion caused them to turn away in embarrassment.

As soon as I was able to compose myself, I sat down on the sofa.

"It's not just happening here," Kenji said. "It's happening in America, too. Some other people have been arrested. It's all because of John Cummings. He got arrested in November and he told the police to arrest others."

I considered what Kenji told me, but it did not make sense. Could I get arrested for anything Cummings said in the U.S.? No, my problem was caused by the Thai police. Of that much, I was sure.

"Kenji, thank you for being here when I needed you," I said in earnest. I didn't know how to express further the appreciation I felt at that moment. Ineptly it came out, "I'm dying for a beer. Will you go with me?"

Although he was exhausted from working the National Travelers Insurance program, he could see I needed to be with a friend. We walked across Phaholyothin Road to Foremost and had a drink. Afterward, I invited him to a movie, but he wanted to call it a night.

When we returned to his apartment, Kachon was there and I talked him into going to see "The Rain Man" with Dustin Hoffman. It was a wonderful film, but I couldn't focus on it. Too much had happened in my own life to escape reality.

Only my body had been freed. They still had my soul. When we got back, I asked Kachon to lock the door from the outside so that if the police came, they would think I wasn't home. I went to bed, but couldn't sleep. My fear of being hauled off in the middle of the night was indelible. `What if they come?' I thought again and again. `If they come through the door, where could I hide?' I climbed into the closet and piled a bunch of blankets over myself. At long last, exhaustion overtook me and I fell to sleep, locked in my apartment and hiding in the closet.

* * *

Ken and Maureen had returned from Koh Samui, so the next morning the three of us met for brunch. I thanked Ken for obtaining the letter from the Embassy and credited him with securing my release. When I described my fear of the police and how I had spent the night in my closet covered in blankets, I started to cry. I surprised myself. I had not realized how fragile I'd become. Or how willing I was to show it.

During my incarceration, one of my competitors had faxed the Thai newspaper articles about my arrest to Joe Vieira, a client from San Diego who had just arrived in Bangkok with his people from KGB radio. I should have been outraged by this stab in the back from a colleague, but I wasn't. When you're in the ring and you get hit 50 times, you don't necessarily remember the 36th blow.

A Glimpse of Freedom

Vieira had written to me after receiving the fax, requesting a meeting at the Royal Orchid Hotel. As emotionally difficult as it was to meet with him, I decided to go through with it.

I arrived at the hotel a few minutes early and spotted him in the lobby having drinks with a Turismo Thai representative. When I walked up to them, Vieira jumped up. "You're early!" he screeched. "Did you do this on purpose?" His reaction caught me by surprise. I interpreted it as a further indication I was no longer a respected colleague. I was now nothing more than an embarrassment.

The Turismo Thai representative excused himself and I sat down. Vieira did not bother offering a perfunctory drink. He made it evident that he simply wanted to sever our relationship as quickly as possible.

I swallowed my disappointment and assured him that my company would do whatever was necessary to assist the transition to another destination management company as expediently as possible. I told him that I didn't want either him or his client to suffer as a result of my personal problems. Then I stood up and excused myself, trying to retain as much dignity as possible. I had expected the meeting to be difficult, but it really drove home the message that things would never be the same for me.

After a second scared and restless night locked in my apartment, I had to find another place to stay. I called Lu, one of the escorts, and asked if I could stay with her for a short while. She lived at Pratunam, less than a mile from Victory Monument, and I thought she was westernized enough to be comfortable with such an intrusion. She welcomed me, but when I moved in, she moved down the hall with Al, another female escort.

The first night, my driver Vic and Lu and Al took me to dinner. Then we went to Al's apartment to play Scrabble. They were doing everything they could to cheer me and I loved them for it, but I couldn't snap out of my state of mind. I was so emotionally devastated I found it impossible to fake a smile, much less concentrate on a board game. Lu and Al continued to invite me for Scrabble, and every night I lost spectacularly, then excused myself early to go to bed.

Soon after my release, my mother called. I assumed she had had news of my situation from either the Embassy or the media. Instead, she had called merely to reconfirm Ken and Maureen's return flight. I think I shocked her when I apologized for all the worry I must have caused her. She didn't know what I was talking about. Ron Fry, the officer from the Embassy who had promised to telephone her the day he obtained my signature on the Privacy Act waiver, did not follow through. Instead, he and other Embassy officials had left it to my mother to discover my plight by reading some outlandish account in the press. Fortunately, she never did. And though ABC had carried the story in the San Francisco Bay Area, neither she nor any of her friends had watched the news that night.

The following evening, I joined Ken and Maureen at a Mexican restaurant near Patpong for a farewell dinner. We bid each other adieu and they left on a tuk tuk for their hotel.

In the past, anytime I was in the Patpong area at night, I would have visited one of the gay bars. Patpong was essentially a legalized red-light district with two types of clubs — those with bar girls or bar boys for sale, where a "john" paid the bar for the prostitutes, then, later "tipped" them — and those similar to American clubs that simply provided a common place to meet singles at inflated drink prices.

If I did end up spending time with someone, I usually rented a hotel room for a couple of hours. There was just too much activity at the apartment and I preferred my privacy.

But when Maureen and Ken left, I simply found a taxi and went home. I had no desire to visit any of these places. A 100-baht drink was a luxury I could no longer afford. The previous two months had changed my life radically.

I struggled to retain some semblance of normality. Although emotionally I was not prepared to work with the National Travelers Life group and did not see them off, Kenji and Kachon handled it well. Two Unisys incentive programs were due to arrive soon and I began spending most of my time in the office working on the details of the itineraries.

A couple of days after my release, Kenji took me aside to tell me that David Groat had told him where to find nearly $2,000 he had hidden in a box in the apartment on the sixth floor. Without actually suggesting that Groat had stolen Bob's money from the safe, Kenji made it clear he believed that to be the case. It was almost the exact amount of cash in U.S. currency that had disappeared.

My stomach turned over. It was David who first suggested we go to the police station for fingerprinting. Was it to draw suspicion away from himself? I didn't want to suspect him but who else *could* it have been? No one but he and I had keys to the safe.

I again was overcome by a feeling of helplessness. I was certain I had brought nothing but misery to everyone surrounding me, and especially to the boys. It was as if I were swept up in a dark dream, just fl-oating from occurrence to occurrence. Nothing felt real.

But one afternoon, Chat's mother, Nu's mother and I caught a bus at Victory Monument for the two-hour ride to Pakred children's prison. When the boys appeared in front of me, I fell apart. I don't know how a father feels knowing he has let his kids down but I imagined what I was feeling was pretty close. They were too embarrassed by my emotional outburst to speak, but at least they knew how I felt. And the message somehow was communicated that I would continue to try to get them released.

A sympathetic prison counselor allowed me to give Chat and Nu enough money to pay for the upcoming semester and gave her word that they would be permitted to attend school again.

After they left the visiting area, an older man appeared. He identified himself as the supervisor. "The boys tell me that you are a good man," he said in English. "Will you continue to take care of them when they are released?"

"I hope so," I replied, "but after all of this is over, I don't know if I'll be able to."

"They love you," he said. "They want to go back and live with you. We know now they are only here because of the police. The police at Din Daeng are no good!" I was so grateful for his words that I had to bite my lip to keep from losing control. This was one of the few times I'd felt validated about anything in months. Finally someone in an official position saw what I so desperately needed the world to see.

* * *

The first of the two Unisys programs was scheduled to come to Bangkok several days after my release. When my entire staff of six people arrived at the office dressed in their company uniforms; when the hostess with her flower garlands was busily arranging them for transfer to the airport; when everyone was scurrying preparing the beer and soft drinks for the arrival transfer, my adrenalin jolted me out of my malaise. Everything suddenly seemed normal, as if the events of the past two months had been a terrible dream and reality was there for the taking, just like it had always been.

My escape, however, was short-lived. While the hotel and transfers had been prepaid, the client contacted another tour operator to take care of the planned activities. When we learned that the lucrative part of the program had been given away, the nightmare and how it was affecting my life and everyone around me hounded me again.

Soon after the departure of the first program, a client and longtime friend from Universal Skytours, the incentive house responsible for the Unisys programs, called to tell me that his wife and the wife of the Unisys meeting planner were coming to Bangkok. I mustered all of the courage that I could muster and went to the airport to meet them.

We had arranged for them to stay at the Shangri-La Hotel, and when I arrived there the next morning to take them for a cruise of the canals, the hotel's catering manager spotted me. I watched as he dashed behind a pillar, then peeked out from the other side, astonished at seeing me. When I caught him watching me, he turned quickly and scurried off in the other direction.

The two ladies were very pleasant. I thoroughly enjoyed the four days that I spent with them. They acted as if they knew nothing of my recent predicament and I certainly didn't volunteer the experience. I did say that their program would be the final one my company would handle in Thailand. When they asked why, I skirted the issue, but indicated that I had some problems with corrupt police officials. Otherwise, I did my best to maintain the glittering image and to pretend that I was still in control of my fate. I think I even had myself fooled.

I was scheduled in court on the Friday following my release. I appeared with Kachon and one of the soi lawyers. The three of us sat in the visitors area discussing my case when, suddenly, I realized that there had been a communication breakdown. My lawyer hadn't understood that a warrant had been issued for my arrest in America after Ed Wehrli's letter was written. I jumped up and quickly left the courthouse. The lawyer was baffled by my sudden behavior, and asked what I was doing.

"He doesn't even know what's happening!" I cried to Kachon. "Tell him that I'm going to wait in the restaurant in front of Wat Pra Keow until I'm sure the police aren't going to re-arrest me." A little while later, Kachon found me and reassured me that all was well. Everything had been extended for 12 days. I simply had to sign a paper acknowledging that I would return on May 4th.

The realization that my own lawyers didn't understand what was going on was unsettling. "Tell them to come to the office, so that we can discuss everything. I don't want any more mixups," I said to Kachon.

I added 50,000 baht ($2,000) to the 60,000 I had previously given the attorneys when they arrived later that afternoon. As usual, Kachon translated. Afterwards, I felt much better about their grasp of the issue and was confident they would do a good job.

The second Unisys program arrived a week after the first. I went to the airport with the staff to greet the group. An escort accompanying them had called earlier from Singapore and insisted to Kenji that she be allowed to set the prices of optional activities. I wanted to meet her and make sure she was happy, even though I knew that Universal Skytours had approved the activity schedule and she did not have the authority to change it.

Kenji went to the Regent Hotel to make sure everything had been properly arranged. When he arrived, he met with the Director of Sales, Malcolm MacKenzie, a colleague from S.I.T.E., and told him that I would shortly be arriving with the group. Malcolm collared me just after I walked in the door. "What is this all about?" he asked. "Come into my office and tell me." I dutifully followed him in and repeated my oft-stated denial. "What do you plan to do now?" he asked.

"I don't know," I said. I really didn't. I couldn't think past the Unisys program. I had flirted with the idea of trying to keep my business alive by doing legitimate night club tours, but that would be a difficult venture at best. Lu, Joi, Al, Kenji and the others had no idea of what a legitimate night club tour might entail. Bangkok had a number of Jazz Clubs and live entertainment night spots, but no one had ever attempted a night club tour of anything except sex clubs. If anyone mentioned night clubs in Bangkok, everyone thought Patpong or Soi Cowboy.

The second Unisys program was going much more smoothly than the first. But on the third evening, during a cocktail party on the terrace at Sala Rim Naam, which was to be followed by a dinner and show, Kenji reported to me that the accompanying escort had negotiated on her own with the jewelry store. She had told the shopkeeper to make sure all the commissions from the sales went to her. Normally, commissions were split among all the escorts.

126

As everyone was going in for dinner, I pulled the woman aside and explained to her that all escorts split commissions. "But they don't need the money as much as I do," she had the temerity to say. "They don't have car payments and house payments." Of course my escorts had just as many financial obligations as she did, but her arrogance and insensitivity was so odious that I refused to argue. I simply decided I would visit the store the next day and tell the owner the commissions should be split among my company escorts and this woman.

Because of what lay in wait for me, that was not to be.

Eight

Liars and Lawyers

*"The first and last aim of the law and
lawyers is to defeat justice."*

— Mark Twain

May 4, 1989 to June 21, 1989

T he morning after the dinner at Sala Rim Naam, I appeared for
my scheduled hearing. Mykel, a friend whom I had met in San
Francisco a few years earlier was passing through Bangkok
and agreed to accompany me. The soi lawyers met us at the
courthouse and told us to wait in the restaurant until I was called. So
we waited. The morning turned into afternoon. And we continued to
wait. I was getting antsy about heading off the greedy Unisys escort at
the jewelry shop.

At 4 PM, the lawyers finally led me into a small courtroom. The
judge was absent, but a clerk called me to the front, told me to report
again on the 23rd, and asked me to sign a paper. As I was signing,
one of a team of three officers handed my lawyer a charge sheet, then
walked up behind me, grabbed my arm and clasped a handcuff to my
wrist.

My heart jumped to my throat. I looked at my lawyer and a scream
escaped my lips. "Why?" I cried, frantically searching the faces of the
policemen. They were laughing. They thought my outburst
humorous. The officer who had handcuffed me shoved me into a
chair. A minute later, he snapped the other bracelet on a Thai man and
ordered us to follow him.

I dragged myself into the waiting room and looked at my friend. He smiled. I held up my arm to show I had been re-arrested. "Oh no!" he exclaimed. "What happened? Do you want me to take your things?" I started to give him my wallet which contained over $1,000 in cash and traveler's checks, but the guard shoved me along.

As we headed to a holding cell, the guard said, "U.S. police want you. Every day we talk. Every day they send telex."

I was put in the same holding cell I had previously inhabited before my transfer to Bangkok Special Prison.

"Steve," someone yelled to me from another holding cell. I looked up and saw David Groat. He was smiling from ear to ear. "What happened?" he asked.

"I don't know."

Just then, the lawyers and my friend Mykel appeared at the window across the hall. "We talk to judge. Everything okay. One hour you go out. Just wait," one of them yelled.

The lawyers disappeared, then returned a few minutes later. "Bail now 300,000 baht ($12,000). You have?"

I had already given my Tweedle Dee and Dum legal team 60,000 baht to bail the boys, which they had not been able to do; added 50,000 baht to cover their fees; and put up 200,000 baht to bail me three weeks earlier. "No, I don't have another 100,000 baht!" I shouted. Then I looked at my friend. "Do you have a hundred thousand baht?" I implored. "I'll pay you back."

"I'm sorry, I don't have anything," he said.

I began pleading frantically. "If I don't get out now, I won't get out until after the trial. I know it."

"I'm sorry," he said again.

Where was I going to get another 100,000 baht?

"Do you have any cash on you?" David asked.

"About 3,000 baht, plus some American money," I said.

"Hide some in your shoe," he instructed. "Give it to me inside."

"Inside", he said, meaning back in prison. As unbelievable as it seemed, the nightmare was going to recur. Against my will, I was going to act in my own worst interest. With each receding moment, reality became more distant and irretrievable. Without knowing what I was doing, I stuffed a thousand baht into my shoe.

"Line up," the officer growled in Thai. Slowly I moved to comply, repeating the process I had gone through two months earlier. I assumed David had arranged with the prisoner who was checking clothing not to check my shoes. Unfortunately, it was one more assumption I shouldn't have made.

My shoes were, indeed, searched and the inmate who found the secreted cash beamed as he handed the cash to an officer, who started yelling at me. "You go soi!" he screamed, referring to the building where they chain you to the wall. Another officer went to fetch Joe, who told them that I didn't know what I was doing. Since they knew I had been in before, that didn't fly. Joe took me aside. "This will cost you some money," he said.

"How much?" I asked.

"Five hundred baht."

I agreed to pay the bribe and suddenly it was as if the incident hadn't occurred. I was dispatched to Building Four with Joe and the rest of the new prisoners. But I was furious at David for encouraging me to hide currency and at myself for listening to him. All he could say in response was "I thought you'd hide it better".

Because we arrived on Thursday at the beginning of a holiday weekend, processing was delayed until the following Monday. Thus we remained with Joe throughout the weekend. This was very unfortunate for two retarded men who were shackled to each other with their hands behind their backs. They were kept like that for three days and not permitted to eat or drink. When Joe and the guards were preoccupied, I managed to sneak them some food, water and Coca-Colas from the commissary. But I was truly afraid for my own safety.

Joe was as friendly to me as he had been when I first arrived in March. Every day he invited me for coffee and for lunch and dinner. The first night, he told me that David and I would be moved to Khlong Prem Prison at Lardyao because we had received our charge papers, "unless you pay the guards a bribe to keep you here."

"Ask Kenji for 6,000 baht," David said to me, "otherwise, they'll send us to Lardyao. Peter says it's much worse there." I started to hedge about paying money for an obscure benefit, particularly since the money would go to my oppressors. I even resented David's insistence. "After all," I reasoned, "it wasn't his money."

I had visitors the following afternoon. Kenji and Kachon appeared, joined by the entire staff — Lu, Al, Joi, Vic, and two additional freelance hostesses — who had just come from seeing off the Unisys group at the airport. They crowded around the screen to tell me that the Unisys escort had learned of my arrest and had grabbed the entire $8,000 in jewelry commission money, leaving them with nothing. I knew that she would report my incarceration to Universal Skytours, and there was nothing I could do about it. My business was finished, so it didn't really matter any more. But I felt rotten for the girls who had worked hard and were bilked of more than 16,000 baht ($650) each.

After the holiday weekend, Kenji came back with the soi lawyers. "I need 6,000 baht for a bribe to keep us here," I told him. Mahachai (Bangkok Special Prison) was much closer for everyone than Khlong Prem at Lardyao, and I would try to make it as easy for Kenji, Kachon and the lawyers as I could. Unisys was the last program for which we had received deposits before my arrest. All other groups had cancelled, and no more payments would be coming in. I wanted to close the office honorably. "Take the 200,000 baht for my bail and pay the bills," I told Kenji.

The lawyers continued to insist that I could bail out again for 300,000 baht, Finally, I asked Kenji to call my mother and see if she would contact friends in America who might be willing to help. "Tell

131

her to call Warren," I said. Warren had been my first employer in the travel industry and often told me that I was like a son to him. By his own admission, he was worth millions of dollars. If anybody could afford to loan $12,000 for a year or two, he could. I had called Warren in April when I was out on bail, but he insisted that he was on his way out the door, headed for three weeks in Europe. "We can talk about it when I get back," he had said.

Kenji relayed the message to my mother and she telephoned him. His terse reply was that he had discussed my request with his wife and, together, they decided that my case had generated too much publicity. They did not want to get involved.

I was assigned my former room cell in Building Three and asked for the return of the things I had given away when I left.

Soon after, anticlimactically, Chat and Nu were released from children's prison and moved back to my apartment. Kenji moved in to supervise them, making sure they returned to school. I suspect the reason they were finally freed had to do with pressure on authorities from their parents, perhaps the lawyers, and perhaps, to some smaller degree, the brief contact I had had with the children's prison supervisor. Unfortunately, Thep's father never showed to sign the proper papers and the poor kid had to remain there. I asked Kenji to see what we could do about it.

Once they registered for the new semester, Chat and Nu came to visit. It was great to see them out and free, really the first good thing to happen since the start of this nightmare.

My re-arrest made me realize that my lawyers didn't really know what they were doing. They had assured me nothing would happen unless I were found guilty during the trial. Then, the week following my re-arrest, they called me to the lawyer's room to ask what I thought of the charge.

"What charge?" I asked. "You were handed the charge sheet, but you never gave it to me. Where is it? What have I been charged with? Give me a copy and I'll get someone to translate it!"

They just shrugged. They had come to discuss my charge, but they hadn't brought it with them. A week later, Kenji brought one that was nearly illegible. I took it to one of my friends within the prison and asked for a translation. Finally, two-and-a-half months after my arrest, following the big police press conference and front page stories that suggested I had been involved with child pornography, pedophile sex tours, and operating a child sex and prostitution ring, I learned that I had been charged with a single count of masturbating Nu.

The next time I saw my lawyer, only Tweedle Dee appeared. I asked what they needed to fight the case. "Two hundred and fifty thousand baht more," he said.

"I know what your fee is," I snarled at him in Thai. "I mean what information do you need? What do you need to fight the case?"

He looked at me as if I hadn't understood him. "Three hundred thousand baht," he said this time.

My first court appearance had been set for the 23rd of May. Again, I had to dress in a brown shirt and shorts with my ankles chained, and ride the caged bus to the courthouse.

On this occasion, Tweedle Dum showed up without his other half. The two evidently hadn't spoken following Tweedle Dee's visit the previous day because the first thing T. Dum asked for was a postponement. He told the judge I hadn't yet chosen an attorney. And he didn't know how right he was! His request for a delay, after I stressed that my re-arrest had changed things and that I wanted to expedite my case, was the final straw.

The next time Kenji came to visit, I told him to contact the Australian Peter Bailey's attorney, Sombattsiri Nabadalung. The trial hadn't even begun and I had already gone through two law firms and 140,000 baht.

Peter had warned that Sombattsiri was a crook, but I had decided that if I was going to hire a crook, at least I'd hire a competent one. I had given up hope that I could find an honest law firm to win a court case in Thailand. Everything that had happened since my initial arrest

133

indicated that the entire system operated on corruption and nothing was done unless one joined the parade. Honesty in Thailand was not the best policy. It didn't even seem like a viable option.

One day in late May when David and I were exercising in front of the building, word came that the Embassy had sent someone to see us. It had been almost three months since my impassioned pleas to talk to an Embassy representative and I had given up hope on that score too.

David grabbed me and said, "Don't say anything. Treat them the same as you would cops."

"I won't say anything." I intended to let them do all the talking.

We entered the lawyer's room and took seats. Two middleaged women came in from the other side of the screen and sat down. One introduced herself as Marcia Pixley. The other was introduced as "just a friend who came along to keep me company." David then introduced himself and Marcia turned to her friend, gesturing toward me and said, "And *this* is Steve Raymond."

I was taken aback. I hadn't really prepared myself for open hostility. I thought Embassy people would be more subtle, but Marcia made her feelings obvious. She threw me off guard and bruised my sensitive ego so much that I overreacted. I wanted her to like me, so that she would question the validity of the accusations against me. My resolve not to say anything quickly crumbled and I gushed forth with a barrage of information, intended to elicit sympathy.

David sat in stunned silence as I gave Marcia all the details of my case, the location of my passport, the date of my next court hearing, and even my plan to have my lawyers delay court proceedings and keep me in Thailand until I could learn the details of the charge against me in America. Once David tried to kick me to shut me up, but to no avail. It was like a dam had burst. I wanted desperately for someone to know that we were not guilty and had not done any of the things we had been accused of doing.

When we finally walked out of the lawyer's room, David began a tirade of verbal abuse. "You fucking idiot! Are you fucking nuts?" he screamed. "She represents the enemy! You only tell her what you *have* to tell her. Nothing more!"

I considered what he said and felt rather stupid. On the other hand, I asked myself, how could I think that the Embassy and the United States government were not my allies?

I already knew that Embassy officials had done all they could to make my situation more difficult. I knew in my heart that their actions had been reactions, a personal revulsion over the alleged cause of my arrest. It probably never dawned on them that the accusations were untrue. Or that they were treating me as guilty until I could prove myself innocent.

In short, I knew David was right, but I didn't want to accept that he was right. I wanted to believe what I had learned in civics classes that the U.S.A. really did stand for human rights and liberty and justice for all.

Because I had naively revealed to Marcia Pixley my original strategy of delaying the case, it wasn't long before the Embassy dispatched a letter to the court asking that it be rushed. I stupidly gave her the whereabouts of my passport, and the Embassy sent someone to Din Daeng Police Station to confiscate it, thereby insuring that I could not be bailed out again. The U.S. government wanted to dig my grave, and I gave its representatives a shovel.

Kachon succeeded in contacting Sombattsiri, who came to see me at the prison. He was a short bug-eyed little man with a round face and a nervous energy, more than a little reminiscent of the late actor Peter Lorrie. I asked how much he needed as a retainer. "Thirty thousand baht," he answered. That figure sounded refreshingly reasonable, so I instructed Kenji to give him fifty thousand, assuming that would take care of him for a good part of the trial.

Sombattsiri's English was good and he assured me that he was quite competent. "I used to be the top prosecutor in the government," he said. "My brother is one of the top policemen in the country." He was making the point that he had the connections if I had the money. I wondered about all the poor people in Thailand who had no political connections. Were they always found guilty? I surmised that the wealthy, influential men in my building must have crossed people even wealthier or more influential. I also suspected, however, that none had been as wealthy and influential as my own adversary, Uncle Sam.

My next court session was scheduled for June 15th. Sombattsiri had 10 days to prepare and said he would be spending them working full time on my case. The following afternoon, he returned to the prison with my personal bank book. "What are you doing with that?" I asked flabbergasted.

"Kenji gave it to me because there wasn't enough money left in the company account," he answered. I was dumbstruck! Although I hadn't yet received a financial accounting, I calculated that after paying all the bills, the company account should have held twice what I had authorized Sombattsiri to receive. I was upset that Kenji had not only failed to provide me with the records, but that he had given Sombattsiri my personal bank book. I reluctantly signed a withdrawal slip and he left with it after reassuring me.

I had kept both Kenji and Kachon on the payroll and hoped to continue with at least one of them until my trial was completed. But if all of my company funds were disappearing, I wouldn't be able to do even that.

Although newspapers were banned inside the prison, my room leader, a former Thai military officer, received a Thai newspaper every day. However, by the time the news was read, passed on, and translated by someone who might not speak English well, it was even more distorted than it was when first printed in the newspapers.

For example, when the Chinese government crushed the student demonstrations in Tiananmen Square, we heard that Taiwan had declared war on China, had bombed Beijing, and was attacking with a naval force.

At about the same time, some Thai workers had been picked up in Singapore for illegally working there. For punishment, they were beaten with canes. The Thai newspapers and television networks made the incident the headline story of the day and the Thai government — putting on its public face — accused Singapore of brutality and barbarism.

The very same day, in Bangkok Special Prison, a prisoner fell asleep under a table and didn't wake up in time to report for lockup. When he was discovered, the guards beat him into unconsciousness. By the time they were finished "teaching him a lesson", he was a bloodied pulp, had undoubtedly suffered internal bleeding, and had at least one broken bone. The following morning, as a "humanitarian gesture", the two-faced Thai government sent a navy ship to Singapore to pick up the Thai nationals who had been treated so "brutally" by Singapore.

On June 14th, the day before my court appearance, Sombattsiri returned with Kachon to ask for additional funds. Kenji had told him that we had just received a 30,000-baht check as final payment from one of the programs we handled in April, and he wanted it. I was incredulous. We had not had a single court session and Sombattsiri was coming back for more money. But even more unbelievable was that Kenji would continue to tell him about my company and personal finances. I wanted to give him a tongue-lashing but, for this at least, Sombattsiri's presence was all too constant.

When I tried to talk about the case, he refused to discuss anything except the check. I smoldered. I was stuck and he knew it. Tomorrow was the beginning of my trial and he represented my only hope. Sure, I could have looked for another attorney. But that would take time. And where would I begin looking? It wasn't as if I could dig through the yellow pages.

Reluctantly, counter to good common sense, I signed the check over to him while demanding to know if he had given Chat and Nu assurances they could tell the truth in court without fear of reprisals.

"I was planning to talk to the boys today," he said without a shred of guilt.

"You mean you haven't talked to them yet?!"

He told me that he planned to go to my apartment with Kenji and meet with the boys when they returned from school.

"Have you talked to the boys' parents?" I asked. "Do you know if the prosecutor plans to call them to testify?"

"It's standard," he said. "The prosecutor will call the boys, the parents, and the police."

"You promised that you'd talk to the prosecutor. You said you were going to take him to lunch. Have you talked to him?"

He ignored my question. "We have to go now," he said, "so that we can meet the boys when they get home." At that, he and Kachon got up. I watched them walk out of the room, shook my head, and slowly returned to my building.

The following day, I went through the whole process of dressing, being chained and waiting in the holding cell. I was eventually summoned and made to squat in front of a desk. I looked out a window, hoping to see Chat, Nu, their mothers, Kenji or Kachon. Then I heard my name. I picked up my chains and dragged them into the small courtroom.

Nu was sitting with the prosecutor behind a table on the left. He was looking down at the floor and he refused to look up. "Nu," I called out. He looked up briefly, shot a glance at the prosecutor, shook his head, and looked back down.

Chat's mother came over and put her hand on mine, as a gesture of support. "What's wrong with Nu?" I asked. She just shrugged and walked out. Then Sombattsiri sat down alongside me. "I'm going to ask for a postponement," he said. "I don't know what Nu is going to say."

"Haven't you talked to him?" I asked incredulously.

"Not yet," he said. "Nu went to a friend's house after school yesterday, so I didn't get to see him."

The judge accepted his request for a postponement and set the date of the next hearing for June 22nd, a week later. I returned to the prison dismayed by my inability to find a decent lawyer.

When Kachon and Kenji came to visit, I elicited a commitment from them to press Sombattsiri. I was still upset with Kenji over my bank book, but I had to remind myself he was young and naive and I couldn't afford to alienate anyone who was trying to help me.

Believing that the boys would, indeed, tell the court of their torture at the hands of the police, I asked Kachon to contact the newspapers and have them attend the next court session. Kachon knew a reporter at Thai Rath and I was anxious for an impartial journalist. He promised to contact him and to do what he could to make sure Sombattsiri was prepared for the next session.

A few days later, Sombattsiri appeared in the lawyer's room. "I need 200,000 baht," he reported.

"Two hundred thousand baht," I choked. "What on earth for?" He had already robbed me of nearly 100,000 and had gone to court but once to ask for a postponement because he had not been prepared.

He looked at me with a straight face and said, "I need to pay the boys for their testimony and I need to pay to get some witnesses."

"What!?" I couldn't believe my ears. This man obviously hadn't even read the details of my case, nor had he talked to Kachon or Kenji since committing — nearly three weeks earlier — to "work full time" on my case for 30,000 baht. "You don't need to pay the boys, goddammit, all you have to do is assure them that the police won't hurt them if they tell about the torture. They love me. I know they do. And you don't have to pay for witnesses. I have all the witnesses you need who will testify on my behalf." My anger was so intense that my eyes became glassy and reddened. "You're not getting any more money from me until I get some positive results!"

I stormed out of the lawyer's room convinced there was no such thing as justice in Thailand.

* * *

139

> *"Governments show how successfully men can be imposed upon, even impose on themselves, for their own advantage."*
> **— Henry David Thoreau,**
> ***On the Duty of Civil Disobedience***

June 22, 1989 — August 4, 1989

Although I didn't know it at the time, June 22nd was to be a pivotal day. As chains were clamped to me and I was herded on and off a bus and tossed in a holding cell at the courthouse, I still wasn't sure if Sombattsiri had talked to Chat and Nu or if the newspapers would cover the proceedings.

Again I was forced to squat in front of a desk while I waited for a deputy. Thirty minutes later, one appeared. I stood, gathered my chains, and followed him barefoot through the guard's station and upstairs.

I entered a much larger court room — about 50 feet long by 30 feet wide — than in previous appearances. Five people whom I did not recognize were seated on benches in the rear. I hoped they were reporters.

The prosecutor appeared with his assistant, donned his robe and sat behind a table opposite me. Then Sombattsiri walked in, set his briefcase down, and took out his robe.

"Did you get a chance to talk to Chat and Nu?" I asked.

"Yes, yes," he said impatiently. "I took them to my house last night so that the prosecutor wouldn't be able to get to them and scare them. I told them that the police couldn't do anything else to them. Don't worry. Everything is okay."

The judge entered and took his seat behind a raised desk. A court recorder followed and sat to the right at a small table with an antiquated typewriter.

The judge asked my lawyer and the prosecutor if they were prepared, then instructed the prosecutor to call his first witness. Nu's father entered the courtroom. He was unsteady and I knew instantly he had been drinking. The prosecutor asked if he knew that I had a sexual relationship with his son.

"I don't know anything about that," he responded. "The first I knew that there was a problem was when I read about it in the newspaper, so I went to the Din Daeng Police Station to find my son." He continued by telling the court that Nu had been happy living with me and that he was one of the best students in his class.

"Did you go into Mr. Raymond's apartment to visit Nu?" the prosecutor asked.

"I went to his apartment a couple of times to do some work for him," he replied.

After Sombattsiri asked a couple of questions, Nu's father was dismissed. Instead of taking a seat in the courtroom, he asked to be excused so that he could get a drink. He returned to the courtroom a few minutes later.

The judge told the prosecutor to call the next witness. Nu timidly entered the courtroom and was instructed to stand behind the podium in the center, facing the judge. After pledging to tell the truth, he looked at the prosecutor.

I could only understand part of what was being said, but I wasn't really trying. I was so angry that a good kid like Nu was being made to go through this indignity that tears welled up in my eyes.

I wanted to scream. Then Nu suddenly turned and pointed at me. I tried to control my emotions and listen to his testimony, but I couldn't. The prosecutor completed his cross-examination.

Sombattsiri picked up his notes and stood in front of Nu, then asked Nu to describe his treatment by the police at Din Daeng. A shy boy, Nu spoke so softly that the judge asked him to speak up in order to be heard. He recounted the incident in detail, stating that the police had picked him up at his school, taken him to the Din Daeng Station, forced him to undress, then applied electric shock to his genitals and told him they would continue until death if he refused to sign their statement. He said he signed the statement only because he had been forced to do so. He said that he loved me and that I was very kind to him.

When Nu completed his testimony, Chat was brought into the courtroom. He was angry. "I love Khun Steve," he said. "He's like a father to me. The Din Daeng police shocked me with electricity so that I would sign their statement." Then, during the cross examination by Sombattsiri, Chat continued, "He didn't run a sex tour business. I worked for him in the office and I helped with the luggage truck when his groups arrived."

I could understand Chat much more clearly. I knew that he was releasing some of the anger that had built up over the past four months. He was not behaving at all like the demure, quiet boy I had known in February.

Kachon had always been dilatory. He often arrived at the office late, but when it was extremely important that he be on time, he had always come through. Yet he was tardy today for what seemed to me the most important assignment I had ever given him. He and another man entered the courtroom when Chat had finished his testimony. The man with Kachon was the reporter from Thai Rath. He had missed all of the testimony.

My anger was visible. I glared at Kachon and again tears clouded my eyes. I had been constantly thwarted in my attempts to get the truth known.

Fortunately, the judge read the witnesses' statements at the conclusion of the session. It did not have the dramatic impact of hearing the testimonies from the boys, but it was better than nothing. I could only hope it would sufficiently motivate the reporter.

Following the court session, I was returned to Bangkok Special Prison. A couple of hours later, a directive was sent to the commander of my building and I was called to see him. He explained, as I squatted, that he had been instructed by the commander of the prison to lock me up. "You have a new case in America," he said. "The U.S.

government says that you are a security risk, so we can't let you leave the building during the day. You must remain inside."

"What? What new case?" But the commander had no answers, only orders that I could no longer exercise outdoors, go to the commissary for food, or visit Daeng Six to teach English to the vice commander.

That afternoon, David Lyon, who had replaced Ed Wehrli as Consul General at the Embassy, wrote a directive revoking my United States passport.

The following day, my room cell leader brought me a tiny article that appeared on the bottom of page 8 in Matichon newspaper. It mentioned that Chat and Nu had testified about the police torture and concluded with a short, terse comment about the inefficacy of the police actions. Nothing was printed in Thai Rath or the Bangkok Post, or the others.

Through handwritten letters to the Embassy and verbal messages via Marcia Pixley, I continually requested an explanation of the charges against me in the United States. When I confronted Marcia she said she was not authorized to say anything about it. Again, this struck me as straight out of Kafka's *The Trial*. When I said as much, she agreed to bring in someone who could explain, and even wrote me a letter in July to assure me that someone would come within the month. No one ever did.

During one visit Marcia made a cavalier remark about Bangkok Special Prison looking like a country club in comparison to Khlong Prem. Her comment made me feel like inviting her for a prolonged stay at the "country club" — you know, to kind of get her input from the inside. On the one hand, I supposed it was fortuitous I had paid the guards to keep from being transferred. On the other, I wondered why, if this prison was so much better, had foreign governments vigorously protested the conditions here and why the Thai authorities had since been so diligent about moving foreigners to Khlong Prem?

On June 29th, Marcia handed me the letter from David Lyon which informed me that my passport had been revoked. The reason given for the revocation was the issuance of the California State warrant on March 14th. Yet the Code of Federal Regulations that had been copied and presented to me along with the letter specifically stated that passports *could only be revoked based on federal warrants* of arrest, not state warrants. The regulations also stated that I could appeal the revocation, if I so desired. I sent Consul General Lyon a letter requesting a hearing on my passport revocation.

In July, Marcia came to the prison with a man named Lowell Strong who identified himself as an FBI agent. I asked him to explain the details of the charge against me, but he refused. "Your charge is a State of California matter," he said. "I am a federal agent, so I cannot comment on it. There is no federal warrant for your arrest... yet," he said ominously. Marcia looked surprised at his last comment.

Strong began to talk about my return to prison in the United States. After recalling David Groat's horror stories, I told him that I'd rather be in a Thai jail. "We're going to take you back," he said flatly.

"Not if I don't want to go back," I snapped as I stood up and walked out of the lawyer's room. I was sick of being pushed around and having my life trampled on by people who would not know the truth if it stood up and hit them in the face.

"You shouldn't have said that," David castigated me after I told him what had happened. "Don't tweak them. Act like you're going to do what they want. What you did was dangerous. They're the enemy and they're holding all the cards."

Again, I knew he was probably right, but I really didn't know how to respond. I wished that I had an American lawyer to help me through this mess.

Just after the visit from the FBI, a prisoner arrived in Building Four covered with bruises. He had been charged with raping, then killing a three-year-old girl! The police arrested the man in the Khlong Toey slum, then beat him until he confessed he had murdered the girl while high on heroin. Deputies told prisoners what the man had been accused of doing. They set upon him and beat him senseless.

When he regained consciousness, Joe and the guards beat him again and kept it up throughout the night. The next day, the man was transferred to Building Two and chained to the wall. The following week, the inmates in his room bragged that they had burned off his pubic hairs with a cigarette lighter. When this sadistic act had been completed, 14 of the 15 prisoners in the cell sodomized him. The physical abuses persisted every day. Finally, at the end of the week, the guards boasted that they had given the prisoner a rope and released the chain from the wall. While a couple of inmates helped, the unfortunate man hung himself from a ceiling fan.

Sombattsiri came to visit one day in early July to tell me that he had just spoken to my mother. Kenji had given him her phone number in California and he called to ask her for more money. "She said that she sent you a check for $3,000," he snapped. "She said to tell you to sign the check over to me."

The man was like a rodent, sniffing up and down the cracks and corners in search of bugs. I had just received the check from Kenji and hoped to use it for personal expenses and for rent on the apartment so that Chat and Nu could continue to live there and remain in school. My mother had unwittingly placed me in a difficult position by telling Sombattsiri that she had sent money. He had done an excellent job the one time he had come to court prepared. But he had spent only a few hours on my case and would soon have received more than 150,000 baht ($6,000). But I believed that if I didn't pay, Sombattsiri would quit and the system would destroy me.

My next session was held on July 20th. Just before 9 AM, I was brought into the courtroom as the prosecutor was donning his robe. The only other person present was his assistant. Outside in the hallway, the investigators from Din Daeng Police Station were waiting to testify. Through the doorway, I saw Lieutenant Chanasithi, the one the boys said had tortured them. I glared at him, but he averted his eyes.

The judge entered the courtroom, though Sombattsiri still had not arrived. We waited. The judge seemed to keep himself busy with paperwork for a while. Finally, at 9:45, he told the guard to return me to the holding cell.

Dejectedly, I sat on the floor in the filthy cell, wondering what had happened to my lawyer. A few minutes later, a deputy called me out. I picked up my chains and followed him back to the courtroom. This time, Sombattsiri and Kachon were waiting.

A woman whom I had not noticed earlier stepped up to the podium and took the pledge of verity. I looked questioningly at Kachon. He took out a small notebook, wrote something on a piece of paper, and handed it to the guard to give to me. The note said: "Woman from hospital. She check Chat and Nu. She say nothing show about sex."

When she stepped down and the judge had finished paraphrasing her testimony into his tape recorder, a police officer took the stand. He identified himself as Police Sergeant Wasant Ngarmsompong, one of the investigators who arrested me and searched my apartment. He looked scared and nervous. He told the judge that he and his fellow investigators had been instructed by Police Major Tharin Chantaratip to arrest the "foreigners" at my apartment and David Groat's apartment. He testified that there had been no complaint and that *they found nothing in the apartment*. However, he also told the judge that Chat and Nu were in my apartment when he and the other officers arrived there. Unfortunately, I was not able to follow his testimony and was unaware that he was not telling the truth.

Then Sombattsiri cross-examined him and asked why he had sent the boys to prison and why he had taken my passport. He claimed to know nothing about the boys' incarceration and he also denied taking my passport. When he stepped away from the podium, he was visibly shaken.

146

Kachon passed another note to me after Ngarmsompong's testimony. It read: "His boss tell him to say Chat and Nu in apartment. He say he sorry." I thought Kachon was referring to the press conference and that the police sergeant was testifying he had been instructed by his supervisors to tell the media that the boys had been in the apartment. I didn't realize Kachon was telling me that the man had just perjured himself because his supervisor had instructed him to do so.

Next, Lieutenant Suthep Chanasithi entered the courtroom, stepped to the podium and identified himself. I glowered at him as he spoke, but he would not look at me. He told the judge that he arrested me because of the Matichon newspaper article, that he searched my apartment and *found nothing*. He talked about interviewing the boys and he, too, perjured himself and told the court that the boys had been in my apartment at the time of the arrest. He neglected to mention that I had been arrested while working in my office.

Like his predecessor, he seemed to be very nervous during his testimony. Sombat asked him why the boys had been taken to Pakred and he denied any knowledge of their incarceration. Yet, according to Chat, Nu and the children's prison supervisor at Pakred, Lieutenant Chanasithi had been the man who brought them in. He said that he had not taken them there and didn't know who had. From this, I guessed he had overstepped his authority when he asked the Child Welfare Department to imprison the boys.

Chanasithi stepped down, still averting my glare, signed his statement, and took a seat in the rear next to Ngarmsompong. I turned to Sombat and asked him to meet me downstairs in the lawyer's room to discuss the testimony that had just been given. He agreed as a guard stepped up to return me to the holding cell.

Only a few minutes later, Kachon appeared across the hall from the cell and held up a bag of fried rice that he had purchased for my lunch.

"Where is Sombat?" I asked.

"He not come," Kachon said. "He go already."

Sombattsiri did not come to the prison the rest of the week. My next court date was scheduled for the following week and I wanted to discuss what had happened in the last session. When Kachon finally ambled in, I asked him to go to Sombat's house and bring him to me. "I need to talk to him," I said with urgency.

The next day, Kachon came to report that my mother had spoken with Sombat and that she was going to send him bail money. Sombat told her that he thought he could bail me out — even though I had no passport — for 200,000 baht.

I was frantic. I had already grown to mistrust the weasel and I believed now he was poised to take my mother's money. "Tell her not to send *anything* to Sombat," I said sharply. "Tell Kenji to call her right away!"

The day before I was scheduled to appear again in court, Sombat came to the prison. I was relieved to see him and anxious to discuss the case.

"Kenji says you want to sell your computer," he said as I took a seat. "I'll buy it."

I ignored his comment and asked him who the next witness would be. He, in turn, ignored my question and said that if I gave him the computer his fees would be totally paid.

The company computer was the newest generation IBM clone, was less than a year old, and was selling in Bangkok for 150,000 baht ($6,000). I had already given Sombat nearly 150,000 baht and I didn't plan to give him any more, at least not until the trial was completed.

"Okay, I'll pay you 70,000 for it," he said bargaining like a street vendor.

"We can talk about the computer when the case is finished," I growled. But he wasn't interested in discussing the case at all. He acted as if the case were irrelevant. When I refused to agree to his terms, he detachedly listened as I read my notes about the trial, then stood up and said that he would give me some cash and credit the remainder. Then he was gone.

That afternoon, Mark Morgan came to the prison. I had previously asked him to try to sell the computer for me.

"I've checked around," Mark said. "Your computer is not worth 100,000 baht ($4,000). A friend told me that it was only worth 25,000. I'll give you that much for it."

"What? Sombat says he'll give me 70,000 for it and he hasn't even seen it. I know it's worth much more than 25,000 baht."

"Does he know that it's broken?" Mark asked.

"Broken? Since when?"

"I tried to use it the other day and it wouldn't bring up data. I've sent it to be repaired."

"Kenji said it was working all right when you came and picked it up from the office," I fired back. I was suspicious and irritated that people were picking over the carcass of my business assets like a bunch of chop-licking buzzards.

"Something funny is going on at the office," Mark said, abruptly changing the subject. "Kachon hocked your typewriter the other day and I had to pay 5,000 baht to get it out of hock. And I wouldn't trust Kenji if I were you." Then he offered to pick up my office equipment — a fax machine, a copy machine, a fridge, the telex, the safe, and the computer and printer — and take it to his shelter.

"Will you try to sell everything for me?" I asked.

"I'll try. But at least if the things are at my house, you'll know they're safe."

"Okay," I sighed, "but I want to talk to Kenji before you do anything."

I left the visiting area wondering whom I could really trust. Mark said that I couldn't trust Kenji, but I was wondering if I could trust Mark. It seemed to me that he was undervaluing my computer so that I would sell it to him for next to nothing. Meanwhile, Kachon was taking office equipment to a pawn shop. That night I couldn't sleep at all. I wondered if anyone's motives were honorable, or if prison was turning me into a mistrustful cynic.

When morning broke and it was time to prepare for court, I was a nervous wreck. I hadn't closed my eyes all night. I wearily dragged myself to the courtyard, had the chains clamped on again, had my fingerprints taken again, squatted in line again, stood for the National Anthem again, climbed into the crowded bus again, dragged my chains to the holding cell again, waited on the filthy floor again, picked up my chains again, squatted in front of the deputy's desk again, straggled upstairs to the courtroom again, and again waited for Sombattsiri to arrive.

Everyone else was ready to go and, this time, instead of sending me back downstairs, the judge — visibly annoyed at Sombattsiri's tardiness — announced that the trial would proceed whether I had a lawyer or not. I thought my ears were deceiving me.

The prosecutor called one of the officers from Din Daeng Station to the stand. Not only was there no interpreter to explain what was happening, but the prosecutor was being allowed to proceed without anyone in attendance representing me.

"What kind of legal system is this?" I wondered as the officer began his testimony. He told the court that I was arrested after a Matichon article appeared which stated that a boy had been raped at Victory Monument. The prosecution had never produced this mysterious victim, but the infamous article was once again being presented as evidence that I had committed a crime. I couldn't follow the officer's testimony. When he had finished, the judge asked if I had any questions. He evidently assumed that I understood what the man had said. "I want an English translator," I said.

This confused the judge. He had heard me speak Thai to Kachon and assumed that my language ability was sufficient to understand court testimony. "I want a translator," I repeated.

The judge said something to the clerk, who stood up and left the courtroom. After a few minutes, she returned with another woman.

150

The judge said something to her and she turned to face me. "Do you have any questions?"

"Yes, I have a question," I said. I looked at the officer in front of the podium and angrily asked, "Who made up all the stories?"

Everyone just stared, so I repeated my question. The interpreter turned to the judge and told him that I wanted to know what evidence the police had. I understood her. "No, who made up all the stories that were in the newspapers," I said even more forcefully. "Who made up all the stories about me?"

The judge stared at me bewildered, not knowing what to say. At that moment, Kachon and Sombattsiri walked into the courtroom. They were two hours late. There was no mistaking the smell of Mekhong whiskey on both of them. "Where have you been?" I said through set teeth.

Sombattsiri ignored my question and asked for a transcript of the officer's testimony. The clerk handed it to him. He read the first few lines of the transcript, then put it down and asked this officer the same thing he had asked at the last hearing — who took the boys to Pakred prison and who took my passport.

The officer claimed to know nothing about either the boys' incarceration or my passport, so Sombattsiri excused him. "Ask him who made up the stories!" I demanded.

Sombattsiri looked at me and spit, "I told the judge that one of your competitors made up the stories about you."

"What!? I don't care what you told the judge," I scowled. "I want to know where this whole thing started. I want to know the truth!"

He turned away and refused to say anything else. The truth was unimportant to him, but my unanswered question had been haunting me for months. Where had this whole thing started? "The police will know who told the stories to them. Who did all of this to me? Ask him where it all came from!"

"Matichon," Sombat replied tersely. Communication was almost impossible with him. "Will you please come down to the lawyer's room and talk to me?" I pleaded.

Again he promised and again I waited for naught. I could have strangled the man. I was taken back to the prison, with no idea what would happen next.

Soon after that strange day in court, an article appeared in the Bangkok Post about the police at Din Daeng Station. It said that the police there had used a cattle prod on a Thai man named Samnao Khamthawee to force him to sign a confession. The man had gone to the newspaper and exposed the practice. The article opined about how barbaric and unbecoming it was of a developing democracy like Thailand.

A few days later, someone wrote a letter to the editor of the Post reminding readers that torture had also been used by the Din Daeng police to collect evidence against "two Americans charged with committing indecent acts against teenagers." The author of the letter went on to say that "regardless of the fact that these two Americans did not fit the description in the (Matichon) article, the police in their quest to find a suspect arrested the two Americans who lived in the area."[10]

Kachon visited and left me with news that Sombattsiri had received a check from my mother for 200,000 baht. Kenji had been unable to reach her in time to divert payment per my instructions. I was upset, but Kachon calmed me down and said he would make sure the money was used to apply for bail.

On Monday of the following week, Sombat came to the prison and saw David Groat. "Why didn't he ask to talk to me?" I wanted to know.

"He only came to have me sign some papers," David replied.

Groat had yet to pay anything, while Sombattsiri had received 350,000 baht from me and that alone made me realize how incredibly naive and stupid I'd been. Furthermore, Kenji had just gone with him

to pick up my computer from Mark's h
in the hands of my lawyer. Sombattsir
for all he could, so evidently in his mind
me anymore. Now he was setting his si
to wring something out of him.

An American in his mid-40's named
medical doctor with a physique like Arno
a clinic in Bangkok that served the city's
had lived quite modestly, as he only cl
afford to pay. Under pressure from her r
him to bring in much more money, his
leaving him and would return to her family l
only child.

When she came with a female companio
snapped and viciously attacked the two wom
almost killed them, he called the police and ga

Now he wanted to know if I could recomr
told him about Sombattsiri and, reluctantly,
Sombattsiri prepared himself for court, he seer

Once again Sombat came to the prison and
Peter, but refused to call on me. Dick and I
headed for the visiting area. A guard stopped
pass, but we brushed past him and said our lav
was unused to such audacious behavior, and
stared. Perhaps he was a bit intimidated by Dick'

When we barged in, Peter and David were ta
They were visibly irritated that we had preempted
their precious few minutes with the elusive lav
angry that I didn't really care. "What about my k
choking.

"Yes, I received the money from your mother,"
"When can I bail out?" I demanded.

't know! I will apply, but the Embassy has your passport,"
This was not a revelation. He knew all along that the
had my passport. Suddenly Sombattsiri's eyes lit up like a
on dollar signs. He had spotted the face of a new farang and
began schmoozing with Dick whom he had not yet had the
ity to fleece. When I insisted on specific answers about my
gnored me as if he were deaf.

r interjected. "He didn't call you," he complained. "And I
alk to him." Reluctantly I retreated, waited for Dick to finish,
two of us returned to our building, unimpeded by the guards.

ji arrived for a visit the next morning. "Mark came in the
of the night and cleaned out the office," he said. "There's
left in it."

took everything?" I asked incredulously.

erything."

old him that he could take the equipment to sell, but I hadn't
m to remove the desks and everything. And I said that I wanted
speak to you first."

nji said, "Everything's gone. I don't really trust him."

, wonderful, I thought, now Kenji is telling me that he doesn't
Mark, the week after Mark told me not to trust Kenji.

en, remembering Mark's accusatory comments I asked, "Did
on hock my typewriter?"

Yeah," Kenji answered. "He was going up country to try to talk
's father into coming down to Bangkok to get Thep out of
ed, but he didn't have the money, so he took the typewriter. I told
about it and he went down and got the typewriter back."

he bell rang to announce the end of the 15-minute visit. "Tell
to come and talk to me," I yelled at Kenji.

was feeling like bait at feeding time for sharks. First it was the
ce and prison guards with bribe money, then the lawyers, and
my friends. I had been asking Kenji for a financial accounting
e the middle of April. It was now the 1st of August and I still

hadn't received it. I suspiciously wondered if he had taken what money remained in the company account.

The only thing that kept me going was the constant stream of cards and letters that arrived daily from family and friends in the States. They kept up my morale, because — in prison — it's easy to give up. Despite my efforts, I knew I had lost control of my fate.

The day after Kenji's visit, word came that David and I would be transferred to Khlong Prem. The Din Daeng police demanded to know why I had not been moved to a high security facility after being informed by the U.S. government that I had "fled (the U.S.) to avoid prosecution". I was, obviously, a security risk.

David scurried about the prison, trying to get the order reversed. He talked to the official who had received our bribe and who was responsible for the list of transferees. "It's out of my hands," he told David. "This order has come from the commander himself."

I paid one of the guards to inform Kenji, Mark and Kachon of my whereabouts.

Nine

The Face of the Monster

"Depression is all-consuming. It eats at the soul until the soul has no composition. It destroys energy and wastes the desire to be energetic; it kills the spirit; it mutilates hope; it annihilates desire. From the residue of all that is good in the human spirit, a festering evil emerges; the evil of desolation, self-pity, self-degradation, self-centeredness.
Depression creates an infertile aura within whose sphere passion, anger, love, ambition and the emotions that are the domain of the human spirit, cannot exist. Depression reaches ultimate fruition when it has enveloped and smothered all light until the only conceivable alternative to the pain, the only escape, is black death. Suicide is its triumph."

August 4, 1989 to September 21, 1989

I wrote these words soon after my arrival at Khlong Prem in Lardyao. Never before in my life had I experienced such an overwhelming desire to stop fighting.

On the morning of August 4th — my last at Bangkok Special Prison — I rolled up my mat, gathered my things and assembled in the central courtyard with six other prisoners including David Groat.

156

While we awaited our transfer, a trustee who worked at the welfare shack delivered to me a letter from Rick Stokes, a friend and attorney in San Francisco. I tore open the envelope and eagerly read the contents, hoping for answers to some of my questions. Rick explained that he was expecting to move to Puerto Rico and would, therefore, not be able to take my case in the United States. He said that my family had met with him and that he had recommended one of his former colleagues, Bruce Nickerson.

The letter went on to say that the charges against me in the U.S. were the result of statements made to the police by John Cummings. It said the charges involved a boy from Sacramento named Pablo Luna and that a Utah businessman named Howard Ruff, the publisher of an investors' newsletter called "The Ruff Times", was apparently responsible for much of what had happened in Thailand.

The letter created more questions than it answered. Why would Cummings have mentioned me to the police? And what could he possibly have said that would lead to charges in America? After all, since Cummings had gotten married years ago and moved to Sacramento, I rarely saw him, though there were times he would suddenly appear unannounced at my doorstep in San Francisco for a weekend "getaway" from his repressive conservative life. Sometimes he came alone, but at other times he brought friends, or foster children. Whenever I was not home, he and his friends usually spent the night with another gay San Francisco acquaintance, the closeted manager of the local Christian radio station.

And who was this Howard Ruff? Why did he want me imprisoned and what had I done to him? The name Pablo Luna was vaguely familiar. He had lived with Cummings and his wife. I remembered meeting him there once with a group of friends en route to a camping trip in the Sierras. But what did he have to do with any of this?

The seven of us were moved to a holding cell at the courthouse. Morning turned into afternoon and then, late afternoon, when finally we were loaded onto another of the caged buses. Everyone, of course, was manacled, some with unusually large and heavy chains.

The bus crawled through Bangkok traffic for two hours, from Sanam Luang, through Dusit, past the King's palace, to Nonthaburi. This town had always held pleasant memories for me. I felt that its aged bicycle samlors and crowded river pier exemplified the exotic and exciting nature of the country. Had I known that just a block off the main street was one of the largest high security prisons in the country, it would have lost some of its charm.

The coach dropped off two prisoners at Bangkwan Prison, then turned onto Ngam Wong Wan Road, and finally pulled up to Khlong Prem, the largest prison in Thailand, housing nearly 15,000 inmates. A massive iron gate was thrown open, and through it, we dragged our chains and our mats and our meager personal possessions, proceeding down a dark hallway, through a second gate, into a large courtyard and on through a third gate. There, we were ordered to squat while everything was searched including valuables which had been sent separately from Mahachai. Miraculously, my wallet still contained the $1,000 in cash and traveler's checks which I had to sign for and then return.

Then we stood and struggled forward, through more iron gates than I could count, before arriving at another large courtyard and a cluster of drab green buildings resembling barracks.

My ankles were chafed and cut from dragging the large chains, my back felt like I had lost a piece of my spine, and my knee which had popped out while I was exercising two days earlier, was throbbing with pain.

David heard that arriving prisoners at Khlong Prem were required to wear chains for the first month. "Don't worry," he assured me, "I think I can get our chains removed. The guards at Bangkok Special told me who to contact here, and they owe me." I didn't quite understand what he meant, but he always seemed to be working on one scheme or another. I couldn't imagine wearing these things for a full day, never mind a month. They were excruciatingly painful after a few hours.

We were marched into one of the drab green buildings which looked more like what I had always imagined a prison to be. Dozens of cells lined the interior on two levels. Catwalks with railings trimmed the upper-level cells, while those on the first floor faced the central courtyard. "Now this is a real prison," David said with some bizarre admiration. "Bangkok Special was a joke."

We were searched a second time by trustees and taken upstairs to a 10 foot by six foot cell. It had an uninviting cement floor and, at the rear, a three-foot cement wall divider setting off a tub filled with rancid water and a dirty squat toilet covered by what looked to be mud. There were no ceiling fans and the air continually hung with a strange rank odor. A weak 25-watt bulb provided barely enough light to see, and a screen which had at one time been installed as protection from mosquitoes was torn to shreds and flapped loosely from the bars on the window.

Five of us crowded into the tiny room. "This was the cell where Abdul Aziz killed himself," a trustee said to me in English as the iron door thundered shut. Abdul was a devout Muslim from Iran whom I had known at Bangkok Special Prison. He had been extremely depressed because his mother, back in Iran, was dying and his arrest had brought shame to the family. He had been sentenced to eight months for a minor offense, but his imprisonment caused him great humiliation and he could not bear it.

Thai prisoners had treated him contemptuously, but I tried to counter that by offering food, postage stamps and stationery, and lending a sympathetic ear. I hoped I had brought him some degree of comfort. He was transferred to Khlong Prem around the 1st of July. Two weeks later, he committed suicide by slashing his wrists.

Evidently, no one had occupied the cell since Abdul's death. Many Thais believe that ghosts live where people have died, so the trustees had been reluctant to enter the cell after the body was removed. The "mud" that I had seen on the toilet and the rear of the cell was, in reality, dried blood. And the odor another remnant of the tragic ending.

David, obviously the most anally-fixated among us, immediately began to clean it while Thai prisoners in nearby cells taunted us. "Do you see Abdul?" they asked. I told them Abdul was with us and was just fine.

Although it was not easy, the five of us managed to find space to sleep. In the middle of the night, David screamed and jumped up.

"What's the matter?" I said after being jolted awake.

"I'm all wet," he cried. "My mat is soaked."

We had failed to notice a hole which was bored through the cement wall of the tub and a spigot that had been left open.

At 6 AM, the noise of the key turning in the lock rousted me. I assumed that, as at Bangkok Special Prison, we were to gather our bowls, soap and toiletries for showers. The others preceded me downstairs and were gone before I could maneuver my aching knee and back, gather my things, pick up my chains and hobble along.

I had difficulty finding the bathing area, but when I finally did, I set my toiletries down and wondered how I would get my pants off with my ankles in chains. "Farang ab thi non, khrap," a prisoner next to me said. He indicated I was in the wrong place and directed me to a small pond behind which stood another tub surrounded by foreigners.

I picked up my chains and painfully hobbled past the pond to a vine-covered trellis that surrounded an entranceway. When I looked in I could not believe my eyes! There was a village — a prison village — bustling with energy. I looked upon a maze of walkways and 60 or 80 open huts, each with bamboo fencing. There was a store, a restaurant, an area for weightlifting, a place to cook, and a "theatre" where one actually paid for a seat to watch a video!

I dragged myself into this frenzy, trying to smile at others, but wincing from the throbbing in my knees and the chafing of the chains on my ankles. When I managed to smile at Thais, they smiled back. But westerners were either outright hostile or suspicious.

Nearby was an open trench filled with sewage so polluted, I was to later learn, that the oxygen level of the water was zero. At last, I came upon the tub and, before it, stood David struggling to get his pants down through the steel anklets that held the chains to his legs. Another prisoner was assisting him. I hobbled over and prepared myself for similar acrobatics. It felt good to wash off the accumulated grime. I vowed to appreciate a long hot shower, if ever again I experienced one.

After drying off, I started back for the cell with a plan to rest, but was stopped in the "village" by a bearded blond-haired prisoner. "You can't go back to the building until 4 PM," he said with a German accent. "In the meantime, you can leave your things in my area."

He introduced himself as Michael Roenisch and welcomed me into his hut. He offered me a chair and said, "Would you like a cup of coffee?"

"I'd love one!" I exclaimed.

"I've been here three years," he said calmly, "and I'm still going to court. I don't know when my trial will finish." Then he quickly changed the subject. "This area is called the `garden'. It's for foreigners only. Everything here is paid for by us. We pay for the huts, the walkways. We even paid to have the water pipes brought out here."

He went on to explain that new prisoners could buy huts as they became available, but there was no more room left to build new ones. Prices started at about 6,000 baht. Once a hut was purchased, the prisoner owned it until he decided to sell or was released. Without a hut, one had no place to go between 6 AM and 4 PM.

"Cells inside the (prison) building may be purchased also," Michael continued. If one wished to move into a cell owned by another prisoner, one had to pay a nominal fee, perhaps 500 baht. However, if one wished to purchase a cell, paint it, put tiles on the floor, put in a fan and a good light, the cost was about 3,000 baht. Once a prisoner purchased a cell, he could choose his cellmates. Michael had purchased a private cell for 15,000 baht, but the prison was becoming too crowded and prison officials no longer sold private cells.

New prisoners were initially placed in the worst cells, thereby encouraging them to spend money to move into nicer quarters. Besides renting cells and collecting money to build huts in the garden, the guards supplied whatever prisoners wanted... for a price.

Several prisoners at Khlong Prem were heroin addicts and constantly high on the drug. Guards sold the heroin, but if the very same guards were to find the powder in a cell during a search, they would beat the prisoner and additional time would be added to his sentence. On the other hand, prison addicts with enough money could make the charge disappear by bribing the commander of the prison.

Expecting Kenji or Kachon to bring money soon, I hadn't really worried about landing at Khlong Prem with only a few hundred baht in my account despite the $1000 in my wallet remaining inaccessible.

Here foreigners only received one free meal a day, sometimes consisting of three uncooked eggs and rice or turnip soup. The prisoners operated a restaurant in the "garden" that offered mid-morning and mid-afternoon meals that were quite good. Meals cost between 20 and 40 baht each, so by the end of my first week I was broke and forced to exist on rice and raw eggs. Marcia Pixley had brought some vitamins to Mahachai and that helped, but I was always hungry.

Not long before my arrival, my few hundred baht would have gone twice as far. Prisoners had been purchasing food from a supermarket that delivered to the prison every day. However, the prison commander had recently realized that he was missing out on a great source of revenue. He opened his own supermarket within the prison, doubled the prices, and banned food from the outside. Prison officials claimed that the change was instituted because heroin was coming in with the food shipments. But everyone on the inside knew there was only one source of heroin — and that was the guards.

David's great scheme to get our chains removed did not materialize. Every day, they became more and more painful until the chafing created sores on my ankles that got progressively worse. I had a pair of wool socks which I wore to prevent my injuries from becoming infected. Others were not so lucky.

My lower back had also become a concern. Dick, the physician, told me that I had spina riffida occulta, which meant that a piece of my spine hadn't developed fully. He had given me exercises that would alleviate the pain, but I was unable to do most of them with my legs in chains.

Besides the physical discomfort, wearing chains 24 hours a day slowly diminished what remained of my self-esteem. Although Thailand had signed the 1955 Geneva accords regarding the treatment of prisoners, it was in direct violation of about half of them.

After the first week, Michael suggested that I try to bribe the building chief to remove my chains. I guessed that if the chief were offered some of the money in my wallet, he might make it accessible to me. I went to his office, bowed at the door, waied him, then squatted down in front of his desk. I offered him 1,000 baht if he would remove my chains. He told me that, because I was still going to trial and had not yet been convicted, he could not remove my chains. His rationale was that I might be eventually convicted. "If you are convicted, you might receive a long sentence," he said, "therefore I am unable to remove the chains."

I reported this rather bizarre conversation to Michael. "What he was telling you," Michael explained, "was that you needed to offer him more money. You should go back and offer him 5,000 baht." The stupidity of this sham bothered me so much that I decided to stick it out. Then, too, I wondered how I would feel moving about freely while fellow prisoners remained shackled simply because they didn't have bribe money.

My isolation from the outside world was complete. It was not possible to receive any newspapers in Lardyao, as it had been in Mahachai. Radios were forbidden and there were, of course, no telephones. Kenji and Kachon had visited at least once a week when I was conveniently located at Bangkok Special Prison, but suddenly the visits stopped. Mail also stopped coming. Family and most of my friends didn't know where I was.

The only visit I received during August was on the afternoon of the 10th from a man named John Ambrose of the U.S. Department of State. He was accompanied by a woman named Lauri Morton from the Embassy. When the message came summoning me and David the other Americans wanted to know why we had been singled out. "Tell Marcia that we want to talk to her," they shouted as we hurried to the visitors' quarters.

Ambrose was sweating profusely. "I just flew in from Washington," he said. "I've come to ask you a few questions." He then handed two sheets of paper to the guard to give to us. I picked up the paper and read it. It was a copy of my Miranda rights. "I'm an investigator from the StateDepartment," he said.

"I won't sign this." I wasn't very savvy about such things, but after what the United States government had done to me thus far, I wasn't about to sign away my Miranda rights without an American lawyer present.

"Well, at least sign saying that you refuse to acknowledge this," he said.

I looked at David. He shook his head, so I passed the unsigned paper back through the bars. At that, the investigator became visibly irritated. "If you don't sign this, I can't ask you any questions!"

"Exactly!" I thought.

That night I was again restless and couldn't sleep. Thoughts crept into my mind about the possibility of the Embassy working against me because of my previous political activities in the United States. One of the legacies that my parents had given me was a social and political consciousness. My father had been a Methodist minister and a conscientious objector, and counseled young men on avoiding the draft during the McCarthy era. After he died in the late `50s, my mother bought a house in an all-white Santa Rosa, California neighborhood for the express purpose of renting it to a black family. She is currently the head of the Stanislaus County chapter of Jimmy Carter's Habitat for Humanity, a past president of the county's Interfaith Council, and founder of the Modesto Center for Senior Employment. She worked for peace during the Vietnam war, and had created organizations to feed and employ the poor and build houses for the homeless.

Since receiving an honorable medical discharge in 1965 as an Air Force cadet, I too had been a social and political activist. Besides founding the South Park Youth Organization while at Sonoma State University, I organized a coalition of peace groups and was very active in the anti-Vietnam war movement.

After Anita Bryant won an anti-gay referendum in Florida in 1977, I became active in the struggle for gay rights. I marched arm-in-arm with Harvey Milk, the gay San Francisco supervisor who was later assassinated with Mayor George Moscone. I became an activist in the San Francisco Gay Democratic Club, later re-named the Harvey Milk Lesbian and Gay Democratic Club. By 1983 the club had become the largest gay political organization in the country and I had served for two years as treasurer.

I had also been a "card-carrying member" of the American Civil Liberties Union, had been a supporter of Amnesty International and had been active in several gay rights organizations throughout the early 1980's.

But wasn't I entitled to join any organization I wanted — as long as it was legal? Was I less entitled to my freedoms than heterosexuals?

I kept probing for a clue — tortured by my inability to find an answer — until my brain shut down, just before dawn.

* * *

My next court session was scheduled for August 15th. As always, I went with high hopes. This time, I hoped to see a friend or two, or perhaps a reporter to tell me that he had discovered the story to be untrue.

I was called from the cell, made to squat in front of the deputy's desk for a half hour, then assigned an officer and taken upstairs to one of the smaller courtrooms. Again, the judge and prosecutor were there, but Sombattsiri was not. It was my turn to present my case, thus the prosecutor couldn't call a witness as he had done at the previous session. At 10 AM, the judge resignedly instructed the guard to take me back down.

About an hour later, Kachon appeared at the window across the hall. "Sombat cannot come," he yelled, "becau he get drunk. He welly drunk. I try, but no goos." Then Kachon disappeared.

A few minutes after he had left, a guard called me out of the holding cell and took me back upstairs. Kachon was in the courtroom telling the judge that Sombattsiri was sick and requested a postponement. The judge agreed and set the following session for five weeks hence. He told Kachon and the prosecutor that we could begin our defense on September 21st.

I wanted to wring Sombattsiri's neck. He had just cost me five more weeks in prison because of his drunk. After talking with Kachon about my options, I angrily dragged my chains downstairs to await my return to prison.

In the days following, I wrote letters to everyone whose address I knew, asking them to exert pressure on Sombattsiri. I had given up on the possibility of bail, I just wanted to finish the trial.

I also wrote a detailed list of instructions to Sombattsiri, giving him names of individuals whom I felt would testify on my behalf. I asked him to subpoena the editor of Matichon so that we might find out who had given the newspaper the "story" that began it all. Because all outgoing mail was screened by prison officials, I would hold onto these 17 pages until Kachon came for a visit.

When the other prisoners heard that my lawyer had not shown up in court, they asked who represented me. "Sombattsiri Nabadalung," I replied and they all burst out laughing.

"Who turned you onto Sombattsiri?" one asked.

"An Australian at Mahachai named Peter Bailey." That brought more guffaws.

Another American prisoner said, "Bailey gets a commission from Sombattsiri for everyone he ropes into hiring that crook."

Everyone, it seemed, had a horror story about my attorney. One Vietnamese prisoner had supposedly given Sombattsiri his family's life savings to bail him out. Sombattsiri never made the application and never returned the money.

An English prisoner, who was slowly dying of an exotic disease, said, "I used Sombattsiri to defend me. I lost the case and because of my health, asked Sombattsiri not to appeal so that I would be eligible to apply for a King's pardon and return to England for medical treatment. He filed an appeal anyway, destroying my chance to get proper treatment. The man is a bastard. Don't trust him to do anything you want." He spoke slowly and painfully. His skin had partially disintegrated over parts of his body. Although he didn't have AIDS, he looked like a man dying of the incurable disease.

One of the buildings at Khlong Prem was used as a school where I was able to take a Thai language class. There were no other foreigners in the school, but because I had some knowledge in both spoken and written Thai, the commander of the school accepted me. Within a few days, I was not only studying Thai, but teaching English to a group of Thai prisoners.

In September, when the school term ended, I asked the commander if I could make it official. He agreed and assigned me a classroom. The announcement was made to the Thai population in our section that anyone who wanted could study English during the lunch break. The commander even offered to extend credits toward graduation to students who completed the six-week course.

Thirty-six men came to class on my first teaching day and, yes, I taught in chains. I soon discovered that they were at very different levels of ability and I couldn't simultaneously teach them all. Eventually the beginners dropped out and the class dwindled to 20 of the more advanced students.

Teaching school became the high point of my stay in Lardyao and almost made life enjoyable. It gave me a purpose and it gave me a fringe benefit. Thais are extremely polite. They are taught from early childhood to respect their elders and those from a higher social status. As a teacher, I quickly obtained status and, therefore, respect from my peers and, to some extent, the guards.

In August 1989, an international agency of the United Nations published a report listing Thailand as the seventh most corrupt country in the world. Any attack on the Thai character is taken by those in power as a personal insult. The Supreme Commander of the Armed Forces, General Suchinda Kraprayoon, reacted to the report by blaming the elected government. As a result, the government, which had publicly lost face, returned the favor and blamed the army. The army, having lost face, then threatened to use force against the government to make its officials apologize for such blasphemies. The government official who had issued the blistering rejoinder was pressured into resigning. Meanwhile, nothing was done to improve the corrupt state of the nation.

On the 1st day of September, I was called outside for a visit. I had not had a visit from a friend since my transfer to Khlong Prem. I was so excited and filled with anticipation, that as soon as I saw Chat and Kachon in the visiting area I had to excuse myself to find a toilet.

The visitors area at Khlong Prem was worse than at Bangkok Special Prison. Instead of being separated by three feet, the distance between the screens was at least 10 feet. Again, everyone had to shout to be heard above the other conversations, only here it was much more difficult.

Chat told me that he and Nu were back in school and that made me feel very good. Kachon claimed that he hadn't visited sooner because he had been arrested and held by the Din Daeng police for impersonating a lawyer. David had asked Sombattsiri to retrieve his personal letters, photos and financial records from the police station. Sombat would not go but wrote a letter on his stationery authorizing Kachon to get them and identified Kachon as a member of his law firm. The police knew better, arrested Kachon, and held him at the jail for seven days.

"Why didn't Sombat get you out?" I asked with astonishment.

"He no hel. He not want to inwolve," Kachon answered. "Becau' he write letter that I working for him."

Before Kachon left, I gave him the lengthy list of instructions for Sombattsiri.

Soon after their visit, Marcia Pixley came to the prison and called for all the Americans. Nine of us went to see her.

"I need some money," I said. "What about my EMDA loans?" The United States government has an interest-free loan program for citizens held in foreign prisons. David and I had both applied for funds in July before we left Mahachai.

"I've lost your applications," Marcia said. "You'll have to fill out the forms again."

"We have no money," I whined, "We can't buy food. We're starving!"

"I have a few baht of my own money. I'll leave it in your account, then bring the rest as soon as the application is processed." I smiled in appreciation. This was certainly a kind gesture on her part.

"Would you also ask the commander to remove our chains?" I pleaded.

"I'll try," she said sympathetically.

Her pledge and the money she loaned had a quieting effect on me. I began to sleep better. I still experienced some rather telling dreams, but overall my state of anxiety and frustration diminished.

In one dream, I was dressed in a hand-tailored double-breasted wool suit which I had purchased in Italy, and was taking clients on a site inspection of the Shangri-La. As we entered the hotel's elevator, I was trying to explain to them why I was wearing chains around my ankles.

Another dream was really a recurring nightmare from childhood during which I would be chased by a monster without a face. In my youth, I had always managed to escape from it. But when the vision appeared to me now while I slept on the floor of my cell, the monster actually caught me. I struggled to escape from the horrible creature and looked into the face of... John Cummings. I awoke drenched in sweat.

According to Freud, the dream represents a common childhood fear. Children often have secrets to hide from either their families or from society. Freud had said that the monster represents that entity from which the child needs to keep his secret. Children who recognize that they are gay at an early age often experience this type of anxiety-producing nightmare.

Kachon and Chat returned on September 7th. This time, they brought Nu, Kenji, and Mark Morgan. I didn't really want Chat and Nu to skip school to visit, but it boosted my morale to see them.

"Did you give the papers to Sombattsiri?" I asked Kachon.

"Oh, yes," he assured me. "Don' worry!"

This was the first time I had seen Mark and Kenji together since they, individually, had counseled me to not trust the other. I berated Mark for taking everything from my office.

"But you said I could," he claimed.

"No, I didn't!"

He turned to Kenji and started to argue with him. "Damn it!" I cried. "I need your help! Please try to get along. It's discouraging to see you two arguing." I asked them to work together to get Sombattsiri to do what I had paid him to do.

A month had gone by since my arrival, yet the building chief still had not done anything about the chains. Those of us who had come together from Bangkok Special Prison met and went to him to demand their removal. He told us to write a formal request to the prison commander. We wrote the request, had it translated into Thai, and waited. A week passed without a reply. Every day that went by shackled to those despicable things seemed like an eternity. Finally, on September 13th, 40 days after we had arrived, seven of us received notice that our chains would be removed. An eighth man, charged with murder, had to remain in them another month as additional punishment.

When I sat on the ground in front of the vise and a prison trustee pulled the wooden handle to pry apart the iron bracelet, I felt like a free man. I stood up and started to walk. The sensation was as if I were floating on air. It was exhilarating. Life was suddenly worth living again.

The day before I was scheduled to return to the courtroom, an Irishman named Dan, a Brit named Simon and the other Americans in the "garden" sat me down for a "heart to heart" talk. "Plead guilty," they said. "Tell the court you'll change your plea. It may not be too late. Nobody ever wins a case in Thailand. All the cards are stacked against you. If you plead guilty your sentence will be half what it will be after they find you guilty. Most Thais plead guilty because they know they can't win, whether they're guilty or not."

September 21 — November 17, 1989

My letters and entreaties finally paid off. Sombattsiri appeared in court, accompanied by Kachon, Kenji, Chat and Nu. As usual, he was in a great hurry and had no time to talk to me. In my letter, I had asked him to call in the Matichon reporter to explain the origin of the article; then Sumate Sudasna Ayudhaya to testify about the type of business I had run; then Mark Morgan to testify that I had never worked or volunteered in his children's shelter; then Chat's sister, Rekha, and Nu's mother to testify about my relationship with the two boys; and finally Kenji and Kachon.

"Did you read the letter?" I asked. "I want you to call the others before Kachon and Kenji."

"What letter?" Sombat looked perplexed.

I turned to Kachon. "Didn't you give him my letter?"

"The letter." Kachon spoke in English so that I was aware he had not let me down. "I give you two week ago. You put is on desk. Lemember?"

"Oh, yes," Sombat replied, avoiding eye contact with me. It was obvious he hadn't even glanced at it.

"I wanted you to bring the witnesses to court to testify," I said angrily.

He looked at me as if he didn't understand. His eyes were vacant.

Just then Chat came and sat next to me on the bench. Nu followed. I hugged them both and they returned the embrace. I hoped that this whole thing wouldn't traumatize them. I desperately wanted them to know that I didn't blame them for anything that had happened, that I understood — they had been victimized just as I had been victimized.

Sombat was talking to the judge. Then he turned to me and said, "You testify now."

"What?" I sputtered. "You haven't even discussed my testimony with me."

He just shrugged and gestured for me to take the stand. I stood up. Chat and Nu returned to the bench at the rear.

Sombattsiri asked Kenji to act as interpreter. I pledged to testify truthfully and faced the prosecutor. "Did you have sex with Nu?" he asked, pointing directly at the 15-year-old boy. Nu stood up and left the courtroom.

I hesitated. "Change your plea," they had said. "It's not too late." "Nobody wins a case in Thailand." "Your sentence will be halved if you plead guilty..." "Nobody wins a case in Thailand..." "Nobody wins a case in Thailand..." "Nobody wins..." What would the boys think if I copped out on them after their courageous testimony? "NO!" I said firmly.

The prosecutor looked me in the eye. "Did you have sex with Chat?"

"NO!" I replied even more forcefully, and stared determinedly at the judge.

The prosecutor turned and looked at Chat. Then he pulled out a copy of my warrant of arrest from California. He read the charge on the warrant and followed with a description of the charge written on United States Embassy stationery. I glanced at the signature at the bottom of the page. It was from Consular Officer Stephen Pattison. The Embassy had refused for six months to tell me anything about my charge in America, but they had given a copy of the warrant and a description of the charge to the prosecutor. The letter was dated June 22nd, the day the boys had testified that they had been tortured.

Who does the United States Embassy represent? I wondered bitterly.

"Get me a copy of this!" I instructed Sombat. If I couldn't get any information about the charges against me in America from American officials, I would get it from the Thais.

Next, the prosecutor presented a copy of a letter from David Copas, Security Attache at the Embassy, dated March 6, 1989, requesting that Thai officials arrest and hold me without bail while the United States government investigated the allegation that I ran a sex tour business. *The letter was dated before any warrant had been issued in America and before Consul General Ed Wehrli had written the letter denying any United States Government involvement in my arrest and incarceration in Thailand.*[11]

173

The judge looked at me and asked when I had changed my plea to not guilty. I didn't understand the question, so Kenji repeated it.

"I never changed my plea. I always pleaded not guilty."

It wasn't until I received a full translation of the police testimony a year later that I understood why the judge had asked the question. I hadn't realized at the time that Lieutenant Chanasithi testified that I had made a "partial confession" at the police station on the day of my arrest, apparently referring to the fact that I had told him the two boys lived with me.

When I sat down, I turned to Sombat. "If you're not going to use the 200,000 baht to apply for my bail, then give it back... and how about the money you owe me for the computer that you took."

"I'll pay you," Sombat said.

"When?" I asked.

"In a week." Then he reached into his briefcase and pulled out a note pad. "If you want the money, you must write me a note asking for it."

In plain English, I wrote that I wanted the money Sombattsiri owed me, indicating his promise to pay me within the week. I dated the note and signed it.

Sombat looked at the piece of paper, tore it up and told me to re-write it, deleting the date. I rewrote the same note and dated it. He tore it up again and told me that if I didn't write the note that he wanted, he would never return my money.

The man was worse than a crook — he was a liar, a thief, a manipulator with the morals of a slug. It was futile to argue with him. I wrote yet another note and signed it, undated.

The judge set my next court appearance for a month later and asked me to sign a copy of my testimony. Chat came over and hugged me when I got up to leave. "Khap khun khrap. Thank you," I murmured.

Five days after my courtroom testimony, Marcia Pixley came to visit. "Why did Stephen Pattison write a letter to the prosecutor?" I asked bitterly. "He refused to explain the details of my charges to me, but he had no problem explaining them to my prosecutor. I still haven't received a copy of the California warrant. Why is the United States Embassy so determined to have me convicted in Thailand?"

"The Embassy is here to help you," she said, apparently believing it. Her remark was laughable but I was in no mood to laugh.

"There was a letter written by a man named David Copas asking the Thai police to arrest me. Why was that?"

"I haven't seen that letter. I don't know anything about that," she said. "I'll go back to the Embassy and see if I can find the letter you're talking about."

On October 3rd, Marcia returned. She had found the letter from David Copas. "We thought you were in prison because of the Thai charges," she said.

"I'm in prison because the American government asked the Thais to arrest me," I snapped. "Ed Wehrli denied any U.S. government involvement in my arrest *after* David Copas wrote the letter. Why had he lied?"

"David Copas was working in a different department," she said without blinking. "Our office didn't know anything about that request."

"Wehrli's letter said that *no U.S. government official had asked for my arrest*. It didn't say `nobody in our department' asked for my arrest."

Marcia didn't know what to say. And that's where it stood. The Embassy had sided with the prosecutor. As far as they were concerned I would remain behind bars until proven innocent.

"I have a letter for you," she said, changing the subject. I followed her to the end of the corridor so she could pass it through. The letter stated that the passport hearing I had requested would be held inside Khlong Prem Central Prison on October 12, 1989. I still hoped to get my passport returned and make bail. I believed as long as I was at the mercy of the United States government and Sombattsiri, I would lose.

But if I could get out and find a lawyer who would work with me, I would win.

The letter allowed that I had the right to have an attorney present my case. My mother had just hired a Philadelphia law firm called the International Legal Defense Council to act as liaison. I wrote and asked her to tell the Philadelphia lawyers to contact Sombattsiri and to advise him about how to proceed with the hearing. I also asked Marcia to remind Sombat about the hearing and wrote to Kachon and Kenji asking them too to make sure that he would represent me.

By the 10th, I had not heard from anyone except Marcia. She said that Sombattsiri had promised he would be there. I didn't trust him. I believed that even if he attended, he wouldn't be ready, so I sat down to prepare my own case.

On October 12th, I impatiently waited for the hearing to begin. I felt that I had a good case whether or not I was being represented by a lawyer. It was pouring rain as I walked out the section gate, through the courtyard to the double gates, through the double gates into the next courtyard, and into the commander's office.

I came in sopping wet but in high spirits. Two Americans were waiting, Consul Stephen Pattison and Eigel Hansen, the legal advisor. Pattison immediately apologized for not having a stenographer. "We searched all over the Embassy but couldn't find one that was available," he said, "so we brought a tape recorder to record the testimony. Should we wait for your lawyer?"

"No, go ahead," I said. "I don't think he'll be here." He was already 10 minutes late.

Pattison turned on the tape recorder, introduced those present, gave a brief description of the nature of the hearing, then asked me if I had a statement to make.

"Yes," I said.

"Please proceed."

I read from my notes, offering a brief history of those actions which the United States government had taken against me that I considered to have been improper. Then I said that the letter from Consul General David Lyon which informed me of the revocation of my passport had stated the basis of that revocation was the California warrant of arrest. Yet the Code of Federal Regulations specifically stated that a passport could be revoked only for a federal warrant of arrest. "Since a federal warrant had not been in existence when the revocation order was issued on June 22, 1989, I contend that the revocation was illegal."

When I was finished, Eigel Hansen pulled out a copy of a federal arrest warrant dated June 22nd and handed it to me. It stated that I had "fled to avoid prosecution" from the California warrant which had been issued on March 14th, *two weeks after my arrest in Thailand.*

I was flabbergasted. I had never seen a copy of the federal warrant and had been unaware that it existed. Lowell Strong, the FBI agent who had seen me in July, had told me then that no federal warrant had been issued. Yet this was dated June 22nd. Either Strong had lied or the government had back-dated it. In addition, the letter from David Lyon revoking my passport had mentioned only the state warrant.

I was incensed. There were no charges against me in California until the warrant was issued. I said, "How anyone could possibly consider that I `fled to avoid prosecution' in California in March when I was in a Thai jail at the time the warrant was issued..."

"The foundation for the warrant is not an issue," Pattison interrupted. "I can't allow you to go too much into that beyond what you've already said."

He can't allow me to go into...?!! So he was going to play magistrate and write the rules too. I was getting railroaded. The U.S. government had stuck it to me once again. I left the hearing vowing to sue. I wanted to force these public servants to abide by the Constitution, to recognize that the Bill of Rights does not exist selectively — for some Americans and not for others — at their option, and that government officials are obliged to honor every citizen's rights, not only inside the United States, but wherever United States officials represent them.

The government had arranged for my incarceration without explaining why, an arrogant dismissal of my right of habeas corpus. American officials had ignored my requests to describe the charges against me in America, yet they were using those charges as an excuse to incarcerate me. They had issued a warrant that was blatantly bogus. They knew I hadn't fled. They had orchestrated my imprisonment, were a party to the administration of cruel and unusual punishment, and prevented me from being released on bond to fight my case on the outside. They had cut me off from the outside world so that I had no control over my business or personal affairs. They had dismissed any pretext of wrongdoing by claiming to be at the mercy of the Thai government. Yet, before the United States interfered in my case, the Thais had allowed my release on bail.

A week after my passport hearing, I was scheduled for court again. I didn't expect my attorney to appear, so I drafted a letter to present to the judge asking for postponement while I looked for a new lawyer. The letter described how I had been lied to and cheated by Sombattsiri.

The session was scheduled for 9 AM on October 19th. When I went to the courtroom, Nu and Chat were waiting but Sombat wasn't. The two boys came over and hugged me. "Sombattsiri yu nai?" I asked them. "Where is Sombattsiri?"

"Mai ru," they responded. "We don't know."

I handed the letter to the judge. He read it and asked what he was supposed to do with it.

"Put it in the court file," I suggested.

He shook his head and started to hand it back to me, then changed his mind and handed it to the prosecutor. I was furious at his indiscretion, but I controlled my ire. He was the last person I could afford to alienate.

The prosecutor read my letter and started laughing. He evidently thought my description of Sombattsiri's manipulations funny. He took the letter outside to show some of the other lawyers in the hallway. They all started laughing.

When the prosecutor returned a couple of minutes later and handed my letter to the judge, he started to give it back to me. Then he changed his mind and put it into his file as I had suggested.

Kachon arrived. He put a copy of the Bangkok Post down on the table in front of me. The headline screamed, "HUNDREDS KILLED IN HUGE SAN FRANCISCO EARTHQUAKE".

I grabbed the paper and attempted to focus on the story. My head was swimming. Was my family all right? What about all my friends there? Where was the epicenter? The frustrations of my own existence suddenly faded next to this. The newspaper railed about the collapse of the Bay Bridge, the Nimitz Freeway, and apartment buildings in the Marina district. I imagined the worst. The world outside had already become unreal to me — but this was unbelievable.

After allowing me time to digest the news, Kachon handed me copies of faxes from the International Legal Defense Council in Philadelphia, dated the first week of October. "I see the fac paper on Sombat desk. I see your name tat why I take." They were copies of the American arrest warrants and instructions to Sombattsiri about how to proceed with my passport hearing. Sombattsiri had received everything a week before the hearing, but hadn't bothered to read the material or attempt to get it to me.

The judge set the next session for the 27th of October, eight days later. He said that I had to tell Sombattsiri in person that he had been fired before I could bring in a new attorney. When I started to leave the courtroom, the guard grabbed the newspapers and shook his head. "Cannot," he said.

On October 27th, I returned to court. Kachon and Kenji had gone to Sombattsiri's house to make sure that he would come. They hadn't

179

told him that I was going to fire him. Instead, they told him that Chat's sister and Nu's mother were coming to testify.

Amazingly, Sombat arrived in court ahead of me. He was looking for the two women so he could call them to the stand. "I thought you were getting a new lawyer," the judge said.

"I am." I was confused. It was the judge who had told me to bring Sombat into court to fire him before I could hire a new lawyer. I turned to Sombat and demanded that he repay the money he owed me for my bail and the computer.

Sombat tried to ignore me. He turned to the judge and started to talk to him in very proper "high Thai". I couldn't follow the conversation. I repeated my demand, only louder. Suddenly Sombat whirled around and said, "I'm not going to give you anything!" With that, he picked up his briefcase and left the courtroom.

I was frightened. I wasn't sure I would ever see one baht of the 450,000 ($18,000) I had given him. What he had done for me would have cost 20-30,000 baht from an honest lawyer.

I turned to the judge and asked what recourse I had against Sombattsiri. He just shrugged. I don't know if he understood my question, or didn't want to understand. `But at least I've gotten rid of the bastard,' I thought. `Now maybe I can get witnesses to come to trial and finish my case.'

Kachon had contacted a lawyer friend who was prepared to take the case. I sat in the courtroom for a few minutes after Sombattsiri stormed out and gave Kachon a list of instructions to give to the newest lawyer. I again requested that he call all of the witnesses whom I had asked Sombattsiri to call. The judge set my next appearance for November 14th. My friends had more than two weeks to contact everybody.

Marcia Pixley arrived for a visit soon after my court session. I asked if the Embassy would be disposed to help retrieve my money from Sombattsiri. "I'll get David Lyon to write to him," she said.

"That won't do any good. He'll ignore your letters like he ignored your request to come to the hearing. Can't you get a Thai government official to take some action?"

"I don't think we can do that," she said.

I wanted to say, "You can get Thai officials to do what you want them to do when it serves your purposes," but I held my tongue, knowing it would only anger her.

Instead, I returned to my section and wrote a 16-page letter to the Philadelphia lawyers, asking that they take action to get my passport returned and to file a lawsuit against the United States governmental agencies that had so blatantly violated my rights.

On November 7th, the nine Americans in the prison were called to the vice commander's office to meet with a top official from the U.S. Department of Justice. He had just come to Thailand to ratify a prisoner exchange program negotiated between the two countries.

Stephen Pattison and Marcia Pixley accompanied the official. When Pattison had the opportunity, he handed me a copy of the warrant that had been issued in California on March 14th. Seven months after the fact, a U.S. official finally gave me a copy of the warrant.

"This is the first time that I have been officially informed of this charge, you know," I said.

"Yes, I know," he replied, without a trace of guilt.

"Have you sent a transcript of the passport hearing to the law firm in Philadelphia?"

"No," he answered. "I lost the address that you gave me at the hearing." I gnarled my teeth together repeatedly. This was not the first time Embassy officials had conveniently "lost" something pertinent to my defense.

The frustration and anger that I felt, was being felt — to some degree — by all foreign prisoners who were entangled in the Thai legal system. It translated into a tension between the various racial groups in the "garden" that erupted the day of the U.S. officials' visit.

A Flemish man was attacked by a gang of Chinese following an argument over drugs.

The Chinese often moved in packs and tried to run the "garden" through intimidation. Several Europeans, fed up with their constant bullying, got together and agreed that if any of them were ever attacked by the Chinese again, they would respond en masse. The next day, some prisoners met with the building chief to discuss the volatile situation and to find ways to reduce the tension.

While they were in their meeting, a Frenchman, walking through the "garden", was set upon by an Indo-Chinese who leapt from a hut and charged at him in a fury. I was no more than 10 feet away when a machete flashed in the air and sliced through his arm. The Frenchman screamed in agony. Within seconds, Europeans, Australians and Americans rushed into battle against the Indo-Chinese and his gang and a full-scale riot ensued. Men pulled apart huts to arm themselves with clubs, seized knives from the kitchen area, and went crazy attacking one another.

Those who spent much of their time in prison lifting weights soon overpowered the diminutive Chinese. The westerners chased them, kicked down their huts and threw their furniture into the ponds. Left in their wake were three groaning, writhing Asian bodies.

As a lifelong believer in non-violence and one who is a bit of a wimp, I had slipped away from the melee to the "garden" entrance. The few guards in the vicinity rushed off to get help. Within minutes, dozens of them, accompanied by the building chief and prison commander, swarmed to the area.

One rather tiny European inmate tried to stop them. "This is none of your business," he said to the startled legion. The guards actually hesitated and stopped, and were facing off with this lone, rather presumptuous farang. It presented such a ludicrous and unreal picture that I started laughing. The building chief broke the logjam, pushing past the prisoner and leading his men inside to break it up.

Five prisoners, including the Frenchman, were rushed to the hospital with serious injuries. Seventeen men were locked into their cells with their legs in chains for months. And the Indo-Chinese was transferred to the highest security building in the prison where violent inmates were kept.

* * *

Michael taught English to the commander of the prison hospital each day and asked if I would be interested in tutoring some physicians. I eagerly accepted. After teaching my usual class at the "school", I would now make my way to the hospital and tutor there as well.

When I wasn't teaching, I was studying Thai or German. Michael set up a language class inside the "garden" for anyone interested in learning his native tongue. By mid-November, he had about 10 regulars, myself included.

Life became somewhat more tolerable inside Khlong Prem. Or perhaps I was learning to make the most of it. As long as I had money to eat and could read or teach, which gave me a sense of purpose, I could survive.

On November 14th, I returned to court. Kachon and his lawyer friend had contacted all the witnesses on my list. I saw my old friend Khun Sumate and pulled up my chains to wai him in gratitude. He shook his head to indicate that a wai was not necessary. After eight months of being looked down upon, his attitude brought tears to my eyes. It was almost as if I had forgotten how it was to be treated as an equal by a member of Thai society.

Chat, his sister Rekha, Nu, Nu's mother, and Kenji were also there. "Where's Mark?" I asked Kenji. He pointed to a young Thai man sitting in the hallway. He was a college student and had been teaching the street kids to read and write as a class project. When Mark opened the shelter and many of the kids went there to live, this man followed and stayed on as a volunteer. He was working in the home almost every time I had gone there to visit. I nodded to him and smiled, but was angry that Mark had not come himself.

"Where is the Matichon reporter?" I asked Kachon.

"She say she don' haf to come," Kachon responded.

"Well, why didn't you subpoena her?"

"The lawyer tell me the jus say she come in the court or not is not importan," Kachon explained.

I angrily told Kachon to ask my lawyer why he didn't think her important when the prosecutor was able to introduce testimony from the police citing the Matichon article.

Sumate testified first. He told the court what type of business I had run. The judge asked if he knew anything about my purported sexual activities and he said he did not. When he completed his testimony, he waited to sign the typed transcript, then left the courtroom.

Next, Chat's sister Rekha and Nu's mother testified that I had been like a father to the two boys. They said that they were not aware of anything negative about our relationship and, through the years, the boys had only said good things about me.

Kachon then testified that he was working with me in the office at the time of my arrest, that he had worked with me for nearly two years, and that I operated a legitimate incentive tour business. He reiterated that the police had picked up the boys at their respective schools the day I was arrested and that they had not been in my apartment.

I asked when the volunteer from Mark's home would testify to refute the allegations made by Howard Ruff and John Cummings about the shelter being a front for child prostitution — allegations that were made by the police at the press conference and later in the courtroom.

Kachon told me that the judge didn't want to hear his testimony, that it wasn't relevant. How could it not be relevant, I thought worriedly.

As my operations manager, Kenji was supposed to testify about the nature of my business. The judge told my lawyer that he had enough evidence and Kenji's testimony was also unnecessary. He said he would announce his decision in three days.

My lawyer, accompanied by Kachon, Kenji, Chat, Nu and the other witnesses went into the hallway to talk to the prosecutor who told them that I had won the case and that he saw no reason to appeal the verdict. When Kachon came in to report the conversation to me, I asked him to call all the newspapers and to bring the reporters to the courtroom on the 17th. "I won't believe I've won until the judge gives his verdict, but I hope so!" I said as the guard ordered me to my feet.

Downstairs, as I again squatted on the filthy floor, chains affixed to my bare ankles, I glanced out the window through the bars and saw Nu. Tears were streaming down his face. I smiled and gave him the thumbs-up sign. He was unable to return my smile. He turned his face and walked away from the window. That was the last time I ever saw him.

* * *

On November 17th I was called to court to hear the verdict. As I was being led into the courtroom by the guard I saw Kachon. "Where are the newspaper reporters?" I asked anxiously.

"Outside," he said, gesturing to the hallway.

I hadn't seen anyone when I arrived, so I asked him to please find them.

He came back in alone. "Not here. I don'no where they go," he said perplexed.

Kenji and Chat stepped over to wish me luck. "Where's Nu?" I asked.

"In school," Kenji replied. "He moved out."

"Moved out!" I exclaimed, "What do you mean `moved out'?"

"He went back to Mark's shelter," Kenji said, adding that Nu had not been getting along with Chat. I found the news very disturbing.

185

They had always gotten along well in the past. Dammit, I thought, why are innocents always the casualties of other people's wars?

The judge entered the courtroom and prepared to read the verdict before an audience of Kachon, Kenji, Chat, the lawyer and myself. The prosecutor was not there.

The judge instructed me to rise and stand at the podium in the center of the room. He began reading the verdict in Thai. I couldn't understand a word. I glanced helplessly at Kachon who was standing just behind me. He was smiling. "You win," he said. "Jus say you not guilty."

I turned around, grabbed Kenji and Chat to hug them and my legs gave way. I held onto the two of them and sobbed with relief. Kenji grabbed me to hold me up. Chat flushed with embarrassment, but kept his composure.

After the decision, I was taken downstairs. Kenji and Kachon appeared at the barred window of the holding cell. "Somebody took all the reporters downstairs to the coffee shop while the verdict was being read," Kenji said.

"Who?" I yelled.

"Maybe the prosecutor. Maybe somebody else who didn't want them in the courtroom," he said lamely.

Someone had stolen my moment of vindication with the media.

"The jus say you go out tonite," Kachon interjected. "He say if you guilty, you sentence six months. You in jail more six months already, so jus say you go out tonite, no matter. I go to Khlong Prem. Fi' o'clock I meet you."

The six hours I had to wait in the holding cell seemed like six days. I wanted to report the verdict to Michael, to Doctor Dick, to David Groat, not to mention my cynical European and American compatriots. "Nobody ever wins a case," they had told me. Ha!

While I was waiting, I saw one of the Thai prisoners from Bangkok Special Prison in an adjacent holding cell. "Tell Peter I won!" I cried to him. "Tell everybody I won!" He nodded vigorously.

186

The Face of the Monster

I boarded the bus for the return transfer in high spirits. Two men from Bangkwan Prison boarded just after I did. They were wearing two sets of chains — one welded around their ankles. As the bus started up, one of the men started crying. His companion told me that their appeal to the third court, the Supreme Court, had been rejected. The sentence was death. They had been found guilty of selling a large quantity of heroin. Within a few days, the two would face a firing squad. I looked into the eyes of the condemned man. He tried to smile at me through the tears.

Their pain was so apparent that everyone on the bus was affected, and I had to view my acquittal from a different perspective. My victory was insignificant compared to their lives. These men were about to die!

When I arrived back at Lardyao, it was 5:30. I looked for Kachon, but he was not there. After my chains were pried loose, I rushed into Building Two and went from cell to cell telling everyone the good news.

"You're the first foreigner to win a case in the four years I've been here," Michael said. I could see in his face that he had mixed emotions. He didn't know whether to be happy for me for my vindication or sad for himself for the friend he would lose.

But the prison had not received orders to release me and, again, I was locked into my cell. I washed with a towel and put on the same clothes I had worn the day I was re-arrested in May. Then I sat on my rolled mattress and waited. An hour went by. I unrolled my mattress and laid down. The two men in my cell, a Burmese man convicted of a contract killing and an Australian convicted of heroin possession, began joking about my "release." As the evening wore on, I became more and more worried that something had happened. Finally, at 10 o'clock I fell to sleep.

* * *

187

November 18, 1989 — November 20, 1989

I woke up the next morning and went outside to bathe, just as I had done every morning. "We thought you were getting out," my friends kidded.

"I thought so too," I said softly.

I sat down with Michael in his hut for a cup of coffee. At that moment, two trustees walked up behind me and told me to gather my belongings. "You go home," they said excitedly, "Go! Go!" they yelled as I bid Michael farewell. "Hurry up!"

The trustees followed me back to the cell and, while I was trying to put on my pants, kept yelling at me to hurry. I gave away my mat to a Thai man, gave some utensils and things to David, and rushed out the gate to the Administration Building.

Another trustee met me there and escorted me through the prison to a building in front of the entry to the "foreign section". "Wait here," he ordered, leaving me standing alone.

On the ground I placed two paper bags filled with my few clothes and waited. And waited. I wondered if Kachon was outside waiting for me, and why I had to be rushed here to wait. Hours later, I was still standing there waiting.

At 11 AM, a farang Catholic priest in a white robe appeared and walked past me to the foreign section. I went over and introduced myself to him. I was anxious to learn if anything had appeared in the newspapers about my acquittal. "Yes," he exclaimed. "There was an article in the Bangkok Post this morning. It briefly mentioned that you had won your case in Thailand, but that you would be extradited to the United States to face similar charges there."

My heart sank like a stone. Whoever had taken the newspaper reporters from the courtroom had evidently made sure that any news of my victory would be tempered by reports that I was being accused of similar acts elsewhere. It didn't matter that I had been acquitted.

When people of power believe you are guilty, the belief becomes the "truth."

In the mid-afternoon, I was joined by a Filipino, who was also being released and, at long last, a deputy arrived and took us through a huge gate to the visiting area, then through a courtyard to a guard's station near the main entrance.

As the guard filled out the release papers, I asked for my wallet which presumably still contained more than $1,000.

"Cannot," the guard said.

"What!" I cried. "You cannot give me my wallet?"

"Mai dai," he repeated. "Today is Saturday. Your wallet is locked up. We do not have the key."

I grew noticeably irritated — but inasmuch as the Filipino was already following two deputies through the long dark corridor to the front gate, I was not going to stand there and argue. I hurried after them.

When the gate was finally thrown open, sunlight flooded my face as if for the first time — it felt gently warm and healing. I closed my eyes against the brightness. I reopened them and saw a disheveled-looking Kachon. His hair was on end and his clothes wrinkled like bunched-up aluminum foil.

"I wait for you all night," he said smiling.

I was overcome with gratitude. Instantly, a lump filled my throat. I did not know many people who would have done that and I was deeply touched. But, I was also unable to say anything more than "thank you". Instead, I kept my feelings at a safe distance and launched into a tirade about my money.

Kachon just stood there grinning. When I stopped talking, he ambled over to speak to the officers and then reported back to me, "Poleet say you mus come back Monday."

"How can I come back on Monday?" I grumbled. "I'm going to either be in jail here or on my way to the United States to face charges there."

The Filipino and I were ordered into the rear of a police pickup. Kachon jumped in with us. One of the deputies closed the gate, then leapt into the cab with a second officer and drove on. About a half mile down the road, the truck pulled into a parking lot in front of Bangkhen Police Station and I was escorted inside and up to the second floor.

A few minutes later, Kenji appeared. "Just sit down," he said to me. "We're trying to work something out with the police."

Kachon came up the stairs jabbering to an officer. I relished the feeling of simply sitting outside a cell and didn't say another word until Kachon had finished his talk and sat down alongside me.

"I want to thank you two for everything you've done for me!" I said. My voice broke suddenly and again I felt my emotions twisting in my throat. "When this is finally all over, I'll pay you guys back, believe me."

Two officers beckoned us to follow them. "We're trying to get you released," Kenji said as we stood up. "Kachon has talked them into taking you to Din Daeng Station."

The policemen led us out of the station and down the street to a corner where they actually hailed a taxi. The five of us rode from Bangkhen to Din Daeng which took about a half hour and I enjoyed every minute of it. "This is a real treat!" I gushed at Kenji. I hadn't experienced air conditioning in nine months and it felt very very good.

At Din Daeng, Kachon tried to convince the officers to release me until Monday. He reminded them I hadn't gone anywhere when I was out on bail. One officer was about to let me go, but another objected. "We should get approval from the Colonel," he insisted.

"Who do they need permission from?" I asked Kachon.

He pointed to a picture of Khongdej Choosri and I groaned. I knew that if my release were up to him, I didn't stand a chance.

I was locked in the cell that, by now, could have had my name inscribed over the door. Kachon went back to Victory Monument to get Chat. They returned together an hour later along with Chat's best friend from the soi. They bought fried rice at a nearby stand and we had dinner together, albeit on different sides of the bars.

When the skies turned dark, I told them to leave. "They're not going to let me out," I said with resignation. As they walked back to Victory Monument, I longed to take that stroll with them and, instead, settled down on the hard wood floor and tried to sleep.

A couple of hours later, Mark Morgan came in, dropped down on the ground, and woke me. "I'm getting married tomorrow," he said.

"What? To whom?"

"To Sujitra," he said, referring to the young Thai woman who had been house mother at the children's shelter for almost a year-and-a-half. "My parents have come for the wedding."

He then told me that Howard Ruff, a blustery businessman from Utah whom Rick Stokes had warned me about in his letter, was waging a vigorous campaign to discredit the home and had made an inflammatory videotape which was getting air time on American television.

Ruff had become involved initially when he read a favorable 1988 Bangkok Post article about Mark Morgan's shelter and decided to raise money for it. Ruff said he was proud of a fellow Mormon doing such good work. But when reports appeared in the press and insinuations were made about the shelter being involved in a child sex ring, Ruff figured he'd been taken for a ride.

Morgan continued, "Howard Ruff has been vicious. He just held a celebrity roast in my honor. He interviewed my ex-wife who claimed that I had deserted my children in Utah, and John Cummings who stated that you ran a sex tour business and that my home was a front for child prostitution — the show aired there on ABC!"

I suddenly felt as if I'd been hit in the face with a club. So it was Cummings after all! I had clung to the belief the whole mess had been concocted in Thailand — anything else just seemed too far-fetched, too outlandish, too unbelievable... fabricating tales about a sex tour operation! And the police believed him. What the hell was the matter

191

with these people?!! Didn't they bother to investigate such deadly-serious allegations from such a questionable source? Didn't they know when they were being conned?

I realized Cummings was crazy — I knew he was sick. But I had not connected it, I had not understood that he could be so full-blown psychotic as to try to ruin my life and Mark Morgan's life and the lives of 30 or so kids with fabrications created from his sweeping guilt and paranoia. Just as Cummings had conned me over the years, he conned the authorities into believing he had reliable information. And I was sure he had determined — in his mind — that destroying our lives could work to his advantage.

Now I understood why, when the police first came to investigate, they had asked only about Chat and made no mention of Nu. It was because Cummings had never met Nu and did not know of him. It also became clear that he misunderstood the name of the Bangkok Children's Shelter to be "Mark Morgan Incorporated", which is how it was initially referred to in newspaper stories about it being "a front for child prostitution".

After the first wave of bad publicity, a sympathetic friend of Mark's had donated to him a parcel of land in northern Thailand where he opened a second shelter in Chiang Mai. A few poor children from the hill tribes came to live there, and some of the kids from Bangkok asked to go "up country". But both places were in jeopardy now.

"Most of the donations from America have stopped," Mark said. "We're running both homes mostly on donations from Thais. They don't believe any of the stories. But Ruff and his people have come over here with that video (transferred to the Thai system) of my ex-wife and Cummings. They are running around now showing it to (Thai) officials, whoever they can get."

Mark and I talked for another hour. He was understandably upset and I could sympathize. I didn't know how Cummings had done this and I didn't know why. But there was nothing worse than this feeling of helplessness when so much seemed to be at stake.

When he got up to leave, he apologized and said, "I've got to get ready for the wedding. I'll come back tomorrow."

On Sunday night Mark returned dressed in suit and tie. "I just came from my wedding at the Dusit Thani," he said, shoving a box through the bars. "Here's part of my steak dinner. Sujitra is waiting in the parking lot, so I can't stay long. She sends her regards."

"Are you going to visit me in the immigration jail?" I asked, assuming that's where I'd be going next. I'd been informed anyone facing charges in another country would have to stop there.

"I don't think so," he said apologetically. "It's convenient and easy to come here and just sit with you. But I don't think it's a good idea for me to go to the immigration jail. You shouldn't be there long anyway."

After Mark left, our conversation of the previous night came back to me. There was so much to think about. I stayed awake wondering what I could do to help keep the shelter open. Howard Ruff had seized on John Cummings' wild allegations and enhanced their credibility by getting them aired on television. They had already hurt too many people needlessly. Besides myself and the employees of my company who had all lost their jobs, they had negatively affected the lives of Chat, Nu, Mark, Thep, Mark's father, the employees at the shelters, and the 30 children to whom Mark had provided a home. I wondered if there was a way to stop moral crusaders like Ruff from doing any more damage. He was like a bull in a china shop, destroying everything, then announcing he's come to help.

Ruff liked to take on causes and this one was great for his tarnished image. Over the years, he became a very vocal doomsday salesman. He appealed to the fear in people and in the late 70's wrote a book predicting the imminent collapse of the American economy. He counseled people to buy gold, get out of the stock market, and stockpile a year's worth of canned food in their homes. Had people listened, it could have precipitated exactly what Ruff was warning against. The market soared right through the '80s, and gold went nowhere. But Howard Ruff sold books.

Those sales enabled him to publish a stock market newsletter called "The Ruff Times" with the same grim doomsday message. As prosperity continued throughout the country, he changed its name to "Financial Survival Report" before later changing it back. In early 1993, he ceased publication without notifying his subscribers, who according to one report in the Oakland Tribune, "became suspicious because Ruff had said nothing" to them. Ruff, who once filed for bankruptcy, claimed he didn't have the money to send notices to his readers. The Tribune quoted him as saying "When you're going through temporary troubles, there's no percentage in telling the world about it and bringing down more trouble."

I didn't realize the entire night had passed until light began to filter in through the hallway. A new week was beginning, my first in a long while outside Khlong Prem. I hoped it would mean a new start. What I didn't know was that I was a long way away from the end and the worst had yet to come.

Ten

I.D.C.

"Virtue itself turns vice, being misapplied;
and vice sometimes by action dignified."
— **Shakespeare, *Romeo and Juliet***

November 21, 1989 — December 7, 1990

By the time Kachon and his lawyer friend arrived at Din Daeng Station at 8 AM, I had finally begun to fall asleep. Kachon slipped a sheet of paper with Thai characters written on it through the bars. "I go to Lardyao for wallet," he said. "You sign name here to say is okay for me."

Kenji arrived as I was signing the paper. Kachon took it and left while the lawyer stayed behind to talk. Kachon had not said what the legal fees would come to, so I told the lawyer I would authorize a payment of 10,000 baht from the sale of my office equipment to pay for the final two court sessions. Then I asked him to file law suits against Sombattsiri and the newspapers, and suggested that he meet me at the immigration jail after the transfer from Din Daeng. He nodded, said he had to talk to Kachon, then departed. Kenji started to leave with him.

"Kenji," I said. "Go with Kachon to Lardyao to pick up my wallet. It has over $1,000 in it."

A few minutes later, two officers unlocked my cell door, told me to gather my things, handcuffed me and led me to a police pickup. Seated between the two of them in the cab, I left Din Daeng Station and headed for the Immigration Detention Center on Soi Suan Phlu.

195

I was brought to the fourth floor during lunch hour and most of the offices were deserted. There was a single immigration officer at his desk. The two policemen from Din Daeng handed him my file and sat down while he opened and read it.

"Why did you bring him here?" the officer asked the policemen. "The papers say he's been released."

It was difficult to follow the conversation, but something was said about the U.S. Embassy, my passport and a case in America. The immigration officer became irritated. He could find nothing in the file about the American request and he questioned why the officers had brought me to IDC. At that point, one of the policemen suggested sarcastically that they drop me at the Embassy itself. The immigration officer impatiently shook his head and said he would allow the Din Daeng cops to check me in and then he would decide what to do.

"Do you have a lawyer?" he asked in Thai.

"Yes," I replied in Thai. "He should be here soon." I said that neither my lawyer nor myself understood why I was being held after the judge had ordered my release.

The immigration officer ignored my remark and told the police to take me to the detention section. They led me downstairs and out the back, across an open courtyard, past a restaurant and through a guarded gate into a compound surrounded by a 10-foot wall topped by barbed wire. Once inside, they removed my handcuffs and turned me over to Immigration Detention Center officials who, in turn, took me to the second floor and through a hallway.

Paint was flaking from putrid green walls. To the right, partially opened windows looked out onto the courtyard. To the left, barred windows allowed glimpses of a large room literally jammed with men, some of them staring at us with somnolent, uncaring eyes. The air was thick with the smell of perspiration and urine.

We came upon an iron door secured by a huge padlock. It was unlocked and pulled from the latch. Then an iron bar was slipped out of the holding clamps with a metallic screech, and the heavy door swung open. I stepped inside and looked around. The door thundered shut behind me.

A cell of approximately 60 feet by 20 feet was filled with faces that turned toward me and belonged to men and boys of all ages and nationalities — faces from Asia, the Middle East, Africa, Europe, Australia and the Americas — nearly a hundred of them crammed into that small space.

A Pakistani sitting next to the door smiled and told me to sit down. I returned the smile and took a seat on the floor.

Seated next to him was an Indian. "Welcome to IDC," he said. He opened a notebook, started asking questions and jotted down my answers. "What's your name? Your age? What country are you from? Where did you just come from? Why are you here?" As he was asking, the Pakistani began snooping through my paper bags, removing the contents.

"Steve Raymond. Forty-four. The United States. Khlong Prem. I have a case in America," I answered, "so the U.S. government has taken my passport."

He wrote "Wanted in America" in his notebook, then told me to pay him 100 baht for "room service". He said, "People without money clean up the dishes and serve the food, so everybody who has money pays 100 baht for the service." That sounded reasonable. Luckily, Mark Morgan had given me 500 baht the night before at Din Daeng. I parted with a crisp purple bill.

"Can I buy a bed?" I asked.

"Yes," he replied. "It will cost 200 baht."

That also sounded reasonable. He returned two red bills as change from my purple note, then handed me a blanket.

"Is this it?" I asked incredulously.

"Yes, we'll give you a nice place. Where do you want to sleep?"

"Any place is fine," I mumbled, starting to lay the blanket down next to a Burmese man in the middle of the room.

"Not there," the Pakistani said. "We'll find you a better place." He picked up my possessions, carried them across the room, and unceremoniously dumped them at the foot of an obese Buddha-shaped Chinese man.

"This is my boss," the Pakistani announced. "He's the room leader."

"My name is Roza," the Chinese said in halting English. "Is everything here?"

"What do you mean?"

"Is everything here? Is anything missing? Did they take anything?"

"I don't think so," I said hesitantly. I was rather befuddled over the question. Like everyone else, he had watched the Pakistani search my bag.

"Where do you want to sleep?"

"Any place is fine," I repeated.

"Find him a place," Roza said to his henchman. Then he gestured to a corner of the room. "This is the coffee shop." Some cardboard boxes were stacked next to four large thermos bottles. Inside the boxes were a few plastic cups, some packages of noodles and a dozen cans of tuna.

"Coffee shop?" I started laughing, then looked around at the somber faces glaring back at me. Obviously no one else recognized the humor.

The Pakistani, whom I would come to know as Djaveed, had me set my blanket down in a space about two feet wide between a Chinese man and a walkway. "I'll be leaving soon," I thought, "so it really doesn't matter where I sleep in the interim."

Once I got settled, the vast population of cellmates resumed their normal activities. There was a lot of traffic moving past my blanket — leading to a much smaller area packed with about a dozen prisoners and, beyond it, the bathroom composed of a number of tiny cubicles lining a watermarked cement wall. Two contained squat toilets.

198

Nearby, faucets were running into four large overflowing cement tubs. I turned them off and stepped into one of the cubicles.

By the time I emerged, someone had turned the faucets on again. I later learned that they were intentionally left running to eliminate some of the diseases that festered from so many people living so closely together.

After meeting a few of my fellow detainees, I spread out on the blanket. The cement floor was very hard, but I assumed I could deal with it for the few days I would be there. I hoped Kachon and my lawyer would appear any moment and report that they had no trouble getting my wallet from Khlong Prem.

At 3:30, everyone jumped up and began yelling, "Cow! Cow!" I had dozed off but the noise jolted me awake. A group of Burmese men and boys quickly lined up in front of the iron door. As soon as it opened, they scurried into the hallway and reappeared within seconds carrying large aluminum trays — there were no plates or bowls — filled with rice and two types of soggy vegetables. The trays were placed on the floor in front of the prisoners and immediately they began to ravenously devour the food. I had no spoon, but I scooped up the rice with my fingers and dipped it into the vegetables — if that's what they were. It was so awful that I couldn't eat it and stuck with rice alone.

After the meal, those detainees in the center of the room picked up their belongings and moved to the side while two Burmese boys appeared from the bathroom carrying a sopping-wet blanket with which they wiped down the floor. Then the detainees scrambled and shoved, trying to regain their former places.

Watching their ignoble struggle for a spot on the floor, I realized the 200 baht I had paid for a "bed" actually secured me a "space". The center of the room was the ghetto of the cell. Those who arrived penniless were forced to fight for a place to sit each time the floor was cleaned following a meal.

I tried laying down to get some rest, but overhead fluorescents made sleeping quite difficult. The brightness in the room remained constant even after the sun went down and the tiny barred windows along the side and rear walls were so high it was impossible to say when the sun was up. I had been thrust into a sort of purgatory in which day was eternal and darkness belonged to another place.

* * *

"Cow, cow, cow!" I was suddenly rousted by the yells which signaled the arrival of another meal and another day. I glanced up at the clock. It read 6:00. Was it AM or PM? I wasn't sure, but I sat up and pulled the bottom of the blanket to me so that no one would trip in the rush to grab the food.

After the meal had been served and the floor mopped, Roza decided that I deserved a better spot. He instructed the Pakistani to clear an area for me against the wall next to a German named Uber.

Just then I heard a scream from the next room cell that made the hairs on my neck stand up. "The Iranian again," Uber said. The screaming continued, accompanied by the grating noise of metal banging against the metal bars.

"Why is he screaming?" I asked.

"He's been here for three years and four months," the German explained. "He can't go back to Iran (because he is anti-Khomeini) and he has no money so he can't get out of here. He's going crazy. He starts screaming when it's time for visitors."

I shuddered at the thought of having to exist in a cell for that length of time.

* * *

Visitors at IDC were permitted to come to the barred windows along the wall and one could actually have a pleasant visit with friends without having to yell across a void. Each day, a few older American

200

women appeared, chatted with a number of the detainees and sometimes did them favors. I learned they were a volunteer committee of Christians made up from the various churches in Bangkok. "We try to make sure that at least one volunteer visits the detention center every day," one of them said.

Three hours after the bell signaled the end of visiting hours, the afternoon meal arrived. I tried once more to eat the vegetables but again gave up and bought some noodles from the "coffee shop".

On the third day, the room leader decided that he wanted me to sleep next to him. A young Portuguese man had been sleeping in the spot, but Roza switched us. He noticed I hadn't been eating the food, and invited me to share meals with him and with the four Chinese men who ran the "coffee shop". The food, which Roza paid one of the cleaning women to bring in from the outside, was a decided improvement over what was being served.

At 9:30 AM, Kenji and Chat appeared at the barred window. "What happened to Kachon and the lawyer?" I asked. "Did you go with them to pick up my wallet?"

"No, he left before I knew it," Kenji replied. "He hasn't come back to the condo. He disappeared. We don't know where he went."

"Do you think he took off with my money?"

Kenji just shrugged.

"The Embassy people may come to take me to America any day. I would like to get lawsuits filed against the newspapers and the police before I leave. Could you please try to get hold of the lawyer? He planned to visit me, but I haven't seen him since I left Din Daeng."

Kenji said he would try to find both Kachon and the lawyer, then left with Chat. It was only at that point I realized Chat should have been in school.

A few minutes later, Khun Sumate and Khun Noo Setabut from Pacific World appeared at the bars. They were both very busy, very successful people and I was touched that they would take the time to visit. "We read the article in the paper about your acquittal," Sumate said.

"Is there anything we can do? Do you want anything?" Noo Setabut asked.

I had a simple request. "How about some peanuts and some of those caramel-covered nuts," I said. "Enough to share with the others?"

That afternoon a huge package arrived by courier. It was filled with candies and nuts, enough for 40 or 50 people. Then, a couple days later, a second package arrived. These gifts continued for the next couple of weeks and actually gave me something to look forward to after opening my eyes in the morning.

Although Roza was pleasant and generous to me, his attitude toward most of the others was less so. He owned the "coffee shop", received all the income from "sales", and took in all the "fees" collected from new arrivals. With this, he paid for his own private security force which was exclusively Chinese, the exceptions being Djaveed the Pakistani and the Indian man who had checked me in.

A few days after my arrival, a Frenchman arrived. He had been arrested in southern Thailand for possession of marijuana, had served a sentence in the prison at Songkhla, and arrived at IDC to await deportation to France. During the 20-hour drive from the southern province, he probably had had too many beers. One of Roza's "security guards" told him to take a shower and pushed him toward the bathroom. He reacted by turning around to face his attacker. Instantly, 10 men leapt up and began beating him mercilessly. I couldn't bear it — all those beatings I had witnessed before flew back at me and I threw myself into the melee between him and Roza's men.

"Stop it!" I cried. "Stop it!"

To my astonishment, the Chinese men backed away. I turned to the Frenchman. Blood was spurting from a large cut above his eye. His face was full of massive welts and bruises and his torn t-shirt exposed cuts and bruises on his chest. He was dazed and seemed to be in shock.

Roza was out of the room at the time of the attack. He had gone downstairs to work in the police office. When he returned, his "security men" told him what I had done.

"You mind your own business," he warned me.

"When someone is being hurt, it is my business," I replied vehemently.

"You don't understand," he said with disgust and shook his head as if he were reprimanding a child.

He was right. I didn't understand. It seemed to be such an arbitrarily cruel act.

A couple of days later another new arrival, a Sri Lankan man, was attacked. This time, when I attempted to intervene, two of the larger Chinese men shoved me violently across the room. I hit the wall and fell to the floor. I looked up to see one of the guards watching the attack from the hallway. He had a smile on his face. Then I realized that Roza operated with the acquiescence if not the encouragement of the immigration police. The attacks were intended to intimidate so that individuals would be obsequious. My successful defense of the Frenchman had sent a mixed message to the rest of the room.

I had expected a visit from Marcia immediately after my release from Khlong Prem to inform me about arrangements for my return to face charges in the states. Everyone else who came through IDC received visits from their embassies within a few days. But two weeks had passed and I hadn't heard a word.

Then on December 9th Marcia arrived to tell me that the prosecutor had filed an appeal of my acquittal and I would have to remain in Thailand until the appeal was heard.

"That can take a year!" I exclaimed. "Do you mean I have to stay in this place for a year? There's not even enough room to exercise in here."

"Do you want to return to Khlong Prem?" Marcia asked.

I wasn't sure what I wanted, other than out of jail. "Why hasn't the State Department reached a decision on my passport hearing so that I can wait for my appeal on the outside?"

"I'll send an inquiry to Washington," she said. "If we hear anything, I'll let you know."

They were at it again! Instead of being brought back to face charges in the U.S. which I was anxious to do because I knew I would win, I had been made to wait two weeks while the prosecutor changed his mind about appealing my acquittal. Something smelled of conspiracy. And while I had no concrete proof, I knew the Embassy had to be behind the appeal, working with the prosecutor. They wanted it both ways — they wanted me in prison but they weren't willing to take their chances in an American court. And it struck me that all those little guarantees in the Constitution — the right to due process, the right of habeus corpus, the right to a phone call, the right to legal representation, the right to a fair and speedy trial — of which most of us think nothing — are far more important than I could have ever imagined.

This much was certain: First, they knew they had no case against me back home and they were willing to let me waste away in prison while they tried to hunt something up. Second, had I been convicted of the charges in Thailand, I would have already served more time than the maximum sentence. The prosecutor knew that and there was no way in hell he would have appealed on his own. He had nothing to gain!

When Marcia walked away, the optimism I had felt following my acquittal was gone. And into that void sprang my unexpressed anger, turned against myself, in the form of a spiraling depression.

Kenji came to visit right after Marcia left. He thoughtfully brought some of my clothes, thinking I would need them for my trip. "I'm not going anywhere," I said dejectedly. "The U.S. is forcing me to stay in this hell-hole."

Kachon came rushing into the hallway just after Kenji walked down the stairs. "Where have you been?" I asked, "and where is my wallet and money from Khlong Prem?"

He was gasping for breath. He shook his head as if he were confused and frustrated. "I don'no you still in Thailand. Khun Sumate say to gib you this." He handed me a fax which had been sent to me in care of Sumate. It was from Bert Van Walbeek, the former president of S.I.T.E. Thailand, congratulating me on my acquittal. Kachon had gone to Sumate's office to ask for a job and Sumate had told him that I was looking for him.

"Sombat try to kill me," he cried. "He sen some men who tae' me up country by car. That why I not come. I fine the wallet at Khlong Prem, but no money."

I felt the air go out of my chest. I was crushed. I didn't know whether to blame him for the missing $1,000 and I didn't know whether to believe his fantastic story.

"Give me the wallet at least," I said.

He ran downstairs, then returned moments later and handed it to me. His story sounded so incredible, but with all that had happened and all I had witnessed in the previous nine months, anything seemed plausible. Prison officials could have taken my money. Someone could have actually tried to kill Kachon. But... I didn't really believe it. He had come to visit only after Sumate had told him that I was looking for him. All my money was gone. I couldn't even afford to buy a cup of coffee now. And what hurt even more was that Kachon was one of the people I trusted most.

I asked Marcia Pixley to check with the office at Khlong Prem to find out what had happened to the money. She later told me that prison records showed everything had been returned.

Because we were considered "detainees" and not prisoners, we were allowed to read newspapers and listen to the radio. The Christian group had been paying for a daily delivery to us of the Bangkok Post and the local Chinese language newspaper. I hungrily devoured every piece of news and trivia, then passed the paper around to others.

Kenji visited once more in December to tell me the police had been to the apartment twice since my acquittal to search for something they could use against me. "They are very angry that you won," he said. "They kept asking me things about people in America who I don't know. They wanted the computer from the office. I told them to go get it from Sombat. They said they're going to get David and Mark now."

"Mark? Why Mark?" I asked.

"Mark better watch out!" Kenji said. It was a prophetic warning.

The longer I was in IDC, the more I hated Roza's gang of Chinese thugs and their partners-in-cruelty, the immigration police. Both groups seemed to get sadistic pleasure out of lording over new arrivals, particularly poor Burmese students who had poured into Thailand to escape a brutal regime. Sadistic beatings were almost daily occurrences and they made the atmosphere ever more oppressive.

I had not received a single card or letter since my acquittal and began to worry about it. I had been in IDC for nearly a month, had written dozens of letters to family and friends, and nothing had come back from the outside. I wondered if the letters I had given to a Thai U.N. official in charge of mail had actually been sent.

On December 15th, the organization of Evangelical Christian women (formally called the Missionary Committee of Christ Church Bangkok) presented a Christmas show, brought a magician inside the cell to perform, sang Christmas carols and passed out packages of food and toiletries to everyone. I asked one of the ladies to post some letters for me when, suddenly, another woman snatched them from her hand and shoved them back at me. "They don't want us to take any mail from *him*," she barked.

Dejectedly I returned to my space on the floor and sat down. Who didn't want them to take my letters, I wondered. Who was "they"? Was it the Thai police or was it the U.S. Embassy? The combination of the rejection and the reminder that I would spend Christmas in this evil place without a word from home was too much for my fragile emotional state. When the Chinese men with whom I usually ate my meals called me to join them, I started to cry uncontrollably. "It's okay," one said sympathetically. "I've been in here for almost a year."

But he didn't understand. Bangkok — Thailand — the world that I had so fervently believed to be a wonderful place had become a living hell and I was unable to do anything about it. I just laid down, buried my head in my pillow and let myself go. The tears poured from my eyes like something in the rainy season. Every time I tried to stop, it just welled up inside and started again. The holiday program intended to bring a little cheer had had on me the opposite effect.

Six days later, a few days before Christmas, Sombattsiri appeared at the bars of the cell accompanied by two immigration officers. He looked ghostly-pale and bedraggled, and more nervous than usual. He hadn't shaved in a couple of days and his clothes were unpressed.

"I tried to give this check for $8,000 to the Embassy but they wouldn't accept it," he said, pulling a cashier's check from his pocket. "They said they needed authorization from your mother."

I scowled at the man who had caused me so much misery. "It's all right," I said. "I'll take it."

Sombattsiri looked perplexed. "I can't give it to you," he said, glancing at the officers hoping they wouldn't allow me to take the check. When they did not interfere, he said, "I need authorization from your mother, but I have the 14,000 baht that I owe you for the computer. I can't give it to you here."

"Yes you can. You can give it to me."

He glanced at the officers again. They nodded their heads and told him it was all right. He looked confused and upset. He was obviously used to dealing only with prisoners in regular prisons. Had he known I could accept the money, I doubt he would have offered it. Even though it was far short of what he had stolen from me, I was broke and needed anything I could get.

The front page of Matichon newspaper (Feb. 12, 1989) with the headline that started it all: "Hunt for Victims All Over the City, 'Play Back Door Game', Foreigners Gather Boys, Set Up Gang for Child Sexual Abuse."

Victory Monument

photographs by Eric Schniewind

Victory Monument condominium where Steve Raymond lived and worked.

Puttri Kuvanonda

Kenji Poonsawasdi

Typical street traffic in an area of Bangkok near Victory Monument.

Suchat (Chat) Sriboonrueng

Pipop (Nu) Sonthi

Din Daeng Police Station

The warrant charging Steve Raymond with unlawfully fleeing the U.S. "on or about March 14, 1989" to avoid prosecution despite the fact he had been living and working in Thailand since 1987.

Bangkok Special Prison

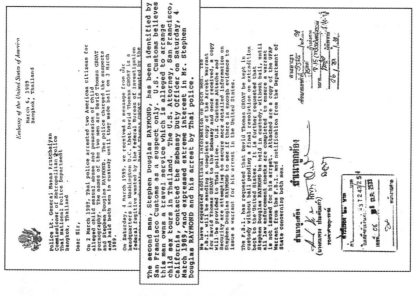

We will keep Thai police authorities informed of any new information received concerning these two men. It would be most helpful to know whether Thai police have enough evidence in the two cases to prosecute. If Thai police authorities prefer to have the suspects sent to the United States they should request that the Embassy revoke their passports and issue travel documents good for travel to the United States only due to the charges against them. The Thai authorities could then declare both men undesirables and eject them from Thailand on a U.S. Aircraft. If this were done we would attempt to have either U.S. Marshals or F.B.I. agents travel to Thailand to escort the two men back to the United States.

In the case against Stephen Douglas RAYMOND it would be helpful to know if Thai authorities found any information during his arrest that shows his travel service is used to arrange sex tours to Thailand from the United States. If such evidence was found it would be most helpful to U.S. law enforcement authorities in making a strong case for issuing a warrant for his arrest in California.

As always your cooperation and assistance in this matter is greatly appreciated. We are most anxious as these are most disturbing for the Embassy and we have every desire to assist Thai authorities in seeing that justice is served.

Sincerely,

David M. Copas, Sr.
Security Attache
Diplomatic Security
American Embassy Bangkok

Embassy of the United States of America

March 6, 1989
Bangkok, Thailand

Police Lt. General Manas Kruchaiyan
Commissioner of Metropolitan Police
Thai National Police Department
Bangkok, Thailand

Dear Sir,

On 2 March 1989, Thai police arrested two American citizens for alleged child sexual abuse and possession of child pornography. The names of the two men are David Thomas GROAT and Stephen Douglas RAYMOND. The police charged the suspects and held both men in custody until they made bail on 3 March 1989.

On Saturday, 4 March 1989, we received a message from our headquarters in Washington D.C. that David Thomas GROAT is a federal fugitive wanted by the Federal Bureau of Investigation. David Thomas GROAT is wanted by the

The second man, Stephen Douglas RAYMOND, has been identified by San Francisco Customs as a suspect only. U.S. Customs believes this man owns a travel service which is alleged to arrange child sex tours in Thailand. The U.S. Attorney, San Francisco, California, contacted the Embassy Duty Officer on Saturday, 4 March 1989, and expressed extreme interest in Mr. Stephen Douglas RAYMOND and his arrest by Thai police.

We have requested additional information on both men. The F.B.I. will be sending a complete copy of the Arrest Warrant for David Thomas GROAT to the Embassy and once received, a copy will be provided to Thai police. U.S. Customs Attache and Security are attempting to secure more detailed information on Stephen Douglas RAYMOND to see if there is enough evidence to issue a warrant for his arrest in the United States.

The F.B.I. has requested that David Thomas GROAT be kept in custody without bail pending a final resolution on extradition back to the United States. It is further requested that Stephen Douglas RAYMOND be held in custody, without bail, until all law enforcement checks are completed to ensure a warrant is not issued for his arrest. We have attached a copy of the UFAP Warrant from the F.B.I. and notification from the Department of State concerning both men.

Embassy Security Attache David Copas' March 6, 1989 letter to Bangkok police requests that Steve Raymond be held without bail and is in contradiction with a March 15 letter given to Ken West by Consul Ed Wehrli *(opposite page)* denying any involvement in Raymond's arrest.

Embassy of the United States of America
Bangkok

March 15, 1989

To Whom It May Concern:

The Embassy recently checked with United States Government law enforcement officials to determine if an American citizen, Mr. Stephen Douglas Raymond, age 42, was the subject of any outstanding federal arrest warrants in the United States. We have not received any information in response to these inquiries to indicate that there are any outstanding arrest warrants in the U.S. for Mr. Raymond at this time. We cannot rule out the possibility, however, that additional information to the contrary might become available in the future.

The Embassy has been advised informally that state law enforcement officials in the United States may wish to meet with Mr. Raymond on his return from overseas.

The United States Embassy in Bangkok has not submitted a request to the Thai National Police Department that they take Mr. Stephen Douglas Raymond into custody. The Embassy believes that decisions on Mr. Raymond's arrest case are matters for the appropriate Thai authorities.

Edward J. Wehrli
Consul

United States Department of State

Washington, D.C. 20520

MAR 2 2 1990

In reply refer to:
PPT/C - Raymond, Steven Douglas

Richard D. Atkins, Esq.
International Legal Defense Counsel
24th Floor, Packard Building
111 South 15th Street
Philadelphia, Pa. 19102

Dear Mr. Atkins:

I refer to your letter of March 12 concerning the passport revocation of Mr. Steven Douglas Raymond.

This Office is in the process of preparing Mr. Raymond's case for submission to and decision by the Assistant Secretary of State for Consular Affairs with respect to the findings and recommendations of the Hearing Officer. We expect a decision will be forthcoming in the immediate future.

As you may be aware, the scope of the hearing accorded to Mr. Raymond in his case is limited and designed to determined if he is the subject of an outstanding warrant of arrest which, under applicable regulations, would call for passport denial or revocation action. It is not the forum for challenging the validity of the warrants upon which the adverse passport action is predicated, issues which must be addressed to the judicial authorities which issued the warrants.

Meanwhile, on March 14, the Department authorized our Embassy in Bangkok to issue Mr. Raymond a travel document in the form of a card of identity or limited passport, for direct return to the United States. Since however there are no direct flights from Bangkok to the U.S., the travel document will not be issued to Mr. Raymond until U.S. escorts arrive to return him.

The U.S. Department of Justice is in charge of escort arrangements, and they have been alerted.

Sincerely,

William B. Wharton, Director
Office of Citizenship Appeals
and Legal Assistance

Below: State Department official William Wharton's letter indicates the Embassy had authorization to grant Raymond a limited passport as early as March 1990.

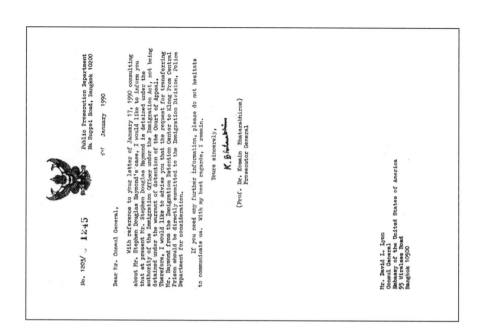

Public Prosecution Department
Na Huppei Road, Bangkok 10200

No. 1205/ ง 1245

5th January 1990

Dear Mr. Consul General,

With reference to your letter of January 17, 1990 consulting about Mr. Stephen Douglas Raymond's case, I would like to inform you that at present Mr. Stephen Douglas Raymond is detained under the authority of the Immigration Officer under the Immigration Act, not being detained under the warrant of detention of the Court of Appeal. Therefore, I would like to advise you that the request for transferring Mr. Raymond from the Immigration Detention Center to Klong From Central Prison should be directly submitted to the Immigration Division, Police Department for consideration.

If you need any further information, please do not hesitate to communicate us. With my best regards, I remain.

Yours sincerely,

K. Bhatarabhirom

(Prof. Dr. Komain Bhatarabhirom)
Prosecutor General

Mr. David L. Lyon
Consul General
Embassy of the United States of America
95 Wireless Road
Bangkok 10500

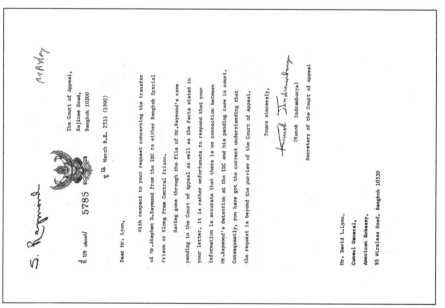

S. Raymond   MAxley

The Court of Appeal,
Rajinee Road,
Bangkok 10200

57885

8 14 March B.E. 2533 (1990)

Dear Mr. Lyon,

With respect to your request concerning the transfer of Mr. Stephen D. Raymond from the IDC to either Bangkok Special Prison or Klong Prem Central Prison.

Having gone through the file of Mr. Raymond's case pending in the Court of Appeal as well as the facts stated in your letter, it is rather unfortunate to respond that your information is accurate that there is no connection between Mr. Raymond's detention at the IDC and his pending case in court. Consequently, you have got the correct understanding that the request is beyond the purview of the Court of Appeal.

Yours sincerely,

(Kanok Indramharya)
Secretary of the Court of Appeal

Mr. David L. Lyon,
Consul General,
American Embassy,
95 Wireless Road, Bangkok 10330

Top: The Thai prosecutor indicates to David Lyon in January 1990 that Raymond was not being held because of the appeal. Nevertheless, Lyon and the State Department insisted that was the case. *Below:* The Thai Court reiterates what Consul General Lyon already knew, that Raymond could get out of IDC if the Embassy would issue him a travel document.

Embassy of the United States of America

March 01, 1990

Sopon Ratanakora
His Justice of The Court of Appeals
Thanon Na Hap Phoei
Bangkok 10200

RE: CASE OF AMERICAN CITIZEN, STEPHEN DOUGLAS RAYMOND
Black Case No. 3564/2532; Red Case No. 6633/2432
Date of Appeal: December 14, 1989

Dear Justice Sopon:

I am writing to you on behalf of Stephen Douglas Raymond, an American citizen whose case is currently being appealed to the Court of Appeals by the Department of Public Prosecutions.

Mr. Raymond was arrested by the Royal Thai Police on March 1, 1989, charged with indecent acts with children, and incarcerated in Bangkok Special Prison. The Embassy revoked his U.S. passport on June 22, 1989, because of pending federal and state arrest warrants in the United States. In August 1989 he was moved to Klong Prem Central Prison.

On November 17, 1989, following the recantation of testimony against Mr. Raymond by key witnesses, the Criminal Court decided to drop the charges against him. The Department of Public Prosecutions then appealed the Criminal Court's decision to the Court of Appeals.

Following the Criminal Court's decision, Mr. Raymond was transferred to the Immigration Detention Center due to the fact that he is not in possession of a valid national passport.

Mr. Raymond, who is suffering from several medical ailments, has repeatedly requested that he be moved from the IDC to either Bangkok Special Prison or Klong Prem Central Prison. Given the fact that the IDC is not intended to house long-term residents, the Embassy has supported his efforts to be transferred.

The Embassy has been advised by officials in the Public Prosecutor's Office and the Immigration Detention Center that because Mr. Raymond's case is currently under appeal, and he is being held solely because he is not in possession of a valid passport, he must be held in the IDC.

Embassy of the United States of America

Bangkok, Thailand
June 26, 1990

Mr. Stephen Douglas Raymond
Immigration Detention Center
Immigration Division
Royal Thai Police
Soi Suan Plu
Bangkok

Dear Mr. Raymond:

I refer to your letter to me of May 25 and to your letter to Embassy Parconsul Marcia Pixley of June 15. In those letters you have made several statements concerning the alleged role of the U.S. Embassy in your arrest and continued incarceration in Thailand which simply are not accurate.

I would first like to state categorically that neither the Consular Section nor any other part of this Embassy had any advance knowledge that you were going to be arrested by the Thai police on March 1, 1989, or had any role in your arrest. The Embassy first learned of your arrest on March 1, 1989, when we were notified by the Thai authorities that two Americans had been arrested and were being held at Din Daeng police station. I subsequently read of your arrest in the paper on March 2 which was the first time I had heard your name. As Consul, I never did later make a request that your preliminary bail be revoked but this was done at the request of Department of Justice officials in the United States.

You state further that your incarceration for the past sixteen months has been wholly due to the actions of U.S. authorities. This is not true. You are being held here due to the decision of the Department of Prosecutions to appeal a lower court ruling to dismiss your case to the Court of Appeals. It is true, however, that you are being held in the IDC, as opposed to a regular prison or being eligible to apply for bail, due to the revocation of your U.S. passport. The decision to revoke your passport was not made by this Embassy but was done on the receipt of specific instructions from the Department of State which was acting in response to a request from the Department of Justice.

Top: Despite acknowledging to the Bangkok Court of Appeals that Raymond "is being held solely because he is not in possession of a valid passport", Consul General Lyon and the State Department indicate in letters to Raymond *(below)* and to senators and congressmen that he was being held due to the prosecutor's decision to appeal.

A detainee rendered this drawing (for which Steve Raymond paid 80 baht) of the Immigration Detention Center during a rare less-than-capacity morning.

"I need a receipt," he said somewhat flustered, and handing me a piece of paper and a pen, he fumbled in his pockets and out came a wad of purple bills. He had been trapped. I did not know why he felt obliged to come to IDC, but I was sure he expected to leave with the same amount he came in with.

"Don't think I'm a bad person," he pleaded. "Your mother is a good person and she loves you."

"She is," I agreed. I was intrigued by this exchange. What had happened to this man to force him to my cell? Had he heard I'd written to the Lawyers Council of Thailand? Had an unknown emissary physically threatened him? Had he read Dickens' *A Christmas Carol?*

When he left, I was bewildered. I was holding 14,000 baht in my hands and Sombattsiri had actually uttered something of an apology to me. The money represented a small fortune. At most I spent between 50 and 100 baht a day for coffee and noodles. This money would last me for months.

I immediately gave 2,500 baht to a friend from Bangladesh who would use it to get home, and sat down to write to David and the others at Khlong Prem to tell them of Sombattsiri's strange change of heart.

A man from Sri Lanka who had seen Sombat give me the money asked if I'd buy his suitcase for 500 baht so that he could pay the police to take him to the airport for a flight back home. Even though the man was a stranger, I felt that if I could help free him from this horrible place for a lousy 500 baht, I would do it. I gave him his asking price, then put the rest of my money in the suitcase and hung it on the wall over my head.

Christmas was very depressing. I hoped that something would happen, but the day came and went like any other. The Chinese men who ran the coffee shop for Roza had grown jealous that he allowed me to eat with them without doing any work, so they got even by having Christmas dinner while I was in the shower. As a result, I went to sleep hungry.

Roza appointed Isa, a man from Oman, to be his "chief of security." Isa's chief qualification for the job was his bulk. His lack of intellect and education was blatant. He walked around the room with a large stick constantly intimidating everyone and, because his gait resembled that of an ape, invited the nickname "The Monkey".

Two days after Christmas, two Burmese arrivals became embroiled in a skirmish over food. The Chinese gang attacked and beat them into submission. Then Isa lined up all the Burmese, grabbed the first in line who was a dwarf by comparison, and lifted him off the ground. "You Vietnam?" he shouted into his face. The Burmese man was bewildered. He didn't understand.

"I don't like Vietnam," Isa growled, dropping him to the floor and slamming a fist into the man's head. The Burmese staggered dizzily but Isa kept at him. "You like to fight?" Punch after punch came flying at him until he was dazed and bloodied. Then the "chief of security" moved on to the next man. The second Burmese was more than a foot shorter and a hundred pounds lighter than Isa. He tried to deflect the Monkey's blows, but Isa threw him into a headlock and beat him senseless. He dropped his bloodied victim to the floor and continued along the row of terrified men.

We were helpless to stop it. The sight of such insane brutality sickened everyone, but we knew that if we tried anything the Chinese gang would attack. Since Roza had appointed Isa and Roza had been appointed by the police, it was futile to complain.

New Year's Eve was celebrated with a great deal of effort. Those who could afford to pay Roza 300 baht for a bottle of Mekhong spent the evening drinking whiskey and coke, while addicts gathered in the small room to snort heroin. Isa drank whiskey, snorted heroin and passed out, which gave the rest of us half a night of peace.

On January 2nd, an immigration officer came to the cell and called my name. The door was unlocked and I was instructed to put on a pair of thongs and follow. It was the first time I had been out of the room in 40 days. It was exhilarating just to be able to walk out the door and through the courtyard.

The officer said that someone had come to see me and that he was waiting in the colonel's office on the fourth floor of the immigration building. I relished the exercise and persuaded the officer accompanying me to walk up the stairs rather than ride the elevator.

We entered the room where I had spent my first moments at IDC. A young, rather thin American couple stood and introduced themselves. "Steve, I'm Bob Pisani and this is my wife."

I took their outstretched hands. The handshake was awkward. I hadn't clasped anyone's hand in months.

Two or three months earlier, my mother had written to tell me that an attorney from the Philadelphia law firm she had engaged to assist me might come to visit. Nevertheless, I was still shocked to see him. He and I sat down on a bench in the outer office while his wife chatted with the colonel in charge of IDC.

"I've been trying to contact Sombattsiri," he began. "But I can't reach him. He won't return my calls."

I wasn't really interested in Sombattsiri. I wanted to know what his firm had done about getting my passport returned so that I could get out of IDC. And I was more interested in whether or not he had filed a lawsuit against the United States government to force them to either return the passport or return me to the United States. "Didn't you receive the letter I wrote you in October?"

He looked puzzled. "What letter?"

My heart sank. My hopes for getting out of IDC depended on his receiving this information. "The letter I wrote describing and chronicling the abuses of U.S. authorities. I had assumed that you had already filed a lawsuit."

"We've been hired only to get your passport returned. I suggest that you have your family get another lawyer for the lawsuit."

I was devastated. I returned to the room and thought about writing my mother, but was too depressed. I lived day to day with this thought in mind: Someday, I would be able to confront those who were responsible. I had thought that my October letter would have precipitated some action. But Pisani now said that he did not think he could even get my passport returned. What good was a lawyer who was pessimistic about his ability to accomplish the only thing he was purportedly hired to do?

* * *

Roza frequently worked outside with the police and, one day, appeared at the barred window to talk to me. "Are you Mark Morgan?" he asked, knowing what my name was. I assumed he was confused and that Mark had come to visit.

"No, Roza. Mark Morgan is a friend. Is he here to see me?"

He shook his head. "I'm looking for an American named Mark Morgan. You're the only American in IDC now. Somebody says there's a Mark Morgan here."

"Morgan isn't a prisoner."

Roza shook his head again and said, "Mai ru ruang. You don't know the story." Then he turned and walked away.

That afternoon there was a commotion in the hallway. I stood up to see a group of police officers leading Mark Morgan up the stairs to the floor above. He was handcuffed. "Mark!" I shouted. "What are you doing here?"

He glanced back but the police pushed him forward and wouldn't let him talk. Roza followed the entourage. "Where are they taking him?" I yelled.

"Room Four," Roza answered.

"Why Room Four?" I asked. Farangs were never taken to Room Four.

"How can I get up to see him?"

"It will cost you," Roza said.

"How much?"

211

"At least 200 baht. I'll ask the police." He turned and went back downstairs.

A few minutes later Roza returned with one of the officers. "You can't move to Room Four no matter how much money you pay," the officer said.

"How about bringing my friend down here?"

"Cannot. U.S. Embassy told us not to let the two of you talk to each other."

I returned to my blanket, but Roza called me back to the bars. "You can't have any visitors. The police told me not to allow anybody to visit either you or your friend. Instructions from the Embassy."

I was furious. The Embassy was treating me like some kind of international terrorist when, in fact, they had done everything in their power to persecute me. `They're the terrorists,' I thought. Even those *convicted* of the worst crimes imaginable can have visitors — but here in detention, the Embassy was dictating that a man found innocent could not.

The next day during visiting hours I asked one of the United Nations workers why I was being singled out for this kind of persecution. "I don't understand it," he said. "Not even murderers have their visits cut off."

The week after Mark Morgan's arrival in IDC, the center was humming with activity. He was taken out of the cell daily for interrogations and press conferences. CBS television network had even sent a film crew to interview him. The stories in the newspapers were almost as sensational and distorted as those that appeared when I had been arrested 10 months earlier. Not only were John Cummings' stories repeated over and over, but with increasing frequency he was mentioned by name — John Cummings, the star witness.

Nevertheless, the Bangkok Post made some attempt at reporting the facts. It said that Howard Ruff had been carrying on a campaign to try to close down Mark's children's shelter and that police had investigated the home but had not found any improper activities being conducted by Morgan, his employees or volunteers. That didn't matter to Howard Ruff who, the Post said, went to his friend Senator Jesse Helms and got in to see the Thai ambassador in Washington, D.C. At Ruff's bidding, Helms asked the Thai ambassador to order police in Bangkok to close the shelter.

The Post story said that Mark was then arrested for operating children's homes without the proper government permit, both shelters were closed, the children from the homes were taken to welfare centers, and Mark was brought to IDC to be expelled from the country. The paper stated that Mark Morgan was now being investigated for child molestation.

One day, while Mark was to meet with police investigators, he called to me to come to the bars. "I can only talk for a minute," he said. "The police want me downstairs."

"What's happening?" I asked excitedly.

"The police have been interrogating the kids."

"Are they using electric torture like they did with Chat and Nu?"

"No," Mark said. "After the newspapers picked up what Chat and Nu said in court, and Din Daeng got in trouble, I don't think they'll try that again. Anyway, the police couldn't get any of the kids to say what they wanted."

I felt sorry for Mark. I knew that with all of the publicity that had been generated, the police were now obliged to find him guilty — and it would be for something more than running the homes without a permit.

* * *

Eleven

At Knifepoint

*"In the corrupted currents of this world
offences gilded hand may shove by justice;
and oft tis seen the wicked prize itself buys
out the law."*
— Shakespeare, *Hamlet*

W hen Mark was brought back later, he was too depressed to talk. For the next few days, I sent numerous messages through Roza and the missionaries, but the only response I received was a verbal message that he was too distraught to write anything.

Finally, after about a week, I received a note. "Howard Ruff is the winner of at least this round," it began, and said that Ruff had presented a copy of his videotape featuring John Cummings to Thai police and they bought it — lock, stock and barrel.

He ended the letter by saying that some of the kids went back to their home provinces and that Nu went to live with Wasana, the Thai woman who had been the cook at the shelter, and her son. The 30 kids who had been living at the shelters would now be forced to leave school and return to the streets or end up in welfare centers.

Meanwhile, Ruff claimed he had obtained proof from police in California that Morgan was offering kids to pedophiles and he traveled around the United States bragging about the success of his efforts to close down the "Thai sex ring". A number of American radio stations and magazines echoed everything he fed them, praising him as if he should be accorded knighthood. He announced he had set up a new shelter to replace Mark Morgan's, hired someone to run it, and made pitches for donations. But after operating for more than a year, "The Ruff House" as it was called, was closed even though Howard Ruff continued to raise funds for it. In April 1991, CBS television in Los Angeles ran the story of the "child prostitution ring" the week of the ratings sweeps. Ruff was interviewed and the announcer asked that donations be sent to support the replacement shelter which no longer existed.

In 1984, Ruff raised money for radical-turned-conservative Eldridge Cleaver's congressional race. Cleaver charged Ruff in the press with keeping $60,000 and "spending my campaign funds on their friends in Utah — $15,000 for a consultant I don't know anything about; $15,000 for a survey I don't know anything about." Cleaver's campaign went nowhere, while a spokesman for Ruff denied Cleaver's accusations.[12]

In 1993, after Ruff had suddenly ceased publication of "The Ruff Times", the press reported he had "lost his shirt in a two-year-old venture selling memberships to a discount merchandise club called Main Street Alliance."

In what sounded like a pyramid scheme, the report stated, "Memberships were sold to a network of wholesale buyers who could earn commissions by selling memberships to other strata of buyers..." The structure collapsed in late 1992, but Ruff apparently plans to resurrect it through a computer bulletin board after he gets his latest scheme afloat, the selling of software programs that he hopes will enable parents to educate their kids at home by computer.

* * *

Throughout the month of January, no one was permitted to visit me in IDC. I had trouble getting mail out and hadn't received any correspondence since November. It was obvious the U.S. government was making a concerted effort to isolate me from the rest of the world. My frustration, anger and depression were beyond description. I was being tortured. The one thing that provided a link to

215

the outside world (and possibly my sanity) was being able to read newspapers. But even there, stories about the "foreign sex gang" continued to pop up in the press, scoring my exasperation. I wrote to the Bangkok Post pleading with them to send an investigative reporter to talk to me. Because neither Kenji nor Chat were allowed to visit, I asked the Christian missionaries to deliver it. Most of them refused, but one charitable lady said that she would.

The more time passed at IDC, the more I understood what freedom meant to me. I had always believed deeply in personal freedoms — freedom of expression, freedom of ideas, freedom of choice, freedom of movement — but also took them for granted. I thought about how often in my life I had griped about what seemed now to be the most trivial things — a friend who is late, a difficult client, financial pressures. In the world of things that count, what did any of these matter? Freedoms seem meaningless until they are gone, and then there is nothing more meaningful.

Prior to my arrest, I was blessed with everything anyone could reasonably want — my own business, a steady income, intellectual challenges, a sense of family — and, to most of it, I rarely gave a second thought. But if this humiliation and persecution had taught me anything at all, it was that I could survive with but two essentials — the support of family and friends; and a sense of purpose. Since my mail and my visits were being cut off, there was a danger I'd lose the first. But the second, a desire to have the truth known, they could never steal from me.

* * *

On January 22, a small Jordanian with graying hair arrived clutching his chest. As soon as the guards closed the door, the man let out a scream and fell to the floor. Roza's assistant, a Chinese man named Louie, who was checking in the new arrivals at the time, felt his pulse. There was none. He put his ear to the man's chest and listened for a heart beat. He heard nothing. Quickly, he put his hand over the chest and whacked it with the fist of his other hand. Suddenly, the man wheezed and started to breathe again, but remained in a stupor woozily mumbling about being hit.

I frantically banged on the bars, shouting to the guards for help. Meanwhile, Djaveed the Pakistani who had searched my things when I arrived went rummaging through the man's wallet. "He doesn't have any money," he complained. Luckily, I thought. At least he can't be robbed while he's having a heart attack.

At last, one of the officers appeared at the bottom of the stairs. "Pen Arai?" he yelled, "What's the matter?" It was obvious he had had too much to drink as he began staggering up the stairs.

"That man is having a heart attack," I cried. "He needs to go to the hospital."

The officer looked irritated. "He's not in my section," he snarled. Then, after thinking a moment, he asked, "Does he have any money?"

"His wallet is empty," the Pakistani griped again.

"I can't take him to the hospital without any money." Then the immigration officer mumbled, "It doesn't matter if he dies anyway, he's a prisoner."

I said to Louie, "I'll pay for his transfer to the hospital. That man can't stay here."

Louie turned to several Chinese and said something to them. Within seconds, a 500-baht bill appeared and was passed through the bars to the officer. He took the money, then unlocked the cell door so that we could carry the heart attack victim out to the gate.

Louie's sudden largess amazed me. As a drug addict, he was rarely motivated by caring for a fellow human being.

Because I had not been able to receive either mail or visitors, I asked Roza if it would be possible to call my family in America. "It will cost 1,000 baht," he said, "to pay an officer to take you to the international phone booth at the post office." The post office was adjacent to immigration. "If you want to make a local call, you can call from the phone in the office. That will only cost 200 baht," he added.

Before I was able to find an officer who would take me to the post office, I was summoned one afternoon to the office of Colonel Sathaporn, the commander of the detention center.

"Sit down," he said as I was led into his private room by one of the officers. "Would you like some tea?" I couldn't believe I was hearing this from the commander. It only added to the bizarre nature of everything I'd thus far experienced.

I waied him, seated myself on the chair in front of his desk, and gladly accepted his invitation. "Your lawyer is causing problems," the colonel began. "I wouldn't let him visit one of the women detainees in Room Five one day after visiting hours were over. Now he has sent a letter to the general complaining about me. I have to write a letter explaining my decision. Can you tell me anything about Sombattsiri that might help? Have you had any problems with him?"

I couldn't believe my ears! Was this karmic law at work? I was only too delighted to tell the colonel all about Sombattsiri, about how he had taken my money, my computer, and my mother's money, then repeatedly refused to visit me in prison to discuss my case, or failed to show up in court, or missed my passport hearing. I suggested that the colonel contact other prisoners in Khlong Prem who had also been swindled by Sombattsiri.

"Will you write that down and sign it?" he asked, handing me a sheet of paper. He had started to take notes, but decided it would be better if it were in my handwriting.

When I was finished, I asked if he would allow me to call my family in the United States. He agreed and gave orders to an officer to take me to a telephone at the post office.

When my mother picked up the receiver, all the emotion I felt at the sound of her voice caused my throat to tighten and constrict. I couldn't say anything for several moments. When I was finally able to compose myself, I told her that I was as well as could be expected under the circumstances. I explained that my mail and my visits had been cut off, but that I would try to find a way to smuggle letters out to her. It was too difficult for me to go on. I didn't want to subject her to my tears. I sent her my love and hung up, feeling I had won a small victory. I had made a phone call, had done it despite the U.S. Embassy's attempt to cut me off from the world, and hadn't had to bribe the police a single baht.

Marcia Pixley visited in January to tell me that the Embassy was trying to have me transferred back to Khlong Prem Prison at Lardyao as I had requested. She said that the consul had written to the Thai authorities and was awaiting a response. On January 30th, the Thai court sent to Consul General David Lyon a letter signed by Dr. Komain Phatarabhirom, Prosecutor General, which stated, "I would like to inform you that at present Mr. Stephen Douglas Raymond is... *not being detained under the warrant of detention of the Court of Appeal.*" [13] In other words, the Thai court was not holding me. Therefore I could not be returned to a Thai prison such as Khlong Prem because I was not a prisoner. I was only being detained at IDC because I had no passport. I could, in fact, leave IDC the moment the United States Embassy returned my passport or issued me a travel document or brought me home to face charges.

After the Embassy received the reply, Marcia came to IDC to tell me that the Thai authorities would not return me to Khlong Prem. She conveniently neglected to say, however, that the reason was they weren't holding me for anything.

* * *

The leadership in the room cell became increasingly brutal. In addition to the 100 baht that each new arrival was forced to pay as a "service" fee and the 200 baht necessary for a comfortable place to sleep, all detainees were now ordered to declare their total monetary assets. Anyone who attempted to hide money was severely beaten and the funds themselves appropriated.

On February 4th, a German man who was scheduled to depart for home the following day was invited by a couple of French Algerians

219

to join them in the small room for a drinking party. Alcohol was technically illegal inside IDC, so the cost of a bottle of Mekhong was six times what it cost on the outside. The police sold the 40 baht bottles to Roza for 150 baht and Roza sold them in the room for 300 baht. Knowing I had money to buy a bottle, Stefan and Philipe, the French Algerians, asked me to join the three of them.

Soon after midnight, I gave them 300 baht and retired to my blanket in the large room.

As soon as I left, Stefan and Philipe demanded that the German pay for all the whiskey too. When the German refused, Philipe and Stefan viciously attacked him.

The German's screams of pain shattered the air and awakened nearly everyone. He stumbled out of the small room toward Roza's blanket, his clothes in tatters, splattered with fresh blood, his money gone. Many of us sat up and watched as Roza called Philipe and Stefan out of the small room to explain. Stefan, the larger and stronger of the two, looked defiantly at Roza and responded that he didn't have to report to anyone. "I'm not afraid of you," he said. Stefan and Philipe had become friendly with Isa, the Omani whom Roza used as his "enforcer", and now the three of them posed a threat to Roza's position as room chief. He was afraid to order his Chinese gang to attack, actually fearing they might lose.

The German left the following morning, limping out the door, his face swollen and blue. Roza gave him 500 baht and warned him not to lodge a complaint. Although he had lost ten times that much, the German knew that reporting the theft would be like spitting in the wind.

Instead of ordering Stefan and Philipe to return the money, Roza appointed them security chief and assistant room chief respectively. Isa was demoted to Stefan's assistant and Louie was cut out completely. Not only was the room cell supervised by the most corrupt, it was being run by the most vicious. Now even using the toilet improperly would result in a beating. You could feel the fear and tension hanging in the air.

The following day, three men were sitting in front of my blanket enjoying a game of dominoes. Without provocation, Isa walked up and ordered them to return to their blankets. I looked at him and said that if I wanted visitors to sit in front of my blanket, that was my privilege. He was suddenly taken aback. He was not used to anyone contradicting him. The surprise wore off and he came at me. But the three men scrambled to their feet and hustled away. Isa stopped — his orders had been obeyed.

I was furious that this goon with the intelligence of a grapefruit was able, because of sheer bulk, to intimidate all of us. I was determined to send him a message, and thus received permission to move my things into the small room where Isa lived.

In my new quarters, I hung my locked suitcase above the ground with ropes secured to the bars of one of the high windows. The following day, I noticed that the suitcase was facing the opposite direction and I guessed that it had been moved while I was asleep. I asked Stefan to help me reach it and take it down to check the contents.

"I'm busy right now," he said. "I'll help you later."

I asked him twice more that day, and each time he had an excuse for not being able. Later, Philipe asked if I would contribute toward the purchase of another bottle of Mekhong. "I'll have to get the money from my suitcase," I replied.

"I'll ask someone else for the money," Philipe said and quickly walked away. At that moment it struck me that my cash was gone. And Stefan and Philipe knew it.

A couple of Burmese boys allowed me to stand on their shoulders, retrieve the suitcase, and find what I had expected. The money was missing, along with a 100-year-old Mexican coin that I had hoped to sell to a collector. I hunted up Roza and told him about the theft. He asked me to describe the coin, then ordered 10 of his Chinese gang

221

into the small room to search for it. Everyone was moved out as they tore everything apart — everything, that is, except the things belonging to Stefan. The shakedown only succeeded in angering my cellmates who were forced to shuffle and rearrange their belongings while the real culprit went about unimpeded. Of course neither the coin nor the cash were to be found.

When this charade was over, Roza just shrugged and said he had done all he could do. Dejected, I returned to my blanket while everyone around me put their things back in order. I laid down on the blanket and closed my eyes.

"Who are you accusing of being a thief?" a voice thundered. I opened my eyes to see Isa standing over me brandishing a knife. "You're accusing me!"

"I'm not accusing anyone," I said quietly and shut my eyes again. I heard a commotion and opened them in time to see Isa lunge at me with the gleaming silver blade. My head exploded trying to think quickly — suddenly, Stefan and John, a black man from South Africa, grabbed Isa from behind and wrestled him under control.

Edmund, a man from Singapore, said, "You'd better leave. Move back to the main room." He stood up and walked toward it, hoping I would follow.

Suddenly, Isa broke from Stefan's half-hearted grip and came at me again with the knife. He slashed at me and the blade cut into my shirt. I could feel the cold steel on my skin just as John grabbed his arm and pulled it away.

"I'm gonna kill you," Isa roared. "I don't care what happens to me."

I picked up my blanket and retreated to the larger room as Stefan and John held him back. I could hear Isa repeat over and over, "I don't care, I'll kill him." I knew he meant it and I believed he was looking only for the opportunity. Like so much steamy air, all of my previous bravura evaporated.

I wanted desperately to contact the Embassy and tell them I was at the mercy of maniacs and thugs and worse, and I wanted out of the God-forsaken place. I certainly could not believe American officials wanted me dead, no matter what they thought I'd done.

The next day, while I was sitting with three cellmates, Philipe walked up to us, pointed his stick at me and said, "Shut up and go back to your area. You don't have anybody to help you. If you say anything about the robbery, I'll set you up with the police and you'll go to Bangkwan." He was talking about planting heroin on me, then paying the police to search my things and find it. I knew he was quite capable of such a thing. "Your Embassy doesn't care about you," he snarled cynically. "Nobody will help you."

Without a word, I rose, walked to my blanket, sat down and did not leave it again, except to go to the bathroom, until weeks after the incident.

That weekend, Mark Morgan left IDC to go to court in Chiang Mai, the location of his second shelter. After all the Howard Ruff hoopla and the "Ruff & Cummings videotape show", the Bangkok police were unable to put together a case for anything more than operating the Bangkok Children's Shelter without the proper government permit. In the Bangkok court, the judge fined Mark 500 baht, but actually took time to commend him for the work that he and Sujitra were doing. Mark assumed he would face a similar conclusion in Chiang Mai. He was wrong.

Upset with the outcome in Bangkok, Ruff's staff dispatched a copy of their infamous John Cummings video to the judge in Chiang Mai. Also, the Deputy General of the Royal Thai Police Department, having lost face by virtue of the outcome in the Bangkok case, pressured the judge and prosecutor in Chiang Mai to come up with something. Obviously, in America, this could have been the basis for a scandal. In Thailand, it was the order of the day.

When Mark left IDC, the ban on visitors was lifted. Kenji and Chat came to see me the Monday following Isa's attack. "We tried to visit twice before," Kenji said, "but they wouldn't let us in."

Their presence was comforting and at the same time, unleashed all my fears. "I'm in danger in this place," I babbled. "Please call Marcia Pixley and tell her to come to visit immediately. I need to get out of here. Please go to everyone that I know in the travel industry and ask them to help me get out. Ask Sumate if he can do anything."

Kenji said he would call the Embassy but was non-committal about my other requests. He felt I was being irrational and that my friends couldn't help me. He was probably right. I had now been incarcerated for nearly a year and had nothing to show for it except an acquittal, which seemed to carry the same influence with my jailers as a conviction.

"I'll be back in a couple of days," Kenji promised as he and Chat walked down the stairs. I never saw either of them again.

Twelve

Discovery

The next day Marcia had me brought downstairs to talk in a more private setting. "Get me out of here!" I said urgently. "I've been attacked and threatened with my life."

"David Lyon is out of town for two weeks," she replied lamely, "but I'll talk to Colonel Sathaporn's assistant."

"How about giving me my passport back!"

She didn't respond to the suggestion and when she stood up to leave, I realized that I really was all alone. The Embassy didn't care what happened to me, and neither did Marcia Pixley. But it always seemed a little inconceivable to my persistently naive way of thinking to continually rediscover they really did not give a damn. I went back to the cell and wrote the U.S. Attorney General requesting an investigation into the actions of the U.S. Embassy.

On March 3rd, 60 Sri Lankans arrived in the middle of the night. The room, which had been overcrowded before, suddenly became unbearably so. We now had a population of 160 men crammed together in a 20 by 60 foot space. It was impossible to lay down and stretch out. The only way that we could sleep unencumbered was to lay in the fetal position with our knees bent, otherwise our feet would tangle up with someone else's.

Stefan had been drinking the night the men arrived. He searched them, slapped them around, pulled their pants down to look for hidden cash, and treated them with contempt. They were terrified of this vicious hulking bully and it made me sick to watch him rob them of their money and their dignity. Roza observed Stefan's careless, brutal attitude and, from that night on, something began to change — slowly and subtly.

Two days after the Sri Lankans arrived, Marcia brought a copy of the prosecutor's appeal. It was 10 typewritten pages long and written in Thai. "Can you have this translated?" I asked.

"The Embassy staff won't do it," she said. "I'll have to send it out and have it done. It will cost about 100 baht a page."

I groaned. After my money was stolen, I asked the Embassy for another EMDA loan. Marcia had brought the first $100 but I only had about $40 left.

"You won't be able to get more money until April 15th," she said. "I suggest you wait until then to get the translation done." She told me she would return then with the loan.

Since my last phone conversation with my mother, my family had been sending correspondence through the Embassy. A Thai employee came one afternoon after Marcia's visit to deliver letters from my family and from the International Legal Defense Council.

"Vichai," I said. "I really want to know what this appeal says. Could you take a couple of minutes to read it to me?"

"Sorry," he said. "I've been instructed not to help you."

After Vichai's comment, I resolved to translate it myself using my Thai-English dictionary. But Thai is a difficult language — it's a derivative of Sanskrit and there are no spaces between words, only between sentences. Even after the word-for-word translation is finished, the meaning isn't always clear.

I had begun to teach English in the room cell to a family of Vietnamese refugees and one of the men, the uncle in the family, had been living in a Thai refugee camp for 10 years. He could read and write Thai fairly well and offered to help me. Thus each day we sat for a couple of hours and translated a sentence at a time, up to a page a day. By April, I had a fairly good understanding of the entire appeal.

The prosecutor had found no new evidence against me but based his appeal entirely on Howard Ruff's videotape featuring John

Cummings' allegations. He stated in the appeal document that the United States Embassy had proof I operated a sex tour business and quoted John Cummings as saying I was a danger to society and intended to pick up street children to use as prostitutes for pedophiles visiting the country. Cummings was viewed as an expert because he was a pedophile — convicted of multiple counts of child molestation and having sex with minors.

Something in my brain clicked. I suddenly understood the "why" and the "how". I began to see clearly the course of the poison river. It started in the deranged mind of John Cummings — a man consumed by guilt and desperate to save his own skin, soften his accusers, and cop a plea bargain. The venom flowed into several police departments like a brook flowing into a large stream. It found an open channel in the San Francisco Police Department with Inspector Tom Eisenman, a man described to me by his own supervisor, Captain Richard Hesselroth, as reactionary.

Eisenman was convinced he needed only a little time before he could find evidence corroborating all that Cummings had said, starting with my having "fled to Thailand". He ignored any and all evidence contradicting Cummings' allegations, including the fact that I had registered myself and my company with the U.S. Embassy in Bangkok, had filed federal income tax in America, and had recently returned to California for a stockholders' meeting at my San Francisco office.

The poison flowed quickly from the stream to the river. John Cummings' stories were sent by police to the Embassy in Bangkok and went from either the California police to the Bangkok police or from the U.S. Embassy to the Bangkok police. A reporter from Matichon newspaper picked up pieces of information from local police and added a flourish or two. It was no accident that the street kid in the original Matichon newspaper article who was purportedly abused and used as a prostitute was never named, never came forth or otherwise ever became an identifiable human being. He probably never existed. No wonder the police had to resort to torturing Chat and Nu to get something with which to charge me.

Cummings had anticipated his arrest from the moment he called his sister using my office phone and, all the while he was still in Bangkok, was scheming for ways to cut his losses. Because he was a law school graduate, he was familiar with the system of plea bargaining. He'd been under my roof in Bangkok for a month, had known me on and off for 20 years, and could give out all kinds of personal information about my life. He would take notes on me and brew fact with fiction, as most astute con men do. And the more he could dangle in front of the police, the less time he himself would spend behind bars.

In his mind, my incentive travel business would become a sex tour operation. Mark Morgan's street shelter would become a home for child prostitution. Cumming's sexual desire for pre-pubescent children would become my desire. My willingness to help Chat and, later, Nu with their education would be made to look like a sinister plot to turn them into prostitutes. And to juice up his credibility, he would tip police about the pedophiles he knew in America.

I wrote a lengthy rebuttal to the prosecutor's appeal and waited for Marcia to visit so that I might have it translated to Thai and sent to the court. When she did not appear as scheduled on April 15th, I asked the missionaries to send her a message that I was broke and needed the loan.

Each day during visiting hours, I watched for Kenji and Chat and Nu and each day, when they did not appear, I felt empty and heartbroken. I had not had a visit from them in more than two months. And as time went by, I accepted the seemingly obvious... even they had given up on me.

* * *

One afternoon, a missionary appeared at the bars and asked for me by name. I was shocked. The missionaries had a list of all the prisoners in IDC and alongside my name, a notation read "child molester". They usually ignored me.

"Your mother asked me to help," the mission woman said. "My name is Monica Taylor." She went on to tell me that my family and friends in America had begun a letter writing campaign to congressmen and senators to force the Embassy to return me to the United States. That was the best news I had received in months. I let out a deep sigh and tears welled up in my eyes. Monica reached through the bars and grabbed my hand to comfort me. For the first time in as long as I could remember, I began to feel that I wasn't completely alone, and that somebody actually cared.

Monica began to visit at least once a week. If she couldn't make it, she would send someone in her place. My mother gave her address to family and friends who sent correspondence through her and she took my return correspondence to send to them.

Although I was thankful for Monica's help, her attitude troubled me. During her first visit, she suggested that I should return to America as soon as possible and stay there. "You don't want to wind up like these people," she said waving at the others inside the cell. "They're just a bunch of losers."

I glanced back at the men and boys behind me. Some had escaped brutal regimes in Burma, Cambodia, Vietnam and China searching for a better life. Some had risked death for freedom. Monica was a Christian missionary, yet she was denigrating many who were poor desperate refugees whose crime was illegal entry into Thailand, and speaking of them as if they were somehow beneath her.

During other visits, she made it clear she did not believe in my innocence. She was very friendly with Marcia Pixley and "other people in the Embassy," and said they had evidence of my guilt.

Finally, at the end of April, Stephen Pattison and Vichai appeared at the bars. "Well, what did I do to deserve a visit by such high officials?" I said, laying on the sarcasm with a trowel.

"Marcia has been out of the country the past month," Pattison said. "Vichai and I came to say hello."

I handed him my written rebuttal of the appeal and asked him to use some of the EMDA money to have it translated. "Tell Marcia that I don't need a translation of the appeal," I said. "I translated it myself. But I do need this translated to Thai to send to the court."

He took the handwritten pages, agreed to give them to Marcia when she returned, and left.

When Marcia visited a couple of weeks later, I was brought downstairs for a more private conversation. "What evidence does the U.S. Embassy have that I ran a sex tour business?" I demanded. I knew no such evidence existed and was anxious to refute whatever they thought they had.

"The Embassy doesn't have any evidence," she replied. "The Thais always say `the Embassy' whenever they talk about any U.S. government agency."

It was obvious she had never seen such "evidence", but it was equally obvious that she believed in its existence. After more than a year, two governments and their police forces and all their investigative agencies had failed to produce a shred of evidence of the alleged sex tour business, yet they all clung to the belief that somebody else had it... somewhere.

The letter writing campaign in America on my behalf was beginning to have an effect. Marcia reported that the Embassy had received a number of letters and calls from U.S. senators and congressmen asking why I had not been returned to the States.

Soon after Marcia's visit, I received a copy of a letter that had been sent by Consul General David Lyon to Harriett McNamara, a business colleague and friend from San Diego, falsely stating that I was being held in Thailand by the Thai authorities because of the appeal.[14] Replies with strikingly similar wording were used by at least five people in the Department of State and the U.S. Embassy and had become so standardized that whenever anybody inquired about me, all someone needed to do was punch in a computer disk.[15]

After reading Lyon's reply to Harriett, I wrote a lengthy response to him in which I said, "Your comments are conspicuously misleading by their omissions." I suggested that his letter was indicative of the type of "stonewalling, evasions and outright lies by Embassy officials that have plagued my efforts for the past year-and-a-half". I placed the blame for my unjust incarceration in IDC where it belonged; squarely on the shoulders of U.S. officials.

In his reply to my May 25th letter which came more than a month later, Lyon wrote, "You state that your incarceration for the past 16 months has been wholly due to the actions of U.S. authorities. This is inaccurate as you are being held here due to the decision of the (Thailand) Department of Prosecutions to appeal a lower court ruling..."[16]

Yet nearly four months earlier, in a March 1, 1990 letter to Thai Justice Sapon Ratanakorn of the Court of Appeals, Lyon acknowledged in his own words that "[Steve Raymond] is being held solely because he is not in possession of a valid passport."[17] The judge agreed and stated in words that could hardly be clearer, "...there is no connection between Mr. Raymond's detention at IDC and his pending case in court".[18] This was the second confirmation in writing (the first being the Prosecutor General's letter of January 30th) that Lyon had received from Thai court officials indicating that, in their eyes, I was free to go. Furthermore, I would later learn in a letter written by William Wharton of the State Department to Richard Atkins of the International Legal Defense Council that the State Department on March 14th had "authorized our Embassy in Bangkok to issue Mr. Raymond a travel document... for direct return to the United States."[19]

My family in Massachusetts had contacted Senator Edward Kennedy, as well as the state's two gay congressmen, Gerry Studds and Barney Frank. Business colleagues contacted Senators John

231

Breaux and Bennett Johnston, both of Louisiana. And family members and friends wrote to Senator Alan Cranston and various California congressmen. All of the congressmen and senators telexed or wrote the Embassy in Bangkok asking why I was being detained. Most of them received letters either from Consul General Lyon or Janet Mullins, Assistant Secretary for Legislative Affairs in the Department of State, saying that I was being detained "under Thai law" because of the appeal. The U.S. Embassy's Lyon and the State Department's Mullins were misleading their own top elected officials.

At least half a dozen letters to them contained virtually the same explanation of my status — in the words of the Embassy and the Department of State, I had not been "acquitted", but rather charges were dropped "following the recantation of testimony by key witnesses", thus implying that there was a strong case against me, if only the witnesses had come through. There was no mention of the torture by police of three teenage boys. This presumption of my guilt seemed not only immoral, it was counter to everything America is supposed to stand for.

I knew that I wasn't required to remain in IDC and wait for the appeal and my family knew it, but we couldn't get anybody to listen to us. The congressmen and senators assumed that we were mistaken and that the StateDepartment officials were correctly interpreting Thai law. Out of frustration, my mother began a petition to President Bush.

* * *

The more crowded the room cell became, the more difficult it became to adjust. One Korean named Kim spoke very good English and carried on a number of intelligent conversations. However, as time went by, his speech became more and more disjointed. A few months later, he was talking to himself every waking minute.

Then an American named Jackie Crosby arrived. He told me in confidence one day that the cell was filled with "Chinese movie stars who want to be here." He and Kim became good friends. They spent most of their time blabbering at each other, neither listening to the other or caring what was said. Their conversations would actually have been quite funny if they hadn't been so sad.

I sent a message to Marcia about Jackie needing Embassy help for his return to America. A month later, he did go back and, according to Marcia, was met at the airport by a mental health worker.

There were epileptic inmates as well and, in one short period, four of them had seizures. Although they created quite a disturbance, the room leaders mercifully did not beat them.

One day a Burmese leper was thrown in with us. His fingers and toes were nothing but stubs and no one would go near him. I bought some noodles at the "coffee shop" and when I offered them to him, he looked at me with eyes so sad and grateful that I felt shamed. I wanted to do more, but did not know how. I was ignorant about leprosy. I had no idea how contagious it was.

The room leaders isolated him and forced him to sit on the wet floor in a bathroom stall used for garbage. Then, in the middle of the night, the police came and took him away. No one ever heard what happened, but I truly worried about his fate.

In a matter of days, a group of construction workers threw up a fence along the hallway in front of the barred windows, so that now visitors would have to stand behind it and shout, just as they had at Khlong Prem or Bangkok Special Prison. The only feature about this vile place had been the opportunity for private conversations with visitors. And now even that had been removed.

One night, an Afghan named Jamie witnessed a group of Chinese pickpocketing several Nigerians as they slept. He woke and alerted them to what was happening. Two days later, Louie, and three Chinese attacked and beat Jamie in the bathroom. He reported the beating to the police, who — in typical fashion — moved him, rather than his assailants, to another room cell.

A few days later, Philipe and Stefan robbed an Iraqi businessman in the small room at knifepoint. During visiting hours the next day, the man told his family. They reported it to the police and to the Iraqi Embassy. Soon after, guards transferred Stefan to Room Four. With Isa having left a week earlier for Oman, the mood improved dramatically.

* * *

"Journalism is a steady stream of irresponsible distortions that most people find refreshing."
— Walter Kaufman

About three months after Mark left IDC, an American woman came to visit. She introduced herself as Lisa Carpenter, a volunteer who had lived and worked at Mark's children's shelter in Bangkok for about six months before his arrest.

Lisa said that she was heartbroken the kids had lost a good chance for something better. She, of course, knew the homes were legitimate and had suggested to Mark's wife, Sujitra, that they take their case to the press. But Sujitra, who worked with the Thai government as a mid-level civil servant, was afraid that if they did that the police might lose face and that would hurt Mark's chances in court.

The strategy was for naught. The judge in Chiang Mai sentenced Mark to the maximum three months for failing to file the proper permit. During that three-month period, the Chiang Mai police took two boys from Mark's home to the police station for interrogation and kept them there for the duration of Mark's sentence. According to Lisa Carpenter, the police then told the boys that if they refused to sign statements that Mark had sexually assaulted them, their parents would be arrested. When one later testified in court that he was not accusing Mark of "anachan", the judge leered at him and told him to stop lying. The court upheld the prosecution's claim and Mark would have to face charges for sexual assault.

Following Lisa Carpenter's second visit, I took a look at that day's Bangkok Post. In it was a two-page story repeating John Cummings' and Howard Ruff's allegations. It made no mention of my acquittal six months earlier.[20]

Meanwhile, the world press continued to report the story as if evidence had been found to substantiate it. Jack Anderson wrote in a syndicated column that federal authorities "have received reports alleging that Mark Morgan was a contact for American pedophiles... Howard Ruff began a campaign to get Thai and U.S. authorities to arrest him. But U.S. authorities had to wait for Thai police to come up with the evidence. He was nabbed last month for having no permit for his foundation..."[21]

In San Francisco, the Chronicle printed a story about the abuse of Asian refugee children in the city's Tenderloin District. The source for the story was Inspector Glenn Pamfiloff, Eisenman's partner at the San Francisco Police Department and the man who had obtained the state warrant for my arrest. Pamfiloff told the reporter, "There is a loosely-organized international ring of pedophiles. Recently with the San Francisco Police working closely with the Bangkok Police there was a big bust of some of these men. The guy who is running the show was Steve Raymond. He's in custody in Bangkok for child molestation charges. The word that we have about what was going on there, and this is from federal authorities, is that they were running a junket where the pedophiles would come to Bangkok and be assigned a boy as a guide to take them around to various places through the country."[22]

Tim Smucker, the freelancer who had written the article in the Bangkok Post about street kids sniffing paint thinner because they were prostitutes, carried his shaky journalism to Canada where the Toronto Globe & Mail ran a piece entitled, "Children Demeaned in Brutal Trade", under the byline "Philip Smucker". The story read as follows: "Last year Thai police uncovered evidence of an extensive prostitution ring headed by an American, Steven Raymond, who tried to use a San Francisco-based company called Destination Services and a false foster home in Bangkok as a front... Mr. Raymond was charged with running a child sex ring in Thailand but was released to agents of the Federal Bureau of Investigation, which wanted him in connection with several child abuse cases in the United States."[23]

It seemed to me Smucker was the worst kind of journalist there is — assuming allegation as fact, throwing in embellishments to goose up the piece, using other newspaper articles as source material without verifying the details, and reporting but one side of the story. He either ignored the fact that I had been acquitted, or didn't know about it. In either case, as a journalist, it was inexcusable. "So what if it's a little distorted," Sandy Ferguson had said to me of his friend's writing. "Tim is just trying to make a living. He writes articles the newspapers will pay for."

The Thai press couldn't let the story die. As late as June 1993, the Nation printed a full page story in the Sunday Focus section written by Wee Soo Cheang in which Ms. Wee reported, "In March 1989, police raided a `children's shelter' set up in Bangkok by David Groat, 36, and Stephen Raymond, 43. From the shelter, police confiscated 11 photograph albums filled with pictures of naked children performing sexual acts — some with the two men arrested. Three teenage boys at the shelter during the raid admitted to police they had performed sexual services for the two men and for other visitors to the shelter. The police also found correspondence that indicated Groat and Raymond had provided paedophile tourists with boys. — After their arrests in Bangkok, both Groat and Raymond told police they had been voluntary helpers at Morgan's shelter."[24]

Ms. Wee quoted from a book published in 1992 by an organization called *End Child Prostitution in Asian Tourism,* which said that "Raymond ... ran a small travel agency, Tour Service Ltd., which provided assistance to paedophiles wanting to travel to other countries."

236

All the poison that John Cummings had created was now spewing out of the mouths of journalists anxious for a juicy story and law enforcement officials anxious for a bust, and this had the net effect of substantiating all of it. The con man had done it again.

I was fed up. I wrote a 14-page letter to the editor of the Bangkok Post, disputing virtually everything in this latest of so-called news stories. I had to vent or I would explode. Not that I truly expected justice to finally arrive, with an excuse for being late.

My dilemma was capsulized by Dr. Richard Gardner in an article titled "Presumed Guilty" and published in Playboy Magazine. Gardner, a clinical professor of child psychiatry at Columbia University and one of the leading experts in the U.S. in the field of child sexual abuse, was quoted as saying, "Here's the problem: We've reached the point on this issue where an accusation is tantamount to a conviction. Thousands of lives are being ruined in this country by baseless charges. What we're seeing now is a repeat of the Salem witch trials ... The attitude is that God and right and the Star-Spangled Banner are always with those who make the accusations" while "...the accused is routinely denied the most basic protections of law. Those who dare point out that fact are themselves subject to vilification."[25]

* * *

Most of the missionaries at IDC came only to preach. There were a few individuals, however, whom I will never forget for their genuine kindness. An elderly Catholic priest brought gifts to detainees every week. I did not even know his name, but he was, indeed, a saint. If someone needed soap, writing paper, toothpaste, whatever, he would bring it wrapped like a Christmas gift in old newspapers and ask for nothing in return. Julia Freeman of Bangkok's Christ Church was another who sincerely and consistently acted altruistically. She always made good on her promises. Most of the others promised, but either forgot or never returned.

237

A woman I knew only as Doctor Garcia, a United Nations physician from the Philippines, was one of the most caring and unselfish human beings I have ever met. She regularly brought gifts of candies, pies and cakes that she had baked at home, exhibiting the type of unselfish compassion that went far beyond the requirements of her job. Whenever I felt depressed, she always found a way to cheer me up. She was a combination of Mother Teresa and Florence Nightingale.

Early in the year, a young woman named Shelli Shultz came often to IDC. She had with her a Thai baby whom she had come to Bangkok to adopt, but as the process was taking months to complete, she spent spare time visiting us as well as prisoners at Khlong Prem. At first, I thought she was one of the missionaries. She struck up a friendship with a British man and, later, with my friends, Ricky from Malaysia, and Albert from Poland. By April, after they had left, she and I began communicating and it wasn't long before she volunteered errands such as making photocopies or posting my mail.

One day, Monica Taylor noticed Shelli taking my letters. She stepped between us, faced Shelli with her back to me, and said, "Don't help this man! Don't you know what he's done?"

I was aghast at her remark. My mother and I had relied on Monica to be a communications link with the outside world. Now I worried that anything I had sent through her had never reached its destination — or, if it had, who had read it beforehand.

Suddenly I said to Shelli, "Would you call my mother tonight and tell her what Monica said to you?"

"I'd be happy to," she replied. "That woman calls herself a Christian? She's no Christian!"

* * *

"Morality is simply the attitude we adopt
toward people whom we personally dislike."
— Oscar Wilde

Because my family and I were aware that either Howard Ruff or Embassy officials had pressured Thai authorities to push the case against me and had been responsible for the prosecutor's decision to appeal the acquittal, my Uncle Chester wrote to Ruff and asked why he was doing these things. Ruff's lengthy response denied involvement, but went on to state, "Steve was arrested with his friend David Groat in David's condo having sex with two nude children and with over 1,000 sexually explicit nude photographs of boys. He was not acquitted of charges by the Thai government. The judge initially dismissed the case when the boys suddenly recanted their testimony. The prosecutor's appeal is based on the fact that even if the boys change their story it couldn't change the fact that the police caught them in the act of having sex with the boys and having all that pornography. I have it on excellent authority that the reason that the boys recanted was because Mark Morgan paid substantial bribes to the boys and their families to change their story. If Steve is acquitted in Thailand he will be deported to the U.S. where he will stand trial in San Francisco where authorities have informed me they have a very solid case. Based on the information which I have, I hope he never gets out of jail."[26]

The utter blind fervor with which Ruff so willingly would send me to the gallows was telling. Had the police "caught me in the act", as he described in his patently blustery manner, it would not have mattered one bit that the boys "recanted their testimony". The prosecutor would have had all the witnesses he needed in the arresting officers. Unfortunately, my uncle died in December 1990 before learning the truth.

Ruff's dogmatism was typical of what I felt I faced on all fronts. In a 1992 Time Magazine cover story called "The Fraying of

239

America", author Robert Hughes expressed the belief that the fibre that binds the nation is beginning to unravel because of "the prevalence of demagogues who wish to claim that there is only one path to virtuous American-ness: paleoconservatives like Jesse Helms and Pat Robertson who think this country has one single ethic... and pushers of political correctness who would like to see grievance elevated into automatic sanctity.

"In the past 15 years the American right has had a complete, almost unopposed success in labeling as left-wing ordinary agendas and desires that, in a saner policy, would be seen as ideologically neutral, an extension of rights implied in the Constitution."[27]

* * *

On May 18th Roza left. He made an absurd speech about continuing to run the "coffee shop" from the outside. Evidently the concession inside IDC was too lucrative to give up without a fight. With Roza's departure, a man named Jose (he pronounced it "Joe-say") from Jamaica took over as security chief and one of the Chinese men, Seituan, became room chief.

One night at about 3 AM, I was awakened by shouts. Louie, the assistant room chief, was talking heatedly to Jacob, a Jordanian heroin addict, and "Little Joe" (also known as Yusef), the Jordanian who had the heart attack in January.

Louie stumbled over to Jose and woke him. "You're trying to cheat me!" he shouted. "You don't know who I am!"

Suddenly Jose jumped up, smacked Louie in the face, dropped down again and went back to sleep. Louie was furious, but he was more intimidated than furious.

The next day, Yusef explained that some American exchange prisoners who had just come through IDC en route to the States, had planned to smuggle heroin with them, but lost their nerve and left it behind. Jose began distributing it to the room's addicts. But after a few days, he decided to charge for their daily fixes. Yusef told Louie where the heroin came from and Louie grew furious. As assistant room chief, he believed that some of the heroin belonged to him.

Two days after Louie's outburst, the police transferred Jose and John, a man from South Africa, to other rooms. It was obvious that the police had been paid off. Louie appointed Djaveed the Pakistani as security chief. Although he was a small man, he made up for his lack of size by wielding a heavy stick and arbitrarily lashing out at unsuspecting inmates. Again, no one would fight back for fear the Chinese gang would explode in retaliation. Seituan was still room leader in title, but Louie was now in control.

I was concerned about the situation and wrote to Colonel Sathaporn asking for a meeting. I gave the note to Yusef to pass on to a guard, but he kept stalling, claiming that he needed to wait for the appropriate moment. I took it back and gave it to an officer myself.

Three days later, the colonel appeared at the bars. "I can't talk here," I said to him. "Could I talk to you downstairs?"

He nodded and instructed the officers to bring Yusef and me to his office. After we had taken seats, the colonel said, "Now, what's the problem?"

I told him that when Jose was security chief, the beatings had stopped and the environment was much more pleasant. Yusef sat beside me but said nothing. Colonel Sathaporn eyed him coolly and then asked, "Is that true?"

"Yes it is," he replied. He seemed reticent about saying even that much. I was surprised. It was as if he didn't want to help.

"Would it be possible to have Jose transferred back to Room One?" I asked.

"Is that all you wanted?"

"Yes," I said.

Within two hours of our meeting, Jose had been returned to our cell and Louie and his henchmen were rolling up their blankets and moving out. I felt a sense of relief. I had accomplished something positive. It wasn't a big victory, but it was significant enough. In a subhuman existence, one is grateful for small favors.

From that day forward, the room leaders — Seituan, Jose and their assistants — held me in high regard, consulting me before making any major decisions. Although occasional beatings did occur after Jose's return, they were at least followed by an apology — and always to me, as if I were some benign guru.

I had asked Lisa Carpenter to find out how Chat and Nu were doing and to see if they were still in school. On her final visit before she returned to the States, she brought a note from Nu. "Don't worry about me," the note said. "I'm doing fine."

She confirmed that Nu was living with Wasana, the cook from the children's shelter, and her son. "But he cries a lot lately," Lisa said. "He'll cry about the slightest thing." In the note, Nu promised that he would come to visit. But he never did.

Following Lisa's departure, I sank into a funk. Before my arrest, Nu had been a happy boy. He was, at times, a bit moody, but he certainly did not cry much. His grades were at the top of his class, which indicated to me he was fairly well-adjusted. But now they had fallen off quite a bit. This whole thing had evidently affected him more than I had allowed myself to realize. I worried that he blamed himself for what had happened to me. I hoped that was not the case, but Lisa's remarks made me think otherwise. I had been deluding myself into thinking this horrible nightmare was not as traumatic for Chat and Nu as it had been for me.

One day in June, Colonel Sathaporn called me into his glass-enclosed office. He was still having problems with Sombattsiri, who apparently had sued him for not allowing a visit to his client. The colonel wanted an additional statement from me regarding the problems I had had with the man. While we were talking, Marcia Pixley and Vichai appeared.

"Have you moved?" Marcia asked cheerily.

"Sure, I sleep here now," I said with a smile and a measure of sarcasm.

"Come in, come in," the colonel said to them.

"We don't want to disturb you," Marcia replied.

"No problem," the colonel said. They stepped in and sat down flanking me as I faced the colonel's desk. Marcia's cheeriness seemed strained.

Vichai made a comment about the letter I had written to the U.S. Attorney General's office requesting an investigation of the Embassy's intransigence and refusal to return me to the United States. "It has caused quite a stir," he said, "a lot of comments."

Marcia handed me a translated copy of the appeal. I looked at it. "I've already translated this myself," I said. "I told Stephen Pattison that I didn't need this translated."

"When did you tell him that?" Marcia seemed dumbfounded.

I looked at Vichai. "Don't you remember when the two of you visited in April and I gave him the response (to the prosecutor's appeal) and asked him to translate it?"

Vichai nodded.

"Don't you remember that I told him *not* to translate the appeal (itself)?" He nodded again.

"This cost 4,000 baht to have done," Marcia said.

"Four thousand baht!" I exploded. "Where's my response to the court?"

"I'll have to check with Stephen," Marcia said. "I don't know anything about it, but you should have told me, or written me a letter..."

"You weren't here in April," I cried. Told her or written her a letter?? Was this my fault? Didn't she communicate with her own boss?

"I've been going to the commissary for you. I've had this translation done for you. I've done a lot of things for you that I don't have to do. They're not part of my job."

243

I said that I appreciated her shopping for me, but I was frustrated with everything. "You wouldn't have to do any of that if you didn't keep me in jail."

Marcia's face turned red with anger. "I didn't put you in jail and I'm not keeping you in jail!"

Colonel Sathaporn sat in shock with his mouth agape. It was extremely impolite for two people to yell at each other in public.

"When I said `you', I was referring to the U.S. government. You are their representative," I said angrily.

"No more!" She stood up. "I'll only do what the law says I have to do! Anything you want, you must put in writing, then I *might* do it!" She turned and stalked out of the room.

"You shouldn't make her angry," Vichai said. "She's trying to help you."

I turned to the colonel. He was aghast. The expression on his face was of a man who had just witnessed something impossible; a lowly prisoner lashing out at a government official! "The American government doesn't even follow its own laws," I cried to him. "They're all talk about human rights, but they ignore them for their own citizens."

Vichai rose and went into the other room to find Marcia. He returned a minute later with a message and a paper to sign. I thought that ridiculous, got up and went in to confront her. She was smoldering. I tried to smile and said, "So now you're not talking to me, eh?"

She glared, turned to Vichai, and made a comment to him. He handed me two plastic bags stuffed with books for me, then abruptly they walked out the door.

I was so disturbed by the argument that I couldn't finish what I had been doing with Colonel Sathaporn. I apologized and returned to the cell, sat down on my blanket and moaned, "I guess that's the end of my care packages."

Yusef overheard me and asked what had happened. I told him about my spat with Marcia. "It's because of your letter to the Attorney General," he said. "The Embassy people don't like that."

Yusef had been in trouble with U.S. officials himself. Although a Jordanian citizen, he one day walked into the Embassy and asked for an American passport. He told Stephen Pattison that he had lost all his identification. Having grown up in the suburbs of Washington, D.C., he had no accent and his knowledge of the U.S. was so keen that Pattison had foregone the rules and issued him one. In fact, Yusef told me he was a member of the Palestine Liberation Organization and showed me newspaper clippings of his arrest in Japan for attempting to route plutonium to Libya's Khadafy. "Imagine," he had said, "the U.S. giving a passport to a P.L.O. member."

The audacious Yusef claimed he knew most of the famous American Protestant ministers and televangelists, from having been a tour guide in Israel. I could never tell how much was truth and how much was bravado, but he always had whopping stories. "You know, sometimes when these holier-than-thou televangelists want to get laid while they're on tour of the holy land, they have me get them a whore. I've had some great times with preachers," he howled.

During Lisa Carpenter's final visit, she ran into Shelli Schultz as Shelli was coming up the stairs to visit me. The two of them went to lunch and talked about my situation and about Mark's shelter. After her visit with Lisa, Shelli dismissed any lingering doubts she may have had about my having operated a sex tour business or about Mark's home being anything but a shelter for street children. She was fully supportive of my family's efforts to have me returned to the United States and spoke of how reprehensible she thought the Embassy's actions had been.

On June 26th, I received a letter from Peter Bailey at Bangkok Special Prison and another from David Groat at Khlong Prem informing me that Kenji and Chat were in jail. Peter said Kenji was at Mahachai and David said he had seen Chat in the courthouse. Instantly

I worried that the Din Daeng police had arrested them for helping me, and I felt my face flush hot with anger. But I was also a little relieved to learn that the reason they had stopped visiting was not because they had given up on me. I sat down immediately to write to Kenji to find out what had happened.

A few days later I received a response. He said that Chat had stolen a motorcycle and gone joy-riding, and that he had been arrested for possession of stolen property. He said that he was not guilty and was fighting his case.

"Chat," Kenji reported, "is being held at the children's court prison at Bangkhen." I thought that strange, as Chat was now 18 and anyone 16 and older usually went to Bangkok Special Prison. It was also uncharacteristic of him to get into trouble. I believed he was "getting back" at the system for all that had happened.

Kenji went on to tell me that the two of them were arrested on February 28th, exactly a year — less a day — after my initial arrest. He said that when they were taken to Din Daeng Police Station, the police "gave us a workout" for telling the court about the electric shock treatment.

"The bastards!" I cried. Hadn't they done enough? I felt enraged — and utterly helpless. I hoped desperately that Chat and Kenji were all right. I cursed John Cummings for all his cruelty and for causing so much pain and suffering.

Thirteen

A Visit From Home

After Sombattsiri's appearance in December, my mother asked the Embassy to help retrieve the bail money he had appropriated. The Embassy threatened to contact Thai authorities and, by July, Sombat had returned all but $300 of the $8,000 my mother had sent him.

Before our argument, I asked Marcia to use part of that money to re-hire Puttri Kuvanonda from Siam Legal Aid. I wanted Puttri to represent me at the Appeals Court, sue the Bangkok Post, and help my family in their efforts to have me returned.

Puttri arrived for the first visit on July 10th. He told me that he could not understand why I had been kept in IDC. He said that whether or not I had a passport was irrelevant, that I should be able to wait for the appeal on the outside. He said that bail had been denied at the request of U.S. Embassy officials and reiterated that the Thai courts were not holding me in the country. He said that I could have left Thailand on November 18, 1989, the day I walked out of Khlong Prem Prison.[28]

"For some reason the Embassy has decided to keep you in Thailand and in jail," he said. "I met with Stephen Pattison. He said that he will not give his approval to immigration to release you for fear you'll abscond. However, he indicated that the agreement between the Embassy and immigration is verbal and he will deny it if confronted. Immigration officials will deny it too."

What Puttri was telling me confirmed what I had suspected for many months now — it was, nonetheless, unsettling. Whether he realized it or not, Pattison had stated to my lawyer that U.S. officials were collaborating with a foreign government to deny me the most basic civil rights, that they were acting above the law, and that they would lie about it if need be. As to the excuse that I might "abscond", he was also aware that both times I had been released on bail I had done exactly what I had been told to do.

"Would you call my mother and Bruce Nickerson, the attorney my mother hired, and tell them what you just told me?" I asked.

"I will call your mother if you wish."

A few minutes after Puttri left the visiting area, Shelli appeared at the top of the stairs. A police officer ran up and grabbed her and they walked back downstairs. She did not return.

I sent her a letter asking what had happened. Her response arrived a few days later. "I went there early," Shelli wrote, "but the guard said I could not go up. He said that people are talking to newspaper reporters and they are cracking down on who could visit. I went to talk to the big boss (Colonel Sathaporn) and asked him why I could not visit. He said because I was mailing letters for you. I asked him when I would be able to return and he said I could not ever!"

I told Shelli to contact Marcia for assistance and she did. She was given a letter which she took to Colonel Sathaporn. He made her wait two hours before allowing a five-minute visit just before the bell sounded for visitors to leave.

About a month after Jose returned, room politics took another bizarre turn. Yusef decided that he wanted to become room chief. Besides being called "Little Joe," he was also referred to as "the fox" and it became increasingly clear why. In a moment of rare candor, he confessed to me that the heart attack he had suffered upon his arrival had actually been self-induced. He took three nitro-glycerine pills which made his heart do strange things. He said that he had his first "heart attack" when he had been arrested in America for a petty crime. The cops felt sorry for him and released him. Another time, he said he used it on the Japanese police. Unfortunately for him, the Thais could care less whether he lived or died so it hadn't worked in Thailand. But I had to wonder if the bane of my existence was to be surrounded by con artists.

Yusef's fellow Jordanian, Jacob, was constantly receiving money from his family, some of which he used to buy heroin. By July, Jacob had bought an airline ticket and while he celebrated his imminent departure by getting high, Yusef relieved him of his wallet containing thousands of baht. When Jacob discovered the robbery and complained to police, Yusef accused Jose who was then shifted back to Room Four. Yusef had not only taken the money, but had used it to bribe the police to get rid of his political rival. It was then that I realized he had orchestrated Jose's previous move from our room. That was why he had seemed anything but anxious to have Jose returned.

Ali, the Burmese chief from Room Four, was then transferred to our cell, along with his Burmese security force. Yusef was appointed his deputy. The Chinese gang was suddenly out in the cold because, for the first time, they were confronted by an equal number of inmates willing to fight them. They retreated to a remote corner of the room. But the tension began to grow steadily, until it became open hostility between two ethnic groups, the Chinese and the Burmese.

Ali worked outside with the police each day and the actual hands-on management of the room was left to Yusef. He actively worked to cause dissension. When my Polish friend, Albert, dispatched a note from Room Four asking that some things be sent to him, Kuresh, the newly-appointed security chief, told me that what Albert wanted belonged in our room. I wrote to Albert, explaining what Kuresh had said, and asked Yusef to deliver the note. Instead, Yusef showed it to Kuresh as evidence that I was "out to get him". As a result, I was in disfavor with Kuresh for months.

The day that Shelli made her five-minute visit, she told me that Yusef had been responsible for having her visits cut off. He had told Colonel Sathaporn that she had taken my letter to the editor of the

Bangkok Post and the colonel evidently assumed it was a complaint about conditions in IDC.

In early August, Yusef's Machiavellian scheming finally caught up with him. He had actually tried to pit the police against their commander, Colonel Sathaporn. The colonel then personally supervised "Little Joe's" transfer to Room Four, where Jose beat the hell out of him for telling the police that he had robbed Jacob. Several others stood by and applauded.

At the same time, Ali returned to Room Four and Seituan again took charge as our room chief. Kuresh stayed on as security chief. With Yusef gone, the environment became as pleasant as possible with 150 people crammed into a small space.

As crowded as we were, those who worked outside told me that Room Two held even more — nearly 200 in a space identical to ours. It didn't seem possible. Because there was not enough space for everyone, they actually had to sleep in shifts. The tension caused by these inhumane conditions unleashed a fury of violence one afternoon. A full-scale riot erupted that police could not quell for almost two hours! When it was over, they paraded a lifeless body past our room cell.

* * *

Puttri filed a lawsuit against the Bangkok Post on August 6th. When he told me, I was ecstatic! After a year and five months, a Thai lawyer representing me had actually done something that I requested. I didn't know if I would win or not, but the mere thought that I had finally gone on the offensive was worth the cost and aggravation of a potentially lengthy trial.

Puttri returned in late August to tell me that the court date had been set for September 4th. Again my spirits soared. Not only would I be able to leave the cell for a few hours — a feat that I had not accomplished since November 21, 1989 more than nine months ago! — but my day in court had arrived at last.

One day a huge muscular Nigerian named Victor arrived. At night, I awoke to hear him crying but didn't want to embarrass him and pretended I was still asleep. The next morning, I asked what I could do to help. He said he had given up on life. No one in his family knew where he had been taken. He had no way to reach them and believed he would remain in IDC until he died. He said that all of his money had been taken by his arresting officers. "I bought 400 shirts and trousers to take to Nigeria to sell," he said. "They're all in my room at the hotel. If I can get to them, I can sell them and buy a ticket home, but the police won't take me unless I pay them."

He told me he hadn't eaten for three days, so I bought him doughnuts and coffee. I then wrote to Colonel Sathaporn explaining Victor's predicament and asked the missionaries to deliver the note. None of them would. Unfortunately, Julia Freeman — the one kind-hearted missionary I had met — was out of the country and Shelli was still personna non grata with the big boss. Eventually, I bribed a guard — but Colonel Sathaporn did not reply and I could not prevail upon the missionaries to go to Victor's hotel. "We won't adopt a prisoner until he's been here for six months," one told me.

A couple of weeks later, Victor became despondent again. Even though I bought food for him each day, nothing was happening to eventuate his return to Nigeria and it depressed him. One day the man who had taken over the "coffee shop" from Roza ordered him to move from his spot on the floor. He refused so the man kicked him in the head. Almost immediately, Victor began to experience terrible headaches. My Afghan friend, Jamie, gave him aspirin but nothing alleviated the pain.

During the early morning hours of August 20th, I was awakened by a noise. I looked up to see three Chinese men punching and kicking Victor in the head. They believed he was trying to steal something from the "coffee shop", though Victor claimed he was only looking for a cup for some water. Despite being outnumbered, with his size and strength he could have murdered his assailants, but instead stoically accepted their blows as if he didn't really care. He grabbed his head following one particularly vicious kick that landed on his ear.

"Stop it!" I cried. "Stop it!" The men finally let up when Victor was nearly unconscious, writhing on the floor.

A few hours later, he went into a coma. I banged on the bars and screamed for the police. The Thai nurse came out of her office across the hall and I begged her to help get him to a hospital. The officers unlocked the cell door and the nurse came in to look at him. She said something to the officers, who started laughing. They closed the door and went back downstairs.

Within minutes, while still in a coma, Victor began to cough up blood and bile. I called for the police again. This time, they grabbed a stretcher, rolled him onto it and carried him to a car. That day Victor died before reaching the hospital. The official autopsy and report printed in the newspapers said he had died of a drug overdose. The news sickened me.

* * *

"Your mother is coming on September 4th," Puttri's assistant, Voratham, said one day. That same afternoon, I received a letter from Shelli Schultz telling me the same thing. My mother was going to buy herself a birthday present and fly to Thailand. I had mixed feelings about her visit. I wanted to see her so much, but she was not a young woman and I wondered how she would take the long flight and the humid heat of Bangkok.

I set up a chess tournament in the room on Sunday to get my mind off her impending visit. But no matter what I did, I could think of little else.

The following day, September 3rd, the day before my court session, Voratham came to tell me to be ready at 8 AM and handed me a statement that we would present in court. He returned the next morning, arranged for an immigration officer to accompany us, then the three of us climbed into his car. We drove to the Southern District Court on Charoen Khrung Road.

When we arrived at the courthouse, Puttri was there to meet me. After a few minutes, a court reporter stepped into the hall to tell us that the Bangkok Post had requested a postponement. Puttri took the opportunity to tell the Post attorney that we would drop the lawsuit if the newspaper would simply print the truth.

"The information that we printed in the article was given to us by the police," the newspaper lawyer said. "They received it from the United States Embassy. Before we can act on this case, we must contact the Embassy to find out what evidence they have."

* * *

"Steve!" It was a woman's voice. I stood up to see Shelli, a young American man whom I did not recognize, and my mother standing in the hallway. A lump swelled in my throat. I had promised myself that I would not get emotional, but my feelings almost betrayed my resolve. All I could do was say to Shelli, "They let you in, huh?"

I was glad for her presence. It offered me a moment to gather my emotional strength.

"You look better than I expected," my mother exclaimed. I was sure that I didn't look as good to her as she did to me. It was wonderful to see her!

In my excitement, I began to talk non-stop, most of it invective directed toward the U.S. government.

"What can I do to help?" she asked when I had finally stopped talking. Her question caught me off guard. I hadn't thought beyond my anger. I mumbled something and started my invective again.

Suddenly my mother wavered on her feet — she felt ill and put a hand to her face and Shelli grabbed onto her. The long journey, the heat and the intense emotions of the moment had combined to make her nauseous. She sat on the cement steps leading to Room Four. Mark Sandlin, the man who had accompanied her from San

Francisco, started to talk to me, but I could not hear what he said. I just stared at my mother on the stairs. Her health was more important to me than all of my predicaments.

"I'm okay," she said, smiling with considerable effort. I knew she wasn't.

"Take her home and to bed," I ordered Mark and Shelli. I watched as they helped her down the stairs. "Please don't let anything happen to her," I said to myself.

That afternoon I received a letter from an Englishman named Colin Churchman, who had befriended me during his brief stay at IDC. He was in Singapore and had contacted an official of Amnesty International on my behalf, informing him of the details of my case. The Amnesty officer was now en route to Australia but, upon his return to Germany, would present my situation to his committee.

"Steve Raymond," I could barely hear someone calling my name. The voice was in a tunnel, or was I dreaming. Then it was repeated. I opened my eyes, stood up and saw Kuresh at the window. "Your mother come," he said. It was Saturday. Visitors weren't allowed on Saturday. How could she be here?

I jumped to my feet and quickly threw on a shirt. The clanging of metal resounded in the hallway, the door swung open and I was allowed to step outside.

"She's downstairs," the officer said. "Go down."

My mother was sitting at a table with Shelli in front of the room where I had sometimes met with Marcia. It was so good to be able to give her a long hug and see her without bars between us. "The Embassy gave us a letter so that we could come in," my mother said. "We met with David Lyon yesterday — Shelli, Mark (Sandlin), Puttri and I."

"He said that he didn't expect an entourage," Shelli added. "I think he wanted your mother to come alone so that he could intimidate her."

I obviously wasn't the only one who had become cynical about the Embassy's actions.

"What did David Lyon say?" I asked.

"Not much new," my mother replied. "He was pretty evasive."

"That's typical."

"Puttri joined us after the meeting got started. Don't you wish that you had kept him as your lawyer?"

She was right. Had I not become disenchanted with his firm's reluctance to apply for bail, I would have saved a lot of money and a lot of heartache. Peter Bailey's comments about Puttri being "one of the only honest lawyers in Thailand" had proved to be more accurate than I could have imagined.

My mother still was not used to the heat, and after an hour she and Shelli left to catch an air-conditioned taxi. They returned again on Sunday and, by Monday, she seemed to be adapting to the weather much more readily.

She again brought Mark Sandlin who had accompanied her to Thailand in exchange for his airfare, which gave him the opportunity to work on a project in Southeast Asia for the Methodist Church.

"You're very angry," Mark observed.

I suddenly snapped at him, "You'd be angry too if you were living a happy life, not hurting anyone, then because of something a self-serving, psychotic criminal said about you, you're arrested, ruined in business, and locked up for a year and a half."

But his comment made me wonder if the river poison had entered my bloodstream. I had never before been an angry person. I didn't want to be angry. People don't like angry, hostile personalities and I wanted to be liked. "I'll try not to sound so angry tomorrow," I said, probably sounding ridiculous to him.

The following day was my birthday, and my mother and Shelli brought a chocolate layer cake and presents. It was my second birthday behind bars. When they left, I took the cake upstairs and shared it with my friends. "Can you have a birthday everyday?" my Afghan friend, Jamie, exclaimed as he stuffed a slice into his mouth.

When my mother visited on Wednesday for the last time before returning to America, she asked, "If you had it all to do over again, what would you have done differently?"

"I would have stayed away from John Cummings," I said.

My mother looked at me and said, "You know, Mark (my younger brother) says that no matter what happens, you always blame it on somebody else. You're always accusatory and negative. Couldn't you tone down your attacks and work in a positive way?"

I did not fully agree with my brother's assessment, but I also didn't want to put my mother on the defensive. "Yes," I sighed. "I'll try to persuade gently without arguing. I'll work on that."

We held each other for a long time and then kissed goodbye. I sat down and watched her leave, fully conscious of the feeling that to me she was the most wonderful human being in the world.

That afternoon, an Indonesian named Paosan arrived from Lardyao. He had served out his sentence and was awaiting a return ticket to Indonesia. He told me that David Groat had pleaded guilty in order to remain in prison.

Even though Thep had been at the courthouse twice during his trial, the prosecutor and the police claimed that they couldn't find the boy to testify against David. The prosecutor had practically given up on the case and assigned it to an underling. To everyone's astonishment, David suddenly pleaded guilty. He asked for a long sentence and was unhappy when the judge only gave him two years and eight months. Apparently, he was enjoying life at Khlong Prem, he liked running the "coffee shop" where he was earning more money than he had on the outside, and he was afraid to be returned to a prison in America. The Bangkok Post reported the story and questioned his mental state.

* * *

On September 19th, Kuresh was moved to Room Four. Moments later, Yusef reappeared and announced to everyone that he would be taking over as security chief. I was shocked. I knew that neither the police nor Colonel Sathaporn liked Yusef. He had to have paid a tremendous amount of money for the privilege of returning in a position of power.

He approached me within minutes of his arrival. "I could go home tomorrow," he said, "but I have some scores to settle." Just then, some noise came from Room Four. "Kuresh must be getting a beating." A wicked smile crossed his face.

Yusef was mistaken. The noise had nothing to do with Kuresh. A man was trying to hang himself from a ceiling fan, but had only succeeded in pulling it down on top of him.

A week after my mother left, I started coughing. Within 24 hours, the coughing became constant. My chest started to hurt, then I developed a fever. My stomach hurt so bad, I could not eat. It felt like I was constipated and the blockage was killing me. The fever caused chills and a cold sweat. I had no energy and couldn't stand without feeling so dizzy that I was forced to lie down. I took every pill Jamie could provide, be it cough medicine, cold medicine, or antibiotics. After about a week the fever started to subside, just as Dr. Garcia returned from her vacation. I told her what had happened and that the pain in my lungs was still very bad. "Pleurisy," she said and handed me 20 ampicillin capsules.

Gradually, the pain went away. The second week in October, I received a letter from home. My mother wrote that she had developed bronchitis after returning from Thailand. She described the symptoms and they matched my own. One of us had evidently given it to the other.

Some time before my mother's visit, a group of about 35 relatively affluent Chinese from Fukien Province was deposited in our room cell. They had paid an agent in China $28,000 apiece to take them to Bangkok, provide them with fake identity papers, and smuggle them into Canada and the United States as citizens. Miss Lo, the wife of one of the immigration officials, was actually part of the organization.

When the Chinese arrived in Thailand, they were brought to IDC so that the agent would not have to pay for their room and board while they awaited their documents. (It didn't matter to the Thais how many of us were housed in IDC because it cost the same for one person as for 100. The United Nations paid for food and blankets and the Catholic Church paid for electricity and water.)

The Chinese group finally departed the second week of October and there was, for the first time in almost two months, space enough to lie down without draping a leg over someone sleeping nearby. Through all this, I was struck by the fact that the Thai government did not seem to mind that IDC was used as a pit stop for this illegal underground railway between China and the western world.

As late as October, articles appeared in the Thai newspapers bemoaning the fact that the children in Mark's Bangkok home would not testify about the "prostitution" that the officials were sure had existed. A woman named Somsri Kantamala, who worked for a children's rights group, was quoted in the Bangkok Post as saying that Mark Morgan "operated a home for runaway boys that fronted for a pedophile sex service. Because both the boys and their families felt grateful for the money, clothes and education he gave them, they refused to provide any useful evidence against him."

I now believed that these people had been so conditioned to their own dogma that nothing could ever change their minds — no confession from John Cummings, no admission by police, no statement from officials, no newspaper story printing the truth. They simply could not accept the fact that there was no evidence because there was no crime.

In mid-October, Yusef left IDC for good and, instantly, the air got lighter. At this point, it should not have amazed me how much one man could poison a river, but it did. IDC, it seemed to me, was indeed a microcosm of society.

* * *

I returned to court again on the 19th. The lawyer from the Bangkok Post said he was prepared and I took the stand. He began asking questions that related to John Cummings' testimony, then about my living situation with Chat and Nu, then about my business. "If you ran a legitimate tour company, did you own any buses?"

Anyone in the travel industry knows that a destination management company seldom owns buses. "No."

"Then where did you get your buses from?" Suddenly I drew a blank. I had been in jail so long that I had forgotten the name of the coach companies we used. "Robinson's was one," I said. We had only used Robinson's a couple of times, but I could not think of the name UMEC, the company we used most often.

"Why didn't you have any Thai employees?" he asked. Obviously he hadn't done his homework.

"I had a number of Thai employees," I answered.

"The United States Embassy has evidence that this man operated a sex tour business for men who like to have sex with children," the lawyer alleged.

"Ask him for that evidence," I said to Puttri. "They don't have any such evidence."

Puttri told the court that since he was alluding to critical evidence, he ought to present it. The Post attorney hesitated. Finally, the judge told him that I had already been found not guilty by a court of law. He asked the man if he was challenging that finding. The lawyer backed down and said that he wasn't.

Later, Puttri assured me that the lawyer for the newspaper hadn't even addressed the issue of the lawsuit. We were suing the paper for reporting that I had been operating a sex tour business and a child prostitution ring, neither of which the lawyer presented evidence to prove.

The next session was set for October 22nd. Puttri's assistant, Voratham, was scheduled to present our case and would become attorney of record. I was dressed and ready to go that morning when

Voratham came to tell me that there were no officers to accompany me to the courthouse. Previously, I had tried to resist paying bribes for things I believed should have been a routine part of their jobs and I guessed that was why no one was available to me now.

"Well," Voratham said impatiently. "What did the Bangkok Post attorney ask you?"

I looked at him aghast. "Didn't Puttri give you a copy of the transcript?" The man was supposed to go to court and represent me, but he had no idea what had occurred at the previous session.

"I haven't seen Khun Puttri," he said. "I can't get a copy of the transcript."

But these guys work together, I thought. Why can't he get a copy of the transcript? I said forcefully, "You must get copies of the (prosecutor's) appeal of my trial, plus copies of John Cummings' comments that the (Bangkok Post) lawyer received from the police so that you can refute them." He looked irritated and glanced at his watch. "Are you going to get those things?" I asked.

"Yes, I will," he said. "It would be better to get a copy of the transcript." Meaning the one he had just said he couldn't get. Voratham was driving me nuts.

"But you said you couldn't get a copy of the transcript. Did you mean you *didn't* get a copy, or you *couldn't* get a copy?" He didn't answer. I wasn't sure he understood the difference in English. Either that or I had him so confused, he didn't know what to say.

"I wonder if I can get a copy of John Cummings' testimony," he said after a couple of minutes of silence.

I looked at him dumbfounded. Wasn't that what I had just suggested? "How did the newspaper get it?" I asked. "You're my attorney. You have more of a right to it than the Bangkok Post."

"He probably got it from the prosecutor and the prosecutor won't give it to me." Then he thought for a minute. "On Wednesday, I will send a letter for you to sign authorizing us to get a copy of the

260

testimony. The person who comes with the letter will tell you when the next court session will be."

No one came on Wednesday. However, Vichai arrived from the Embassy with a letter from the State Department. It was a decision on the passport hearing which had been held almost a year — 51 weeks — earlier! The decision tersely stated that the revocation was proper. It acknowledged that no U.S. warrant had been issued at the time of the revocation, but it said that one was issued soon thereafter, so my argument that the passport had been revoked illegally was not relevant.[29] The letter stated that I had two months with which to appeal the decision. I responded saying that I would appeal.

Voratham appeared two days later with news that the judge ruled we had a legitimate claim against the Bangkok Post. "We can now proceed with the trial," he said.

No sooner had the lawyer left than Marcia arrived with an American friend. Both of them were very friendly. Her friendliness was not strained and her smile was genuine. Since our argument in June, Marcia's visits had been few and very business-like. During one of them, she brought news that Stephen Pattison "couldn't find" my lengthy rebuttal to the prosecutor's appeal and therefore could not have it translated for the court. Had they lost as many documents involving other Embassy business, I was sure none of them would last in their jobs a week.

Although the progress on the lawsuit against the Post pleased me, physically I was a mess. Because I had had no exercise in more than a year my muscles atrophied. For a guy who had once completed an 1,800-mile charity walkathon, this was very unsettling. I now got winded walking up and down the stairs. I had lost a lot of weight. I had always been thin, but now I was gaunt and positively skeletal. I developed a myriad of skin problems, I itched constantly, and a rash covered half my body. But because everyone else in the room had skin problems too, my own seemed less alarming.

Marcia returned in November soon after the U.S. elections. "John Cummings received a long sentence," she said, "and Howard Ruff is dying of cancer."

I'm not usually a vindictive person, but I could summon very few sympathetic thoughts for those two. In any event, Marcia's information about Ruff proved as inaccurate as her information about me.

Several days later, during visiting hours, my "adopted sister" Patti Hall appeared at the window. She had been living in Japan and I hadn't seen her since she visited at Bangkok Special Prison 18 months earlier. It was a pleasant surprise. "Go ask Colonel Sathaporn for permission to visit downstairs," I said immediately. She had a letter from the Embassy authorizing a visit, and Colonel Sathaporn granted the request.

"Your hair isn't red anymore!" she exclaimed as I came down the stairs to where she was seated. "It's white!"

I tried to ignore the remark but I couldn't. It just made me aware of how much of my life had been taken away. Instantly I began talking about my frustration in trying to get out of IDC and go back to the United States to clear myself. I talked so fast she did not have the opportunity to say a thing until I complained that my mother hadn't yet been able to find a lawyer to sue the federal government. "You know how mothers are," she replied. "Their hearts are in the right place, but they don't always deal effectively with these kinds of things."

I took a breath and changed the subject. "Chat's sister, Rekha, visited last month. Chat's in jail somewhere in Bangkhen, north of Victory Monument, for joyriding. Rekha kept asking if I needed more clothes. I told her no, but asked if she would bring some of her home-cooked food. She said she would but never came back. I really want to know how Chat's doing. Could you please find her and give her a letter I wrote to him?"

"How will I find her? I don't speak Thai."

"No problem. Just go to Victory Monument and look for the food stands near the soi. You'll have to ask — just say, `Pi Chat Sriboonrueng'."

"Okay, `Pi Chat Sriboonrueng'," Patti repeated. "I'll go there this afternoon. We'll see each other again in Santa Rosa at Christmas."

"That would be an answer to a dream!" I said.

Patti returned to Japan the following day. Soon after, I received a note from her with my letter to Chat enclosed. "Though I never found Chat's sister, I'm sure I provided several hundred people in the Victory Monument area with some good entertainment for a couple of hours. I had them howling with laughter," she wrote. Apparently, her pronunciation left something to be desired.

Vichai stopped by the window one afternoon after visiting another prisoner. "Marcia will come next week with some good news," he said.

I looked at him dubiously. "When my mother was here two months ago, she said that Congressman Gary Condit's (D-Modesto) office had called to say there would be some news in a week. Last month, Marcia said to expect some news in a week. Now you're telling me that Marcia will come next week with some news. I'll believe it when it happens."

Vichai just shrugged. He had been very supportive of me from the beginning. Months earlier he had told me that he didn't understand why the U.S. government was treating me so poorly.

"Next week" sounded like the U.S. government's version of the Thai expression "prunee" — you know, the one that can be translated, "Some time in the future... maybe."

* * *

On November 14th, the police banned all newspapers in the room cells. Some Burmese students had hijacked a Thai Airways plane to Calcutta to protest the Thai government's amicable relationship with the brutal Burmese regime and the immigration police were afraid the

263

news would presage another hunger strike by Burmese students in IDC. The Burmese had held a hunger strike once before to protest conditions. The resultant publicity had caused the department to lose face.

Puttri and Voratham arrived the same day that the newspapers were banned. We were able to talk downstairs and I expected to discuss strategy for my lawsuit. "I have some bad news," Puttri began as soon as I had taken a seat. "The court dropped the case against the Bangkok Post."

"Why?"

"Because we were supposed to send a summons to the defendants within five days of the date that the judge decided to go ahead with the trial. We forgot to send the summons, so the case was dropped."

The news hit me like a sucker punch. I sat silently, but was practically shaking in my effort to say something. I fought back tears and struggled to compose myself. My singular attempt to strike back had been bungled by my own attorneys. It was three or four full minutes before I was able to speak. And when I did my voice was not my own. I asked Puttri how that could have happened and could we re-file. He answered that Voratham hadn't realized it was necessary to inform the defendants, and no, under Thai law, it would not be possible to file again. I was instantly suspicious and wondered if Voratham had "forgotten" to file as a way of paying me back for my constant abrasiveness.

As the one-year anniversary of my acquittal approached, I received a letter from Ulrich Gunther, of Amnesty International in Germany, informing me that his chapter had voted to adopt me and that my case had been sent on to Amnesty International in London. Unfortunately, Gunther explained, the London office did not ratify the adoption for two reasons: (1) they did not perceive my case as political, which Amnesty Germany disputed; and (2) there was reluctance because of the U.S. government's involvement.

264

My spirits again descended into pessimistic gloom. I had been wasting away in this room for 12 full months and been behind bars for 21! Every day brought new frustrations. What avenue was left open other than to do harm to myself? I was desperate. I sent a letter to Colonel Sathaporn, and asked Dr. Garcia to deliver another to the Embassy, stating that on November 20, 1990, one year after my arrival at IDC, I would begin a hunger strike.

On the 19th, Colonel Sathaporn came to the cell and asked me not to strike. "The U.S. government will take you back soon," he said. "But if you're sick, it will delay your departure. You can't walk on the plane."

"Well, then they'll have to carry me on," I said flatly.

"Why do you want to strike?" he asked. "I have a letter from the Embassy which says you'll be going home. I'll make a copy and give it to you."

"The Embassy lies," I replied with overt cynicism.

"What?" He looked shocked.

"The Embassy lies," I repeated. "A letter will do no good. Why didn't they write this letter a year ago? I'll start eating when I'm released from here."

"If you want, you can stop eating any time," he said, suddenly patronizingly. "Why wait til tomorrow?"

I turned around and walked back to my blanket.

I woke up on the morning of the 20th feeling hungry. I seldom felt hungry in the morning, but my hunger pangs were obvious psychological responses to my decision not to eat. After everyone else had breakfast, some bananas arrived at the "coffee shop". "Why couldn't the bananas have arrived yesterday?" I complained to my cellmate Jamie.

Then, as if I were living a piece of fiction, on this particular day of all days, the wife of a former detainee appeared during visiting hours and offered me and Jamie handfuls of fresh fruit. The demons were trying to tempt me!

When Dr. Garcia came by for her regular visit, she reminded me that Thursday was Thanksgiving. "I've been invited to the Thanksgiving dinner at the Embassy," she said. "I'll bring some turkey back for you."

"I'm on a hunger strike Dr. Garcia. Thank you for the thought, but I'm not eating anything."

That evening, I got a headache. I was very hungry and tried to keep my mind off food. I picked up a book and came upon a story about a Medieval feast. I put the book down and tried to sleep. I dreamt about food.

The next day I woke feeling nauseous and thirsty. After drinking a full litre of water, I felt better though I still suffered from the headache. When I got up to go to the bathroom, I was weak, but not as hungry as I had been the night before. Again, I tried not to think about food, but it was all around me.

Stephen Pattison and Vichai came to visit. They told me that Colonel Sathaporn had called to tell them about my strike. They hadn't received my letter.

"You should eat," Pattison said. "We wrote a letter to immigration asking if it would be all right to release you. We still haven't received clearance."

I couldn't believe what he was saying. The Embassy asking immigration if they could return me to the States was akin to a judge asking a cellkeeper if it would be all right to release a prisoner.

"It will be a minimum of 15 days before anything happens," he said, "and that's awfully long for a hunger strike."

I looked at Pattison, seething inside. I had been in this place a year because of their bullshit. I said coolly, "I'm not going to end my hunger strike until I'm on a plane headed for the United States. I don't believe anything you say. U.S. government officials have lied continuously since my arrest."

"I've been trying to get you out since you arrived here," he replied evenly.

The audacity of the man! I might have laughed had I not been so furious.

"You're stuck in a legal `Catch 22' because of the appeal," he said. He was giving me the same transparent line nearly a year after the court had told the Embassy in writing that they were not holding me, and months after Puttri had told Pattison in a face-to-face meeting that I could leave the country at any time, that I did not have to wait for the appeal.

The third day of my hunger strike was Thanksgiving. I woke feeling very nauseous. I had some gas pains, but after a short nap they disappeared. When I stood, I almost fainted. Prior to the hunger strike, I had been subsisting on a minimal diet and it was obvious I had no reserves, no fat to sustain me. I hadn't expected to feel so weak so soon. I had worried about losing body heat, but my strength seemed to be ebbing before my body heat diminished. I guessed that the tropical heat helped me retain my own. I was not as hungry as I had been on the first day but I was having difficulty finding a book that didn't talk about food.

The population of the room had grown again and was now up to 175. When I first arrived, I thought it was crowded at 90 and I remembered the Sunday when we reached 110 and cleaning had been cancelled because everyone wouldn't fit in the small room while the large one was mopped. Space now was nowhere to be found — and, as a result, the air was heavy and hard to breathe.

On the fourth day of my strike, I awoke feeling exhausted and weak, but the nausea had disappeared. At mid-morning the police came in and escorted me downstairs where I was directed to a bench against a wall. I sat down and waited, not knowing what was happening.

A few minutes later, Marcia appeared in the compound. I was surprised to see her. It had only been two days since Pattison and Vichai came in and I never received two visits from Embassy staff in such a short time.

"Where shall we sit?" she asked. I motioned to the table, stood up carefully so that I wouldn't faint, and shuffled to a bench behind the table.

"Is something wrong with your foot?" she asked.

"No," I said, and looked at it to see if she had noticed something I hadn't.

She opened a file. "The Embassy received a telex last night. Your `friend' Eisenman is coming to get you in two weeks. You're scheduled to leave here on December 7th."

"You've won!" Jamie proclaimed when I told him the news. "Are you going to eat now?"

"Should I?"

"Yes, of course."

My resolve had crumbled. It was weaker than I had thought. I wanted to be pertinacious, but I wanted to eat even more. I peeled an orange and savored it for 15 minutes. A few minutes later Dr. Garcia arrived. "Would you call my mother and tell her I broke my fast," I asked.

She smiled and said she'd be happy to.

Everyone came to congratulate me for my impending release. Other prisoners suddenly decided they would go on hunger strikes as well. A Burmese man tried, but was viciously beaten by the police and forced to eat. The Thais had nothing to fear from the Burmese Embassy.

One of the quirks of Thai law states that those who enter the country legally, but overstay their visas, must leave by plane. However, those who enter illegally can be deported overland to their point of entry. The Burmese who poured across the border illegally after the government crackdown had only to raise 500 baht for their transportation back to the border. Most of them were able to do so in a couple of months. However, one student had entered legally and overstayed his visa and it would cost him five times as much. He had been in IDC for nearly a year, unable to raise the money.

Vichai arrived on November 26th with an application for a travel document. I completed it and, two hours later, a messenger arrived with the papers. After waiting for over a year, the process was incredibly unencumbered... as long as the Embassy wanted it that way.

A Burmese named Salim had been leading a one-man crusade to get rid of the corruption, at least among the prisoners. He obviously could do nothing about the police, but was using his access as a trustee to report thievery inside to Colonel Sathaporn. One day, three of the worst thieves in our room were told to roll up their blankets for their transfer to Room Four. The colonel came to the bars and called me over to talk to him. "Why didn't you tell me what was going on?" he asked. I just shrugged. I had always assumed that, as commander, he knew what was going on and, like his officers, condoned it. I was surprised by his concern and regretted not having given him my trust. Again I had misjudged my fellow man.

The closer it got to my departure day, the more my Afghan friend, Jamie, became depressed and angry. He had escaped from Afghanistan, where he was wanted by both the Mujahadeen and the Communists, by bribing a jailer to release him before his scheduled execution. He had fled through Pakistan and Malaysia before arriving in Thailand. On his second day in the country, he was arrested and taken to IDC.

As with Kuresh, the United Nations recognized him as a political refugee, but until a country accepted him for resettlement, he would languish here. Though happy for me, my departure meant he was losing a friend. He wondered if a hunger strike would help, but I told him that I did not think it would have the same effect in his situation.

The euphoria over my impending release was shattered one day when a letter from my mother informed me that a dear friend, "Bill" Lundy, had died. When I was very young, my father lost his eyesight and while he and my mother spent months at a time in San Francisco with doctors futilely attempting to restore his vision, I had stayed with

"Bill" and her husband, Verl. They had no children and "Bill" always felt like my other mother. The news of her death was devastating, particularly because I hadn't been able to be there for her when she was dying. I put down the letter and cried for the loss of "Bill" in my life and for not having been closer to her in recent years.

In the same way I had taken my freedom for granted before my arrest, I had taken "Bill" for granted. We all tend to forget that life is fragile and ephemeral. The sense that there will always be tomorrow allows us to delay the expression of our feelings. My mother said that I had been mentioned in Bill's will. She remembered me — as she always did — even though I often forgot her. I was surely going to miss her.

The day after Salim arranged for the transfer of the thieves, he gathered everyone together and made a speech. "When a robbery happens," he said, "report it. We can't do anything about the police taking our money, but we don't have to be like them and steal from each other."

Later, he spoke to me alone. "Now I can leave this place knowing I've done some good." I admired him tremendously and thanked him for his efforts. I also wondered how long it would last once he was gone.

My mother had written to ask if I wanted anyone to greet me at the airport when I arrived in San Francisco. I asked Dr. Garcia to phone and tell her, "The more the merrier. She can call the newspapers and the television stations if she wants to."

I reflected on my time in IDC and thought that the outer world had receded to a point where, to me, it had lost all sense of reality. Reality had become that room. The world beyond those four walls only appeared in my dreams and the dreams were simply expressions of a dwindling remembrance of a life I once owned but now barely recognized.

I tried to write about what I had learned and, strangely enough, my thoughts were introspective and positive even though my experience had been negative. I wrote, "Perhaps a true sense of justice can be learned only when one is treated unjustly."

The night before leaving I threw a party — well, as much of a party as was possible without money or freedom. I bought 100 Coca-Colas and 100 doughnuts and bid my farewells to everyone. It was hard to say goodbye to my friends — Jamie and Kuresh, basically good kind people — who, as U.N. political refugees, continued to hang on in IDC with that horrible room their only country. And, of course, the toughest farewells of all would be those I would not have a chance to make — Chat, Nu, Kachon, and Kenji.

271

Fourteen

The Golden Gate

"What is my offence? What is the evidence that doth accuse me? Where lawful quest have given their verdict up unto the frowning judge... before I be convict by course of law."

— Shakespeare, *Richard III*

December 7, 1990

The police were scheduled to come at 5 AM and so I arranged with one of the men who stayed up through the night to wake me an hour earlier. An immigration officer came to the door at 4:30 just as I was walking back from the shower.

"Steve Raymond, leow, leow! Hurry up!" I had not finished packing and expected to use the next half hour to do so. Instead, I threw on my clothes, tossed everything into the suitcase and rushed out. The officer led me downstairs, told me to sit at the table, and disappeared into an office.

Forty-five minutes later, at 5:15, Vichai emerged from the entrance, followed by a Japanese man, an auburn-haired western woman, and a tall gangly farang with a moustache whom I recognized as Tom Eisenman, the officer from the San Francisco Police Department who was convinced I turned boys into heroin addicts. Abruptly, a picture of my re-arrest sprang up in front of me — an officer from Din Daeng shoving a vial of white powder under my face and accusing me of selling it. And I guessed it was Eisenman who had planted the idea — directly or indirectly — with the Thai police.

272

"Well it looks like you've won this round, Eisenman," I said. "But it aint over till the fat lady sings." He offered a rather sardonic smile and agreed that it wasn't over yet.

I was suddenly taken aback by the woman who immediately and aggressively took control, introducing herself as a federal marshal and ordering me to remove everything from my pockets. When she spotted the 700 baht that I had been saving, she said, "You'll want to change that to American money."

"No," I replied. "I want to buy a beer at the airport."

"Sorry," was the no-nonsense response. "No alcoholic beverages. We can't drink and you can't drink."

I looked disbelievingly at her. "Not even one beer with my meal?" I had been looking forward to a beer at the airport for a year.

"No, the airline won't allow it," Eisenman replied.

"The airline?" I said. "You mean *you* won't allow it. I'm sure if I asked for it the stewardess would give it to me." He shook his head.

As the federal agent chained and handcuffed me, Eisenman and his Japanese-American partner from the San Francisco Police Department went upstairs to look at the room cell that had been my world for the previous 54 weeks. When they returned, I was ushered into a van and we drove off.

My resolve not to talk to these people lasted five minutes. Even Eisenman became friendly and loquacious. The three American officers talked about their experiences in Bangkok for the previous two days. No one mentioned my case. I was disarmed!

Vichai checked the four of us in for the flight and accompanied us through customs to the departure lounge. When I finally bid him adieu, my sorrow was sincere. He was the one Embassy employee who had worked wholeheartedly for, not against, my interests.

I was kept handcuffed and chained until seated on the plane.

A short time after we lifted off, the United jet developed a problem with the landing gear which refused to retract. We flew over rural

273

Thailand and dumped a jumbo jetload of fuel over acres and acres of Thai rice paddies before returning to the airport.

How many poor farmers would lose what little income they had because of this emergency landing?

We were soon aboard another flight that would connect in Taipei rather than Tokyo. Eisenman sat next to me and when I complained about being in the smoking section, he said in all seriousness that he assumed I was a non-smoker because "Peds don't smoke."

I laughed at the absurdity of his thinking and asked if he also believed that "all blacks eat watermelons." His bigotry and narrow-mindedness was blatant.

A half hour later, Eisenman asked a stewardess for a copy of the regulations. He turned to the section regarding prisoner transfers and showed me the paragraph forbidding alcoholic beverages. I was impressed that he felt obliged to prove to me that he had not lied.

When I asked to use the bathroom, the federal marshal insisted on accompanying me and standing watch outside the door. Then, when I asked if I could take an aisle seat in Taipei, she quickly retorted, "Absolutely not." Her attitude was so extreme that it amused me. I decided to ask permission for everything. "May I have coffee?" "May I eat an apple?" "May I scratch my ear?" If they wanted an obsequious prisoner, I would be one. After all, U.S. authorities had treated me for the previous two years like I was an international terrorist, so why should I expect a different attitude from a marshal?

When we arrived at San Francisco International Airport, we were met at the plane by three additional policemen and two customs officials. One would have thought Machine Gun Kelly was coming as eight officers escorted me through the terminal.

One said I would have to be taken out the back because reporters were waiting at the main entrance to the customs area. I knew that my family and friends were also waiting and felt very disappointed knowing I would not be able to see them.

274

The federal marshal gave a customs agent the baggage tag and told him to give my luggage to my mother. Then I was ushered outside into a police car and driven to the San Francisco City and County Jail at 850 Bryant Street.

Once in the building, Eisenman took me to meet Inspector Glenn Pamfiloff, his former partner who had obtained the state warrant and had provided a good deal of misinformation to the Chronicle. The two of them were joined by a third man and I was taken into an interrogation room.

Eisenman showed me a tape recorder and told me he was turning it on. Then Pamfiloff asked if I was prepared to make a statement. I was keenly aware that I had not been read the Miranda Rights and that the police actually expected me to make a statement without my lawyer present. "I'm not going to make any statement," I said.

"But you said on the plane... " Eisenman began.

"What I said on the plane was not..." I stopped myself. They were trying to entrap me. On the plane I had said that I was not guilty and the charge was bullshit. Eisenman had then replied something about having the opportunity to repeat the statement in San Francisco.

He picked up the tape recorder and shut it off. The conversation immediately lightened up. After a few minutes of banter about my political views and questions about men they had arrested for child molestation whom they "assumed" I had known, Eisenman made a rather ineffectual attempt to get me to make a statement. "You're acting guilty," he said.

"What?" I shook my head as if clearing it of cobwebs and looked at him askance. I had to wonder how he could defend his strange comment.

"Yeah," he said. "You won't give us a statement. If you were innocent you wouldn't be afraid to talk."

I exploded. "The way you have fucked me over for the past two years...!" I didn't finish the sentence. His juvenile attempt to coerce me into making a statement was not worth a response. I stood up as if to leave, looked at the three men and suddenly remembered I was still under arrest. I sat down again.

Realizing that I would say nothing for the tape recorder, Pamfiloff and the third officer both shook my hand and left. Eisenman then took me upstairs where he signed me over to the Sheriff's Department.

Moments later, I was locked in a filthy holding cell with five other men. My first thought was that at least it wasn't putrid green. A couple of long-haired caucasians and an African-American were lounging on the built-in benches and two young Latinos stood against the wall near a pay phone. A telephone?!! In the cell?!! That was unbelievable.

There was something peculiar about these cellmates. Each time they moved, they didn't step, they strutted. It reminded me of a movie I had seen of birds on the Galapagos Islands doing a mating dance. I had forgotten that young American males also participated in this macho ritual and, right away, I remembered that I could no longer smile at people and expect them to smile back. I also realized that the respect I had been given in Asia by younger Asians would be reversed. America's culture worships youth. Older men are regarded as — "old farts". And now, after two years in prison, I felt like an "old fart".

I began to pace the floor, worrying about my family being left at the airport.

After a couple of hours a black man was put in the cell with us and, without provocation, started yelling at me. "Hey white boy! You! Hey, look at me when I talk to ya!" Then he made threatening remarks. I looked away, thinking that if I made eye contact, it would be taken as a challenge. I laid down on the wall bench. It wasn't difficult to act tired. I had been awake for over 30 hours. Suddenly I was asleep.

The next thing I knew, someone was shaking me. Fifteen minutes had passed. "Lunch," the man said and gestured to the door where small cardboard boxes were stacked on a tray. We were being fed in a holding cell! I certainly wasn't in Thailand any more.

Six hours later, I was brought to a nearby room and asked to take a seat beside a desk. "The news media has been calling all day long wanting to talk to you," a sheriff's deputy told me.

"Good," I replied. "I'd like to hold a press conference and have the truth heard for a change. I'm tired of the lies."

"Tell me something about your case," the deputy said.

I told him about John Cummings, the coverage by the press, and the whole fantastic story. "We'd better put you into protective custody," he said. "There may be a story on television."

After my interview with the deputy, I was fingerprinted and weighed. The scale registered 145 pounds at the time of my initial arrest and I was not overweight. Now I weighed a feeble 120. Next, I was taken into a small room for mug shots and it was just like in the movies. They took my front facial view, then ordered me to turn to the right.

On the seventh floor, I was ordered to strip, issued an orange shirt, pants and socks; then picked up a mattress, sheets and blankets in the hallway. Finally, I was taken to a cell at the very end of a long grey cell block. I put the mattress down on the metal bed frame, crawled between the sheets and fell to sleep within seconds.

"Raymond!" The voice seemed to come from a distance. Then I heard the familiar sound of metal keys in an iron lock. I opened my eyes. "You have an interview."

I had no idea how long I had been asleep or what time it was. I looked out a window across the hallway. It was dark outside. I stepped from the cell and was led into another hallway which was lined on both sides with small rooms, each containing a table and two chairs. In the first room I saw a distinguished-looking man in his 50's, wearing a suit and tie. I didn't recognize him and continued down the hall. No one was in any of the other rooms, so I returned to the first.

"Steve Raymond?" he said. I was still groggy and disoriented.

"Yes," I responded.

"I'm Bruce Nickerson. I just wanted to say hello and get to know you."

I glanced at a clock. It was 11:30 PM. I had no idea why his visit was so late at night or what he had been doing in San Francisco at that hour, but I was impressed that he had come to see me. At this point, we didn't have much to say to each other about the case. I suggested that possibly Pablo Luna, the young witness upon whom the prosecution was relying heavily, had mistaken me for someone else. But the mere fact that Nickerson had come so late to visit me made me feel he was dedicated to the case.

After the visit, I was escorted back to my cell. By the time the longest day of my life had ended, I was fast asleep.

* * *

December 8, 1990 — March 14, 1991

When I awoke once again, something was deliciously different. Not only was it quiet — something IDC never was — but it was dark. I hadn't experienced darkness at night for nearly two years. Lights in Thai prisons were always on. I looked around my expansive cell. I was alone, something else I hadn't experienced for two years. I had really extricated myself from IDC and I felt good about being back in America, even if some of its officials had done me in.

I lay in bed reflecting on my new environment when the lights went on. A few minutes later a tray of food was placed into a slot in the door. I looked at it with astonishment. The amount of food and the quality were not what I was used to. It was mind-boggling: juice, milk, pancakes, cream of wheat, bread, butter. And best of all — no rice!

I ate everything, slowly and with relish. A few minutes later, a deputy came to the cell and said, "Do you want to take a shower?"

"Yes!" I almost tripped in my dash to get out the door. There was another new sensation — hot water.

After drying off, I waited outside my cell to be let back in, when a tall young blond man in the cell adjacent to mine asked, "What's your case?" I was surprised at his question. David Groat had told me that American prisoners don't discuss their cases with each other. "You can tell me," he said. "We're the only white men on the block. We need to stick together. My name is Ted."

I immediately disliked him for his appeal to racial prejudice. "My case is my business," I replied.

"Does it involve children?" he asked.

"Maybe." I always found it difficult to lie, even to a stranger.

"You're a fucking child molester!" he screamed maniacally. I stepped to the door of my cell and shuddered. The hatred in that man's voice was virulent.

When lunch boxes were delivered at 11 AM, Ted yelled from the next cell, "Hey, One!"

Not realizing that he was yelling at me, I ignored him. But he persisted. Suddenly, I understood that I was in cell Number One.

"What?" I said hesitantly.

"Give me your lunch," he said. "They ran out and I didn't get one."

"No, I'm sorry." I tried to be polite.

He started screaming invectives at me. I stepped away from the bars and sat down on my bed to eat.

That evening, the deputy wheeled a pay phone into the hallway. Ted grabbed it immediately and made a call. While he was talking, I asked if I could use the phone when he was finished. I wanted to call my mother. I hadn't been able to talk with her since her visit to Thailand. He ignored me. When he hung up, he shoved the phone to the cell on his left.

279

The following morning, when the deputy came to let me out for a shower, I asked if I could use a phone. "When the phone comes through in the evening, you'll be the first to get it," he said.

Ted overheard us and started screaming. "We have a schedule for the phones!" he yelled. "I get it when it arrives at seven."

"Well, now One gets it at seven," the deputy said.

"Just because this man comes in means that everyone on the block has to change his schedule?" He yelled loud enough for the other prisoners to hear, trying to incite them. They started complaining.

Later, I was standing at the bars of my cell when a tall muscular black man walked past en route to the shower. I had hardly paid him any notice, but suddenly his fist shot between the bars and struck me in the face with such force that I was flung across the cell onto my bunk. I looked up at him, dazed and angry.

"Are you a child molester?" he asked.

"No, I'm not," I said. He smirked, then told Ted that he had just knocked me across the cell. The two of them started laughing.

Following morning showers, a television attached to a six-foot high portable stand in the hallway was usually turned on. I stood at the bars of my cell to watch. Suddenly, I was hit in the face by a torrent of water. Ted started laughing. He had filled his cup with tap water and, while I was distracted by TV, he stuck the cup through the bars just far enough to be able to flip it into my face.

I backed away, dried myself with a towel, and continued to watch the program. That didn't deter Ted. He simply reached around farther and tossed the water on my bunk, continuing on and off for the rest of the day. By evening, the bed was soaked.

On Monday morning, I was scheduled to appear in court for a bail reduction hearing. The guard came for me before I had a chance to shower or comb my hair. I was handcuffed to another prisoner, marched through the cellblocks to the elevator (which in itself was a self-contained cell) and taken to a dirty bathroom-sized cement cell on the second floor where other prisoners also awaited hearings.

The door to the hallway opened and a bearded man in a business suit entered. He rummaged through a number of forms and files and began calling names. He briefly told us what to expect from the judge but if someone asked a question he became noticeably irritated. After learning that I had a private attorney, he skipped over me, went on to the next prisoner, then banged on the door and was gone.

One by one we were escorted by deputies to the courtroom. When I walked in I found Bruce Nickerson waiting at the defense lawyer's table. He signalled me to join him. I glanced to my left and saw a CBS television camera pointed at me. I managed a nervous smile and moved to my lawyer until I stood with him before the judge. All I could think of was that I hadn't washed or combed my hair.

The judge asked me a question. I was dazed by everything and still jet-lagged, and didn't hear him. Bruce told me to answer in the affirmative. A hearing date was then set to review my bail a week from Tuesday, on December 18th. Since there was no proof that I had fled, I hoped to have it lowered to a reasonable level and get out for Christmas. I was soon ushered back to the holding cell while the television camera recorded my every move.

A few minutes later, Bruce appeared and brought with him a copy of the police report of Pablo Luna's testimony. After 21 months behind bars, I was finally able to learn the details of the charge that had kept me imprisoned all that time.

I was so overwhelmed that I couldn't even analyze it properly. In the testimony Pablo stated he had been to my house and described the entrance and the location. He hadn't confused my apartment with anyone else's as I had thought. I tried to rack my brain to remember what the boy looked like. If I couldn't remember what he looked like then I thought it very possible he couldn't remember what I looked like. We briefly discussed the possibility of a line-up to see if he could identify me.

I asked my attorney to bring the transcript back on his next visit when I hoped to feel less muddled. I stood and almost fell down again. "Oh, Bruce," was all I could manage to say. I desperately needed somebody to hug me and tell me everything would be all right. Anybody would have done.

I told Bruce that I still hadn't been able to use the phone to call my mother. A couple hours later, a deputy came to my cell to ask if I had problems getting use of a telephone.

"I haven't been able to make a phone call since I arrived," I said.

"You won't have any more problems," he promised.

As soon as the deputy left, Ted started yelling at me. "Why did you complain to a deputy?"

"I didn't," I said. "I told my lawyer that I hadn't been able to call my family since my return from Thailand."

"If you want something, you ask us. We're not the ones who are keeping you here, they are."

I wanted to remind him that I had asked a number of times for the phone, but I think I realized what I was dealing with — I shut up for the sake of keeping the peace.

On Tuesday, I was allowed to go to the gym along with 10 other prisoners. Ted and his cellmate Brian were playing basketball when I entered the cavernous hall. Some Latino prisoners were kicking a soccer ball around in another area and a couple others were playing ping pong.

I was drawn to the physical fitness equipment and enjoyed a brief workout for the first time since my days at Khlong Prem. While I was resting between exercises, Ted walked over and said, "Why don't you step around the corner, tough guy?" His dialogue was straight out of a schlock gangster movie. "I won't kill you, I'll just hurt you a lot."

I shook my head in disgust and went back to the exercise equipment. "Are you afraid of me?" he asked. He was a head taller, about 20 years younger, and in much better shape.

"Yes," I said.

That acknowledgement seemed to subdue his machismo. He turned and strutted back to the basketball court.

A few minutes later, the prisoners in the gym arranged a basketball game. Seven of them decided to play and they called me to join them.

I declined. I was in such poor physical shape I was afraid the exertion would be too much.

"Come on, man. You make it even," one of them pleaded.

Reluctantly, I removed my shoes and joined the game. When the ball was passed to me, I started to dribble down court. Suddenly, I was struck from behind and the next thing I knew I was sprawled across the floor. To my surprise, everyone except his cellmate Brian started yelling at Ted and condemning him for the attack. I stood up, gathered my strength and resolved to play until our time was up. Although the 15-minute game exhausted me, it was a personal triumph just to complete it. As we were walking back to our cell block, Ted acted almost friendly. "Good game," he said. I took that to be an apology.

That night I telephoned my mother. Ted bitched only a little because I limited the call to 10 minutes. The following day, my mother and stepfather Charles arrived for a visit. The visiting room was on the same floor and at the end of the cell blocks near the conference rooms. Inmates and visitors were separated by a glass shield and we had to speak on telephones. This made it possible to talk with only one person at a time, but it was an improvement over the shouting matches I'd had in Thailand.

My mother said they had come to the airport and only learned they had missed me after customs agents delivered my suitcase. Then on Monday, they had driven 90 miles from Modesto to San Francisco but arrived too late for my hearing and could not see me because it wasn't a visiting day. Today they made the drive for the third time in six days.

On Thursday, Ted was transferred to jail in Sacramento for a court hearing. As soon as he left, Brian called me by name rather than "One" and offered the telephone when I needed it. That afternoon, a volunteer arrived with some books. These things were small, but they

283

improved my spirits and I was better able to prepare myself for the battle in court.

The following Monday, Ted returned. He and Brian began the verbal harassment again but it didn't seem to bother me as much.

Meanwhile, San Francisco was experiencing the longest cold spell in recorded history. The temperatures outside were plummeting to below freezing and I could feel it inside the jail. I asked the trustee in charge of the laundry for an additional shirt, but he replied, "No!" then added, "Do you have a problem with that?"

"With freezing?" I said. "Yes, I have a problem with freezing."

"You aint gettin' another shirt," he snarled. "I don't like child molesters."

On the 18th, a deputy appeared at my cell and accompanied me to the bail hearing. I was mentally prepared, had combed my hair, and felt better about my appearance. There were no television cameras this time. Mom and Charles, my stepfather, were sitting in the gallery. I acknowledged them with a smile and joined Bruce at the defense lawyer's table. He introduced me to a notary public and had me sign the papers for Bill Lundy's will. Then I was ushered back to the holding cell. Bruce followed.

"What are the chances of a bail reduction?" I asked.

"I don't think the judge will reduce the bail," he said with maddeningly quick negativity... or was it a realistic sense of cynicism?

My spirits dropped like a high-speed elevator. Back into the courtroom I shuffled, futilely attempting to smile again. I stood next to Bruce as I had done at the previous hearing. The judge read the police report and made a comment about my "flight to Thailand" and Bruce objected.

"This man is not a flight risk," he said. "He lived in Thailand where he maintained a business. He did not leave the country to avoid prosecution." My lawyer then went on to state that my personal history was testimony to my willingness to work within the system.

In 1984, I hosted a cocktail party at my home on Russian Hill for a former member of the Dutch Parliament who had authored a bill that legalized gay sex in the Netherlands, and whom I had met a few years earlier in Amsterdam. The legislator had come to San Francisco to speak for the abolition of laws that proscribe sexual activity. I learned from my secretary, Susan, soon after the party, that the police had been asking questions about me and that Inspector Eisenman had warned her teenage brother-in-law Rey to stay away from me. Rey said Eisenman had told him that I was trying to turn him into a heroin addict, and that I sold his friends to other men for sex.

Then I learned from my newspaper delivery boy that police had said similar things to him and to a number of his Vietnamese-Chinese friends in the neighborhood. I was upset. Rey and Susan's husband Sonny, whom I had known for years, often dropped in on me.

I called a friend, Ron Huberman, in the District Attorney's office and asked him to arrange a meeting between myself and the officers responsible. I met with then-Lieutenant (now Captain) Richard Hesselroth, head of the Juvenile Division and Eisenman's supervisor. The meeting at the Hall of Justice — ironically the same building in which I was now incarcerated — was congenial. I wanted to know why I was being harassed by the police department.

After I told Hesselroth what Eisenman had been saying about me to my friends, the lieutenant told me not to worry about Eisenman anymore. But in 1985, Hesselroth was promoted and moved out of the Juvenile Division and Eisenman convinced a judge to issue a search warrant while I was in New York at a trade show. Police went through my house and removed all of my personal papers, everything from university diplomas to business files for the Thailand office.

I was forced to sue the city of San Francisco for the return of my property, personal effects, diplomas, photographs, etc. In 1986 a judge ordered Eisenman to return everything he had taken. More than a year later, without having broken any laws, with my U.S. passport in order, with no warrant or police record, I moved to Bangkok to build my business. I had never "fled" except in the minds of those who had assumed my guilt from Day One and created a warrant for my arrest after the fact.

"This will take more time than I have today," the judge now said to Bruce Nickerson. "We'll have to postpone this hearing."

"I have the rest of this week," my lawyer replied.

"My docket is full. The earliest I can reschedule is for the 27th," the judge said. It was remarkable how easily one could be condemned to additional weeks in prison — just like that!

I wanted to say something to my parents, but a deputy hurried me off. I caught a glimpse of Gary Crevallo, the former manager of my San Francisco office, and tried to have him connect with them. But I got pushed through the door.

Outside my cell, the deputy said, "Roll it up, you're going to move." I gathered up my mattress, my books and toiletries and carried them into the hallway.

"Where are you going?" Brian exclaimed as I walked past his cell. "Hey, Ted, your favorite prisoner is leaving."

I followed the deputy to the end of the block, past a guard station and through a locked iron door into a short hallway with three cells. The second and third cells of F Block each held two prisoners, but the first was empty. "In there," the deputy ordered. I stepped inside and the door slammed behind me.

I threw the mattress over the steel bunk and my other things on the floor, then stepped up to the bars of the cell to look around. None of the other prisoners said a word.

Within minutes, I was called for an interview. "How do you like your new cell?" Bruce asked as I took a seat. "I told the sergeant about your problems and he ordered the move. It should be better." He then pulled the transcript of Pablo's testimony from his briefcase and I took a look at it again. This time, I was much more comfortable and alert. Bruce waited patiently while I read the report which must have been typed on a Din Daeng-vintage antique. It stated that Pablo Luna had come to my house while high on LSD on three separate occasions and that during his visit in July 1984, I had orally copulated him.

Pablo's statement as reported by Eisenman said that after having sex with him, I gave Pablo a promotional "break dance T-shirt". He also provided police with a post card that he said he had sent from San Francisco to his mother in Sacramento that weekend. The post card was dated July 1984 and contained a handwritten note from John Cummings to Pablo's mother.

"Pablo said that I gave him a break dance t-shirt when he came to my house in 1984. That was impossible," I said to Bruce. "I held the break dance contest in March 1985. The t-shirts weren't printed until then."

"Can you prove that?" Bruce asked. "Do you have any receipts for the shirts?"

"The contest was a promotion for my company. Get hold of Gary Crevallo or Jake Jue, my accountant. Maybe they still have the records."

"This is good!" Bruce said. "Anything else that you can think of?"

"Pablo said that he took acid, then fell asleep, woke up and `saw' me on top of him. When you drop acid, I don't think you can fall asleep for a while. Also, it's a hallucinogenic. That means it makes people hallucinate and see things that aren't there. We need an expert on LSD to testify. Pablo also said that friends of mine were present. One was Dennis, the other Eduardo, my roommate and companion of several years. Eduardo was so possessive I couldn't look at anybody else in his presence, much less touch someone."

After the interview I returned to the cell, again feeling that everything would turn out all right, even if I wouldn't be home for Christmas.

Three of my neighbors in the new cell block were being held on murder charges. One, a large Tongan named Livai, was charged with killing a white man at a gas station in San Francisco. His was called the "911 murder," because the man had dialed "9-1-1" trying to get help just before he was killed. The second man was a short Mexican-American named Simon. He had been charged with killing his former wife's lover. The third man, Joaquin, was from Cuba. His was a drug-related murder.

The fourth man in the cell block was Rick Parker, a half-black, half-Mexican charged with a number of petty crimes. While the three murder suspects ignored me or were outwardly hostile, Rick let me know he thought the others had no business judging people.

In the morning, my cell was unlocked and I was allowed into the hallway with other prisoners. For the first time in nearly two years, I could actually sit at a table and write. I enjoyed it so much that I sat there for hours.

Then the trustee who had refused me a shirt entered F block to distribute clothes. "Do you have any children?" he asked the others. "Do you know that man is a child molester?"

I walked back into my cell. Joaquin and Simon threw open the door and stepped inside after me. "Are you a...?" Joaquin said something in Cuban Spanish that I couldn't understand.

"What do you mean?" I asked.

He struggled with the English — unsuccessfully — and finally said, "What is your case?" I tried to explain that I was the victim of another prisoner trying to cop a plea to get his own sentence reduced. This totally confused him. He didn't know what to believe, and the two of them turned and stalked out. I followed them into the hall and tried to give them the entire story. They didn't want to hear it. Joaquin whirled on me and said, "Aren't you supposed to be locked up? Look, I'm here for murder. One more isn't going to bother me. I don't want to see you out here with us. You go back to your cell and close the door!"

I thought his suggestion might just be the most prudent thing to do. I felt more vulnerable here than I had in my previous cell.

Here, the five of us were locked together in a small cell block, isolated from the rest of the jail.

The following day, after the deputy had unlocked my cell door, Simon threw it open and walked in as I was writing a letter. "The word is out on you," he said. "You're not going to be safe anywhere in this jail. Nobody here in F block is going to bother you if you do some things for us."

"What do you want?" I asked, and said flatly, "It isn't what you think."

"When you show us something in writing to prove what you say, things will change. Until then, we want some things from you. You get up early and sweep and mop every morning. We've been taking turns doing that, but you'll have to do it every day."

"Okay," I said. It was a small price to pay for "protection".

Then, he continued, "You'll have to pay rent, too."

After two years in Thai jails I was used to that. But I said, "What do you mean?"

"You have to buy $5 a week in things from the commissary for us."

I agreed to his second demand as well, but countered that I didn't have a lot of money.

When Simon walked out of the cell, I breathed easier. I knew that I had just been sold a reprieve. But I also suspected that I had shown my weakness, which to American prisoners was worthy of contempt. Like a shark that smelled blood, they would sense that weakness and move in for the kill.

Even more I resented the need to prove to a judge that I'd never fled to Thailand and to prove to these murder suspects that I'd never in my life done anything to hurt a child. "Hopefully I'll be out on bail in a week," I thought, trying to buoy myself. "So I won't worry too much about what they're planning to do."

In the morning, perhaps fortuitously, deputies realized that I was supposed to be in protective custody and stopped unlocking my cell. The city's Nordic winter continued and the temperature in the cell block never climbed above the 50's. I was able to see the condensation of my breath as I exhaled. Additional clothes were not sufficient. By Christmas, it had become so brutally cold that I spent all of my time sitting on my bunk, wrapped in blankets and shivering. I had to give up reading in order to keep my hands wrapped warmly enough and could do nothing except watch the television in the hallway.

Unfortunately, the others chose the programs — wrestling, cartoons, game shows and pickup trucks with oversized wheels driving over wrecked cars. They also seemed to enjoy police and rescue programs, but always cheered when an officer got shot or was injured. Mercifully, they did watch the news and everyone except Joaquin enjoyed football, which was the one thing I had missed most while in Thailand. I had always been a 49er fan.

Hostility toward me continued, but as long as I "paid the rent" it was not overt. One day, I received a note from Rick Parker, who — like the others — did not openly talk to me. "I don't agree with what they're doing to you," he wrote. "They're assholes. I have no problem with you. I want you to know I'm your friend." As he glanced in my direction, I smiled and nodded a "thank you". Then I promptly tore up the note and flushed it down the toilet so that no one else would see it and take out their hostilities on him.

Bruce arrived for another visit just before Christmas and told me that Gary Crevallo had said he would get proof of the date the shirts had been purchased. Gary also had a shirt that we could present in court to Pablo so that he might identify it and invalidate his own testimony. He also planned to find Rey, my former secretary's brother-in-law. Since it had been Eisenman who interviewed Pablo Luna, Rey's testimony could make Eisenman's credibility questionable in the eyes of a jury.

On Christmas morning, I was called out of the cell for a visit. At first, I didn't recognize the man waiting to speak to me. It was Gordon Elkins, the former director of sales of my San Francisco company and the man who had taken over as president when I moved to Thailand. Since my arrest had presaged the company's bankruptcy, I hadn't been sure what Gordon's attitude might be. He had lost business in San Francisco as a result of all the negative publicity.

I told him that I considered the money he had paid for my stock to be a loan and that I would pay him back, eventually. It wasn't his fault that I had chosen to associate with someone like John Cummings. I walked away from the visiting room feeling much better. I had a tremendous amount of support from those who knew me, even though some had suffered financially as a result of my problems.

The 27th arrived and I was very optimistic about my chances of getting bail lowered from $1,000,000 to a reasonable level. This wasn't Thailand, I thought; American courts will be more rational. When I was ushered into the courtroom, I was greeted by Gordon's smiling face. Behind him sat my mother, who attempted a smile through her pain and my stepfather who sat stonefaced the entire time. I was constantly amazed at my parents' support. They had made six trips from Modesto in a little more than two weeks. Bruce Nickerson and I sat behind the defense table. "Take notes," he said.

Inspector Pamfiloff was the first prosecution witness. From the beginning, his testimony seemed unrelated to the issue of my bail. Assistant District Attorney Cling seemed more concerned with getting the by-now familiar perceptions of me entered into the record and asked about the police investigation of my activities. Completely omitting the harassment I had undergone in 1984 that caused me to contact Lieutenant Hesselroth, Pamfiloff incorrectly stated that the probe began in 1985 when I was in New York and the police were called to my house to investigate a burglary. He went on to suggest that I had fled to Thailand immediately after the investigation began. My lawyer, Rick Stokes, had been given a "power of attorney" which, Pamfiloff said, "proved" I hadn't planned to return to the United States.

It is amazing to me how Cling, Eisenman and Pamfiloff ignored a number of facts available to them because those facts did not support their predispositions. Point one, I did not move to Thailand until 1987. Point two, since there was no warrant for me and I had no police record, there was nothing from which to flee. Point three, I returned to the United States for a visit in 1988, long after I had supposedly "fled". Point four, once I moved to Thailand I registered myself and my company with the U.S. Embassy. People on the lam usually do not record their whereabouts with embassies representing the country from which they are trying to "flee". Point five, nor do they file 1040's and pay federal taxes on earned income.

I was furiously taking notes. I wrote that when I was in New York in 1985 the police had been called to my house at my own suggestion after Gary Crevallo reported to me that a number of people had broken into my apartment. The break-in was not a burglary, but rather involved a group of neighborhood people who knew I was out of town and had, unilaterally, decided to use my apartment for a party while I was gone. The police used Gary's call to them as an excuse to obtain a search warrant and remove all my personal effects. I also noted that Rick Stokes had been given my power of attorney in order to proceed with a lawsuit against the city for refusing to return my belongings.

I wanted desperately to take the stand to expose Pamfiloff's prevarications, but Bruce told me that if I got up there the prosecutor had the right to cross-examine and he had not prepared me for that. All I could think was that, once more, they were getting away with the lies and insinuations. I was beginning to feel as impotent as I had felt in Thailand. I glanced behind me and noticed that Gordon Elkins was waving to get my attention.

"Let Gordon testify," I said to Bruce.

"Who is he?"

"He's the man who took over my San Francisco business when I moved to Thailand."

"Excuse me, Your Honor," Bruce said. "May I call a witness?"

"We'll take a short recess, then," the judge said, "while I deal with some other cases, people who have been waiting."

I was directed back to the holding cell by the deputy.

"Your hearing has been going on this whole time?" one of the prisoners said.

"Yeah, I'm not finished yet," I answered.

Some of them started complaining that they may not make the bus for their return to San Bruno jail. I didn't understand. It was not as if they were trying to catch a Muni to work.

When I went back into the courtroom, Gordon took the stand.

"When did you see Mr. Raymond last?" the prosecutor asked.

"I visited him on Christmas Day."

"Before that. How many times have you seen him since he moved to Thailand in October 1987?" I knew why the prosecutor was asking the question. John Cummings had told the police that I was afraid to return to America after my move.

"I saw him once in October 1988 when he returned for the annual stockholders meeting," Gordon said. "I also saw him in 1988 when I went to Thailand for an agents familiarization tour co-sponsored by our company and Korean Air Lines. Then he was arrested in February 1989." My arrest actually came on March 1st — Gordon was off by a day.

The prosecutor then contended that I had left the country and had broken my ties with America, that I had no family here. Bruce objected. "Mr. Raymond's parents, Mr. & Mrs. Sesser, are in the audience. I'm sure Mr. Raymond can stay with them."

His objection was ignored by the judge who had turned to talk to a clerk. When he turned back, he said that, since I "had moved and broken my ties" in America, he could only see his way to cut my million dollar bail in half. "I know this isn't going to make either side happy," he understated.

I left the courtroom with my heart in my throat. As I was returning to the holding cell, I turned to Bruce. "Will I see you upstairs?" I asked.

"No, I've just got the tapes of John Cummings' testimony and Pablo Luna's testimony. I'm going to listen to them and I'll bring them for you to hear if there's anything interesting."

* * *

The skin diseases that I had brought with me from Thailand were beginning to spread throughout my body. I had been itching for the past year, perhaps a physicalization of my itching to get out of prison, but here I was freezing and itching at the same time. I had hoped to deal with my skin problems on the outside. Now that it was obvious I would be locked up until my trial, I asked for a doctor.

On New Year's Day, my former accountant and my former sales manager, Jake Jue and Karen Friedman, came to visit. After TSU Destination Services (Tour Service Unlimited San Francisco filed for bankruptcy, Karen started her own destination management company and hired Jake. "I have the records of the break dance contest," Jake said. "I'll testify when the t-shirts were purchased, if you want."

"Thank you, Jake. I'll tell Bruce."

When I returned to my cell, Rick Parker was rolling up his mattress. He was being released and I was left with three hostile neighbors.

* * *

"My name is Steve, not Chester," I barked at the trustee who delivered our clean clothes. "Chester" was the name used by prisoners in America to refer to all men jailed on charges of child molestation.

I caught a glimpse of Livai, the Tongan giant who towered over the other six-footers in jail, listening in on this. "Don't smile at me!" he roared suddenly. Of the inmates now on the block, he had previously been the least hostile. "And close the door." A relief guard had mistakenly unlocked and opened my cell when he made the rounds. I pulled the door shut and sat down on the bunk.

Livai walked over to my cell.

"What is your problem?" he asked with an intimidating ferocity. "What did you say to the trustee?"

"I told him my name is Steve, not Chester," I replied.

"Are you calling me a liar?" Livai asked. I had no idea what he was talking about and my face reflected that. He stomped off.

Then it was Simon's turn. "What did that trustee say to you?"

I repeated myself.

"He has no right to call you names or give you a hard time," Joaquin said. His sudden concern for my welfare was amusing. "We'll only ask you for things when we need it. Don't give anything to anybody else."

When the coffee cart arrived in the evening, I placed my plastic cup on the bars. Livai snatched it up and crushed it in his hand. "I guess you don't get any coffee," he said with a sinister grin. "I told you not to smile at me, punk!"

After my transfer to F Block, I hadn't been allowed to go to the gym to exercise. However, on January 5th, one of the guards decided it would be all right. I found myself in the cavernous hall with Simon and Livai.

A guard sat in a booth above center court and watched as I was again drawn to the exercise equipment, used each device for a few minutes, then ran around the perimeter of the basketball court. At some point, I heard Simon and Livai burst into laughter, but the relative freedom of the hall felt good.

When I stopped to rest, Livai grabbed a ping pong paddle and motioned for me to take up the other. He couldn't quite bring himself to speak to me. I took the paddle with relish. I won the first game and he won the second. Our abilities were close to equal and I could feel his attitude toward me shift, ever so slightly.

The following day, we were allowed in the gym again. Livai headed straight for the ping pong table and picked up a paddle, this time verbally instructing me to compete. When we finished two evenly-played games, we tried badminton and he made sniping comments about my lack of ability.

I suggested that Simon join us, but he refused. However he asked me to explain the details of my case to him. I told him about Thailand, about John Cummings, about the whole unbelievable saga. In the half hour or so, I could see him reassessing his thinking.

Later that afternoon, Joaquin came to my cell and asked about my case. Simon had repeated my story to him. When I finished explaining what the U.S. government had done to me, he started talking about my filing a lawsuit. I was home free! All three prisoners were now talking to me. Of course, Simon and Joaquin still expected their weekly rent, but I had survived a ticking time bomb.

I finally got a prison haircut a month after my arrival. The deputy stayed to keep an eye on the barber so that no "accidents" would occur, in case the word was out on me. The man bragged about being a hair stylist, but he wasn't much better than the hair chopper in Thailand. It looked as if he had placed a bowl over my head and snipped around it.

Bruce came to visit one morning at 9. "I haven't talked to Pablo yet," he reported. "My investigator can't find him. The D.A. gave me a new phone number. He's moved. Nothing sinister. The D.A. arranged for a meeting with him and his mother, but they didn't show. They've now arranged another meeting. I thought I'd wait until after that meeting to talk to him."

"I had hoped that your investigator would talk to him first," I said.

"We haven't been able to find him!" Bruce angrily shot back.

"Please don't get angry," I said. "If you don't agree with something I say, let me know in a civil way. I just got off the phone with my stepfather who accused me of taking years off my mother's life and I'm rather depressed about that, so take it easy."

Our talk turned to strategy and brought up something that concerned me. "Pablo stated that Cummings had a `private' conversation with him after he came down from his LSD trip," I said. "Possibly during that conversation, Cummings planted the idea in the boy's head that I had sex with him while he was high. He once tried to convince me that I had made some statements about religion that I know I would have never made, even if I were out of my mind. For whatever neurotic reason, Cummings always felt a need to include me in his problems. I think he had sex with Pablo when Pablo was high, then told him it was me to alleviate his own guilt. When Cummings was in Bangkok a year before my arrest there, he claimed that Pablo had told the police I had sex with him. That was a year before Pablo had ever talked to the police. I told Cummings then that he was crazy and that I had never touched Pablo."

The atmosphere in the cell block had warmed considerably, both physically and mentally. In a two-week period, it went from hostility to ambivalence to congeniality. Even the trustee who had refused me an extra t-shirt and had insisted on calling me Chester, offered to "fix" my haircut. The other trustees were openly friendly and called me "home boy" rather than Chester. The change made my life more tolerable.

On January 15th, bombs started falling on Iraq. I longed to be in the streets with the anti-war demonstrators, expressing my beliefs. I didn't own a company anymore. I didn't have to act straight and apolitical for fear of losing a client. I ached to be outside and do those things. And I felt like life was passing me by.

On the 19th of January, I telephoned Bruce Nickerson at his office. "I have some bad news," he announced. "Pablo won't meet with us. He's refused to talk to us."

The D.A. had told Pablo that he wasn't obligated. But I was furious that Bruce hadn't talked to him *before* the D.A. which we had been pleading with him to do for twelve months, ever since my

297

mother hired him. I wanted him to talk to the boy and find out why he had made up the story. Now it was too late.

"I offered the D.A. a deal," Bruce said, "suggesting that you might plead guilty to the lesser charge of contributing to the delinquency of a minor by letting John Cummings bring the boy into your house."

Suddenly my whole body shook. I was so angry I couldn't speak. "That's nothing!" I finally blurted, not knowing what else to say. I wanted to change the subject before I screamed at him. I hadn't gone through hell for two years just to turn around and plead guilty to some bullshit charge. "Would you be able to cross-examine Pablo in court?" I asked.

"Definitely," he said. "As a matter of fact you should write down questions you want me to ask him. I'll see you on Tuesday and we can go over them."

"I will," I said and hung up the phone.

I had finally gotten medical attention for my skin ailments and was applying something called Quell twice a day. I was also to be issued new sheets, blankets and towels following a hot soapy shower. By the time I rinsed off, nothing had been brought in, and I was forced to sit on my bunk, naked and dripping for an hour waiting for the change. Finally, the trustee who delighted in calling me Chester brought the new clothes and bedding. "What do you have, crabs or something?" he asked.

"I picked up something in prison in Thailand. The doctor doesn't know what it is."

He sneered. "I was in Thailand and I didn't get anything," he said.

I had a problem dealing with the duplicity in jail. One day, Simon asked me about my sexual preference. I suppose that, for the sake of my safety and relationships with those around me, I could have lied. But, aside from the business world, I hadn't denied my sexuality for 15 years. "I've had relationships with both sexes," I said frankly.

Simon ran over to tell Livai who then told Joaquin. They were baffled by my response. I think they expected that, if I were gay, I would lie. Suddenly the climate chilled once again. They didn't become overtly nasty as they had been when I first arrived, but they were noticeably less friendly.

On Tuesday, Bruce arrived to go over the questions he would ask Pablo in the upcoming hearing. He had a written list of questions as I did. Amazingly, they were almost identical.

I was still upset with Bruce for offering a deal to the D.A. But he claimed he hadn't "offered", only "suggested" that he might be able to talk me into it. I had made my point. I was not guilty and I wanted to be found not guilty. No compromises.

The following day, after waiting in a tiny holding cell with two Hispanic prisoners, I entered the courtroom for the preliminary hearing. The gallery was filled with Hispanic faces. I looked around to see if I might recognize Pablo Luna whose testimony seemed to be the linchpin on which the case against me was based.

The judge entered and announced he would hear another case first. I was ushered back to the holding cell. A few minutes later, I was called back into the courtroom and directed to sit in a very comfortable lounge chair behind a table next to Bruce. My mother, stepfather, Gary Crevallo, and Karen Friedman were all in the audience. There were no television cameras. I was relieved.

Pablo Luna was called by Assistant District Attorney Peter Cling, the prosecutor, to take the stand. A young man who looked vaguely familiar stood up and walked to the witness box. Bruce immediately made a motion that all potential witnesses should leave the courtroom. An older woman who had been sitting next to Pablo stood up and walked out. I whispered to Bruce that we might wish to call Gary Crevallo to testify about the break dance promotion.

"Your Honor, this young man's mother just left the courtroom pursuant to the order to exclude witnesses. Are there any other potential witnesses in the courtroom?" Cling asked.

"Yes, I believe Mr. Gary Crevallo," Bruce said. Gary stood up and walked out.

Then Cling began to question Pablo. He asked about his current age, where he lived, how long he had lived there, with whom he lived, and if he lived in Sacramento in 1984. Pablo answered the questions.

"At that time, did you know a man named John Cummings?" Cling asked.

"Yes, I did." Pablo answered.

"And how did you know Mr. Cummings? Who was he?"

"He was a man that just went around and gave kids a good time." He spoke of Cummings almost reverentially. It was obvious that he still cared for him.

Cling then asked Pablo if he had ever come to San Francisco with Cummings. Pablo responded that he had come to San Francisco with him three times that summer of 1984.

"And on those three occasions when you came to San Francisco with Mr. Cummings, did anybody else come with you?" Cling asked.

"No, sir."

"Now, the first time you came to San Francisco with Mr. Cummings during that summer, do you remember about how long you stayed here?"

"About a day or two."

"Did you stay overnight?"

"Yes."

"On that night that you stayed in San Francisco who did you stay with?" Cling asked.

"I stayed with Steven," Pablo responded. I still could not remember his visit.

"Do you see that person in the courtroom today?"

"Yes, I do."

"Will you point to where he is sitting and describe what he is wearing right now."

"He is wearing the orange right there." Not exactly a fashion statement.

"Had you ever seen the defendant before that time that you first stayed there in 1984?"

"No, I haven't." His memory was worse than mine. I remembered that I met him originally in Cummings' house in Sacramento when I stopped there once for a short visit en route to the Sierras.

Cling then asked him to describe my house. His description was fairly accurate, just as it had been in the police report. "Where did you sleep that night?"

"In a little closet by, next to the front door." The closet next to the front door was a small clothes closet. I was sure he had never slept in that tiny space. Besides, it was usually full of clothes. In the police report, he had said he slept in the front room on the couch. His testimony was contradictory.

"Did you sleep in there by yourself or did somebody else sleep in there with you?"

"John Cummings slept in there with me." Now I knew he was mistaken. Why would they sleep in the closet?

"And how was it decided that you and Mr. Cummings would sleep in that closet?"

"Steve Raymond decided that we should sleep in there so that nobody would disturb us."

"And how did the subject of where you would sleep in the house come up?"

"John Cummings came out and said, `We are going to sleep here. Steve Raymond said we could sleep here and nobody won't disturb us.'"

"Before you went to sleep in the closet, had Mr. Raymond said anything to you personally?"

"The only thing he said was that I had a nice figure for a young man... a nice body for a young man." I was rather amused at this comment. I have never seen an 11-year-old with a `nice body'.

301

Pablo went on to say that I had asked Cummings if I could join the two of them in the closet. I was thoroughly bewildered by his statements. My companion Eduardo and I shared a house with two bedrooms and a front room, all furnished with something on which to sleep. Yet Pablo was suggesting that I wanted to sleep with him and John Cummings in a closet. That must have been very potent LSD, I thought.

Pablo said that he and Cummings then proceeded to have sex in the closet.

Peter Cling continued with his questioning. "Now, at some time did you come back to San Francisco with Mr. Cummings?"

"Yes," Pablo answered.

"Anybody else besides you and Mr. Cummings?"

"No, sir."

"During this second trip, did you send your mother any mail or a postcard of any sort?" I hoped Cling was about to torpedo his own case.

"Yes, I did," Pablo responded.

"I have a card that I'd like to have marked as People's One, Your Honor."

"Okay," the judge said.

"Pablo, I'd like you to take a look at this postcard, the front and the back. Do you recognize that?" Cling asked.

"That's a postcard that I sent to my mother when I went to the Exploratorium."

"Now on this second trip to San Francisco did you stay overnight?"

"Yes, we did. At Steve's house."

"How many nights?"

"I think it was one night."

"The trip to the Exploratorium, was that before the evening that you spent at Mr. Raymond's house or after the evening you spent?"

"Before." The police report said that Pablo stated the visit to the Exploratorium had been afterwards.

"The evening that you spent at Mr. Raymond's house, do you remember where you slept that night?"

"Yes, I do. I slept in that little closet room."

"The same room?"

"Yes."

"As of the time you went to sleep was anybody else in the house besides you, Mr. Raymond and Mr. Cummings?"

"No, there wasn't." In the police report, Pablo Luna had stated that another friend, Dennis, was there when he came to visit. But I did not recall Dennis ever visiting without being accompanied by his lover from Santa Rosa, and I knew that Eduardo was still living with me at the time. I did remember that the four of us were sitting around the kitchen table one day having a drink and talking when Cummings arrived with a young boy. Since he remembered Dennis being at my house during a visit, I surmised that the young boy who came with Cummings that day was Pablo.

"At any point in time during that time that you were inside of Mr. Raymond's house during that second trip, did Mr. Raymond himself engage in any sexual conduct with you?"

"Yes, he did."

"What did he do?" Cling asked.

"He went into the room where I was sleeping at and I didn't have no clothes on at the time and then he want to suck my penis."

"Well, did he actually put his mouth on your penis?" Cling asked.

"No, but he was trying to."

"How was he trying to?"

"He was heading for my penis. He was grabbing at my hands to the side."

"And so he had ahold of your hands?"

"Yes, he did."

"Were you able to get your hands free?"

"Yes, I was."

"When you were getting your hands free, what did Mr. Raymond do?"

"He figured that I didn't want to do it so he got up and left."

"Now let's back up. Do you believe that you were given some sort of drug during the time that you were at Mr. Raymond's residence?"

"Yes, I do."

"Who was it that told you they had given you a drug?"

"John Cummings. He said it was acid that he had gave me."

"And despite that, do you recall the events that you testified to that occurred?" Cling asked.

"Yes, I do."

"And why is it that you believe you were given a drug?"

"I didn't feel normal. I felt wide awake, you know, like everything was moving. I am aware of everything, you know." Pablo had just testified that he was asleep when I supposedly came into the closet to accost him.

"I have no other questions, Your Honor," Cling said. He walked back to the table and sat down.

Bruce stood up and walked over to the witness stand. "Mr. Luna, when did you first meet John Cummings?"

"When I was about 12 years old," Pablo answered.

"Now, let's see when you were 12. You were born in '73, and 12 would make it '85." Bruce said.

"No, I had met him sooner than that."

"When did you meet Mr. Cummings?"

"About the year of '81, yes '81."

"In other words you met him about two years before the trip to San Francisco." Bruce evidently hadn't excelled in math.

"Yes, I did." Neither had Pablo.

"You stated that John Cummings gave kids a good time. Did he have sex with these children?"

"No, he didn't. He just wanted to get to know the children better." Pablo was still trying to protect Cummings more than two years after his arrest and subsequent conviction.

"But he had sex with you?" Bruce asked.

"Yes, he did."

"Okay. When did he first have sex with you?"

Cling stood up. "I don't see that that is relevant, Your Honor," he said. "May I cite the Evidence Code section that talks about prior sexual conduct with anybody other than the accused as being irrelevant."

"The prosecutor is right," the judge said. "Okay, let's do this. We are going to ask the witness to step off the stand. I will hear arguments (in chambers)."

Pablo stood up and walked outside to talk to his mother, the attorneys followed the judge into his chambers, and my family and friends took the opportunity to speak with me.

"This is nothing!" Karen said. "This is what this whole thing was all about?" Her mouth was agape as if it were impossible.

My mother came over to hug me. I stood up, but the deputy told me to sit back down.

Bruce Nickerson was arguing in chambers that he should have the right to ask Pablo how many men he had sex with because he had witnesses to testify that Cummings had taken Pablo to many men's houses in the previous seven years. He was questioning Pablo's memory.

"The discrepancies between what Pablo said here and what he is supposed to have said on the police report are absolutely monumental," Bruce argued.

The judge, however, sustained the objection because Bruce had not submitted a written intent to ask the question.

In the courtroom, Bruce resumed the cross examination. "Mr. Luna, you testified that Mr. Cummings gave you acid on that occasion?"

"Yes, he did."

"That's known as LSD, correct?"

Pablo affirmed that acid and LSD were the same, then Bruce asked how many times he had taken acid and to how many houses Cummings had taken him. Peter Cling kept objecting. Pablo said, however, that he couldn't recall being taken to anyone else's house by Cummings. Cummings himself, however, had testified that he had taken Pablo to a number of houses. Bruce had a written statement to that effect.

"Now you testified that the acid, I believe, made you wide awake and aware of everything. Is that correct?" Bruce asked.

"Yeah."

"Didn't you tell Inspector Pamfiloff that it made you sick and sleepy?"

"That is, that's when I was ill at the time when he gave it to me. He bought me a six-pack of beer. I drank it and that's when I began to feel sleepy and sick after I drank it. So he gave me acid after that. The sleepy and sick was because of the beer that John Cummings had gave me."

"You never told Inspector Eisenman about the beer, did you?" Bruce asked.

"No, I just now recalled it right now," Pablo replied.

"On which occasion was that? The first or the second occasion?"

"That was the second. It was the third time..."

"Didn't you also tell Inspector Pamfiloff that you were sick on the first visit?"

"Objection, argumentative," Cling said.

"Did you tell Inspector Pamfiloff that you got sick?" Bruce asked.

"Yes," Pablo said.

"And fell asleep on the first visit?"

"Yes, I probably am mistaken. It was a long, long time ago, so..."

"So then you are not sure?" I was surprised that Cling didn't object to Bruce leading the witness.

"Yes, I am sure. I am sure."

"On the first visit did you take acid?" Bruce asked.

"Yes, I did," Pablo replied.

"Okay. Did this make you wide awake and aware of everything or did this make you sleepy and sick?"

"It made me wide awake and aware of everything."

Cling objected, the lawyers bantered for a while, then Bruce continued to ask questions about the first visit. Pablo said that he had been dropped in Chinatown, then walked to my house to meet Cummings, who then gave him LSD. Bruce asked him where the closet was. He correctly described its location and said that there was a mattress inside it. The depth of my closet was four feet. It would have been a very small mattress. I had stored a mattress in a walk-in closet towards the rear of the apartment, but he was not describing that now.

Bruce continued to question him about the multiple discrepancies between his testimony to the police two years earlier and his testimony under oath on the stand. There were so many differences in details that it was as if two people had given the statements.

Pablo hadn't mentioned the break dance t-shirt which we felt to be a crucial piece of evidence, so Bruce asked him about that: "On this second visit, did Steve give you anything as a gift. Did he give you some break dancing t-shirts?"

"Oh yes, he did," Pablo responded.

"You are sure of that?"

"Yes."

"This visit was the same one where that postcard that you sent. Is that correct?"

"Yes, it is." Pablo had just impeached his own testimony.

Bruce then discussed the LSD that Pablo said he had taken on the second visit and asked if it had made him sleepy as he had testified to Eisenman and Pamfiloff, or if it had made him awake as he had testified to Cling. He decided that it had made him awake, not sleepy.

Bruce now turned his attention to the third visit, which hadn't been addressed by Cling but on which occasion, Pablo had told police, he again took LSD, then refused the sexual advances of my friend Turner.

"Did Turner ask you to have sex with him?" Bruce asked.

"As I recall, no he didn't," Pablo replied.

"Did you tell Inspector Pamfiloff that he asked you to have sex with him?"

"I don't remember if he did or didn't."

"Was one of those people there an Asian?" Pablo had mentioned Eduardo, who is Filipino, in his statements to the police, but had not mentioned him on the stand.

"Yes, he was," Pablo responded.

"Could he have been a Filipino?"

"Possibility," Pablo said.

"Did you see something unusual on this third visit?" Bruce asked.

"Yes, I did," Pablo said.

"And what was that?"

"I had fallen asleep on the couch at Steve's house. When I awakened, they were onto a sexual grouping, Steven, this guy Robin, and those other two guys." Pablo was still having trouble remembering if he was wide awake or asleep while on LSD.

"An Asian and Mr. Cummings?" Bruce asked.

"No, the Asian and I think Turner. I think, I don't know," Pablo said.

"Was Mr. Cummings involved in the group?"

"I do not... I had barely awakened and I do not remember."

"What did you see?"

"I seen 'em... I looked up and I seen Steven and Turner having sexual intercourse, and I looked down to the side and I seen two other people. I did not know who they were. The Asian guy and the other guy was having sex."

I was loving this testimony! Before he was through, Pablo had also linked Dennis and others with Eduardo, my jealously monogamous companion who was terrified of AIDS, and had turned my house into an orgy palace involving a number of friends.

"Okay," Bruce continued. "Everyone present was either over 18 or close to 18, correct, in your estimation?"

"Yes," Pablo answered.

"Do you have hallucinations when you take acid?" Bruce asked.

"Yes, I do."

"What kind of hallucinations?"

"Just like things moving on the wall and that's it. Just little things moving."

Cling objected and Bruce switched his line of questioning. "You had an interview with the police officers. Isn't that correct, officers Eisenman and Pamfiloff?"

"Yes, I did."

"They contacted you, rather than you contacting them?"

"Yes."

"Where did this take place?"

"At my school."

"And what school were you in at the time?"

"Grant Union High School."

"That would have been about two years ago?"

"Two years."

"Did they indicate to you that they thought Steve was a bad man?"

"I don't recall."

"Was there any reason... Was officer Pamfiloff and Eisenman the first people you talked to about this?"

"Yes, it was."

Bruce continued asking questions about Pablo's interrogation by the police, most of which were objected to by Peter Cling. Not being able to pursue the line of questioning about the two officers' investigative techniques, Bruce dismissed Pablo and he stepped down.

I was delighted. I now had plenty of witnesses to contradict Pablo's statements and John Cummings' attempts to corroborate them: Dennis, Eduardo, Robin, Turner.

The two lawyers then approached the bench and discussed the merits of the case against me with the judge. His decision was that the case would stand. "As you know, the standard by which courts make decisions in preliminary hearings is not reasonable doubt, it is simply reasonable suspicion. Therefore, based on the evidence presented, it does appear to the court that there is sufficient evidence for this, at least a question of fact for a jury to decide. Therefore, the defendant is held to answer to those counts against him and is ordered to appear in Department 22 of the Superior Court on February 6, 1991 at 9:30 in the morning."

"The bail remains the same?" the clerk asked.

"Yes," the judge responded.

Fifteen

A New Reality

Bruce arrived for a visit early the next morning. "We've a lot to talk about," he said. "I've spent a lot of time in the law library doing research since I left court yesterday. I need you to do some research for me as well. You say there's a law library in the jail?"

"Yes, but I don't know how complete it is," I said. He gave me a number of things to look up, precedents of similar cases.

"I couldn't believe that testimony," Bruce shook his head as he rose to leave, still amazed at the flimsy case the D.A. had created.

"Why do you write so much?" Simon asked me after I had returned to the cell.

"I write a lot of letters, but I'm also writing a book about my experiences," I said.

"Do you write about everything?"

"Things that are interesting, plus comparisons between the American judicial system and the Thai judicial system."

"Do you use real names?" he asked timidly.

"Usually, yeah," I replied.

"You talk about us, about buying things at the commissary?"

"Bingo!" I thought to myself. "Now maybe the extortion will end." Remarkably, it did. In record time. I was never again asked to purchase things for them.

One of the most bizarre evenings of TV viewing occurred in late January when one program, "Inside Edition", discussed Livai's case and was followed by a made-for-television movie about the prisoner in the cell block directly across from ours. His name was Richard Ramirez and the show was called "The Night Stalker". This wasn't exactly the type of company I had kept on the outside.

"I've got some good news and some bad news," Bruce announced at his next visit. "The good news is that I've found all the cases I needed, Jake has given me excellent records about the break dance promotion, he has one of the shirts, and he and Eduardo have both agreed to testify. The bad news is financial. All of your money has been used up."

Bruce had been paid $10,000 — $5,000 ten months prior to my return, then another $5,000 after my return. He had sent a notice about this to my mother six days earlier, but already was muttering about clients who expected him to work for nothing and complained that he had to borrow money to pay his bills this month. He said that if he wasn't paid by the court hearing in a few days, he would sign off as my lawyer and I would have to use a public defender. I looked at him in amazement. Though I believed he was doing a good job, I also felt he was acting like a jerk. No law firm in the country would expect to be paid in six days. I was helpless to do anything about money — my personal funds had long ago been depleted. My mother had already spent $25,000 to help me. And I had no idea if it were possible for us to come up with any more.

"The D.A. called me," Bruce said. "He decided to add `force and violence' to the charge after Pablo testified that you touched his arm. They're pushing this thing to the limit."

This surprised me. After Luna's testimony, I actually had thought the D.A. might modify the charge to a *lesser* one. I understood none of this. I knew Eisenman was a fanatic, but unless it was to do Eisenman's bidding, I couldn't understand why the D.A.'s office kept pounding away.

As she had so many times in the past, my mother came to the rescue. She paid Bruce by my arraignment date and he was back on the job as if nothing had happened. At the arraignment, I pleaded "not guilty" to two charges; one of aiding and abetting a sexual assault and the other, a sexual assault using force and violence.

As usual, my mother attended the session — this time with her brother, my Uncle Paul, who had taken all of the notes I'd made in Thailand, typed them on his word processor, and sent my descriptions of IDC to family and friends around the country. Gordon Elkins was there as well and handed Bruce a note to give to me.

"Karen Friedman just died," the note said. "A staph infection. She went to the hospital on Sunday and died on Monday." I couldn't believe what I was reading. She had just been at my preliminary hearing.

Everyone loved Karen. She was still quite young — in her late '30s — and even had a brush with fame as the only white backup vocal on the hit song, "Walk on the Wild Side." The lyrics went something like, "And the colored girls sang doo doo doo, doo doo doo doo doo." She had a zest for life, enhancing nearly every life she touched, and was one of the most outgoing women I had ever met. A sinking feeling swept over me. And again I thought that things could never be the same. "This is what this whole thing was all about?" were the last words she had said to me.

In addition to Gordon's note, Bruce handed me a letter from — of all people — John Cummings. The letter began, "My primary reason for writing is to re-establish contact," then continued, "I'm quite sure you've heard a lot about me." Was he trying to be the master of understatement? He asked that I write back and closed the letter with the question, "Where do we stand (in terms of each other) from your perspective?" The man was more insane than I could have ever imagined.

Looking back, I am not sure I could satisfactorily explain Cummings' presence in my life — even to myself. Certainly I'm to blame for my own naivete — for overlooking a million warning signs, for allowing such an individual to disrupt the rather sublime existence I had created for myself. But as a friend said to me later, "it's not totally idiotic or without precedent to have assimilated a college friend into your life without much consideration for the consequences, even if there were a lot of flashing yellow lights."

I thought about what happens to someone who gets bitten by a snake and then goes back a second time. Yet I had a lot of questions that only he could answer, the most urgent being whether he expected to testify against me.

Both my mother and father had tried to teach me to forgive and forget. Even if I could forgive Cummings for what he had done to my life, I could never forgive him for what he had done to those I loved. I sat down in the cell and began composing possibly the most difficult letter I have ever written. It took two days to complete. I kept tearing up and rewriting the pages. I wanted to tell him what I thought of him, but I also wanted answers to my questions, yet still feared what he could continue to do to me. His statements to police did not match anything that Pablo Luna had said in court. But I worried that he would get a copy of Pablo's testimony and then rearrange his lies to fit those statements in front of a jury.

I tried to probe gingerly... like a snake handler, though I could not resist the temptation to include a passage from Shakespeare which I thought appropriate: "Shame serves thy life and doth thy death attend."

Bruce arrived on the evening of February 8th with a tape recorder and the tapes of John Cummings' testimony to Eisenman and Pamfiloff. They were six hours long! As I listened to them in the interview rooms for the next couple of days, a lot more of the pieces fell into place. On the tape, Cummings claimed Mark Morgan's children were being sponsored by pedophiles. With a constant stream of cruel untruths, he managed to generate a frenzy among law enforcement officials and the media and destroy my career and all of Mark Morgan's work and an easier life for all of his kids.

Cummings also told police that, besides Pablo, I had sex with an Indian boy whom he had once brought to my house. One of the tapes was of an interview with that boy who truthfully denied Cummings' allegations. Cummings obviously hadn't coached him as well as he had Pablo. In a better world, I would hope that would have been significant enough to Inspectors Eisenman and Pamfiloff to throw Cummings' credibility into question.

After listening to the rest of Cummings' testimony, I heard tapes of Eisenman and Pamfiloff begging Pablo Luna and the Indian boy to help them "get these professional peds off the street so they can't hurt anybody else." The inspectors actually told them that boys who have sex with men become "child molesters" themselves. Their theory reminded me of the discredited belief about gay men being "created" by overbearing mothers, a theory that I had been taught a quarter century earlier at Sonoma State.

The two officers strongly influenced the Indian boy's attitude about Cummings, the man in whose words they seemed to put so much stock. Initially the boy indicated that he liked Cummings. By the end of the tape, he said, "All peds should be killed in electric chairs!"

I was amazed that, under Eisenman and Pamfiloff's prodding, the Indian boy didn't turn around and accuse me just to "help them put away" another one of those "professional peds."

On February 23rd, news arrived that the elected government of Chatichai in Thailand had fallen to the generals in a military coup. Outrageous as it may sound, John Cummings had told the FBI that I was a personal friend of the prime minister and that the prime minister was a pedophile. Again, I was totally baffled over how these investigators could have ever considered Cummings a credible source. He mixed partial truth with outlandish folly and they took it all for fact. Would I have spent time in Thai prisons if the prime minister were a pal, for God's sake? Then I wondered that if they did take Cummings seriously, was there even a remote chance the U.S. government had passed this "revelation" about the prime minister's supposed sexual preference on to the Thai generals and encouraged the coup? (According to a report by Reuters in April 1992, the leaders of the coup had selected Narong Wongwan as prime minister but eventually withdrew support for him because of American "suspicions" that he was linked to the international drug trade.) If the U.S. had that kind of influence over Thailand, and Cummings had that kind of influence on U.S. investigators, I had to wonder who in reality was running this world?

Bruce came to tell me that Judge Jack K. Berman had been appointed to hear my trial in Superior Court. My lawyer had filed a "995 motion" asking Judge Berman to look at the evidence provided by the District Attorney and rule on whether there was sufficient evidence to go to trial.

The motion began by saying that "defendant Raymond was held to answer... without reasonable or probable cause in that no evidence was adduced at the preliminary examination to show that he performed a lewd and lascivious act upon the victim."

Because of Pablo's testimony that Cummings had sex with him in my closet, the D.A. had thrown in a second count against me of aiding and abetting. Bruce's motion said, "The District Attorney is operating on an aiding and abetting theory but the evidence does not support such a theory. California law defines aiding and abetting as follows:

"A person aids and abets the commission of a crime when he or she acts,

1) with knowledge of the unlawful purpose of the perpetrator and

2) with the intent or purpose of committing, encouraging or facilitating the commission of the crime...

"Mere presence at the scene of a crime which does not itself assist the commission of the crime does not amount to aiding and abetting."

He then used a precedent to further his position and stated, "The facts alleged in count one do not rise to this level as a matter of law. First, there is no evidence to indicate defendant Raymond knew that a lascivious act was going to take place. Second, there is no evidence of `aiding, promoting, encouraging or instigating.' All the defendant did was to put the perpetrator and Mr. Luna up for the night." Bruce strengthened his motion to dismiss by citing legal case histories.

"Count two," he stated, "is at best an *attempt*. California law defines `attempt' as follows:

"An attempt to commit a crime consists of two elements, namely a specific intent to commit the crime, and a direct but ineffectual act done towards its commission..."

The motion mentioned a number of precedents, then addressed the prosecutor's attempt to add force and violence to the charge, stating that, in order to charge force and violence, the crime had to be committed.

March 1, 1991 was set as the date for the judge to decide on the motion.

"Don't expect the motion for dismissal," Bruce warned with his now-familiar-but-still-maddening negativity. "This case is too political. They've spent too much taxpayers' money and effort to let it be dismissed, whether circumstances warrant it or not."

On the second anniversary of my arrest in Thailand — two years to the day — I went to the courtroom to hear the judge's decision. My mother and stepfather were in the audience as usual. While I was still in the holding cell, Bruce appeared and told me that the D.A. had requested a postponement to have time to review the motion. Bruce had submitted it on February 8th, three weeks earlier. I accepted the delay as just one more in a mountain of frustrations. They were determined to keep me imprisoned as long as possible, I believed. Bruce then handed me an eight-page typewritten letter from John Cummings.

"If we go to trial, do you think the prosecutor will bring Cummings in to testify?" I asked Bruce.

"I don't think so," he answered. "His testimony would be impeached so easily."

`But his testimony is why I'm here in the first place!' I couldn't help thinking.

317

When I returned to the cell, I read Cummings' letter which left no doubt in my mind that he was actually insane. He was asking me to provide him with a copy of Pablo's testimony and threatened that if I didn't get it to him, he would get it another way. "Does he think I'm a total idiot?" I wondered.

Although he had already been sentenced and had his sentence reduced in exchange for his testimony, I knew it would still be possible to get the sentence diminished further if he could deliver my conviction as part of an ongoing plea bargain. He had already managed to cut 62 years off his prison term by being "cooperative".

Two years in prison and I hadn't done anything wrong, other than use terrible judgment in allowing Cummings into my life. I'd like to put that two years in perspective for you with one striking example. Former Supervisor Dan White had shot and killed San Francisco Mayor George Moscone and Supervisor Harvey Milk, thereby irrevocably altering the city's political landscape, and had spent just a year longer than I had behind bars.

March 14, 1991 arrived, exactly two years from the date that Eisenman and Pamfiloff had created the warrant for my arrest. I went into the courtroom hoping we might be able to get one of the two charges dismissed.

Judge Berman read from a sheet of paper on his desk. He agreed with the motion that the charge of aiding and abetting had no merit. I glanced at Bruce. He was smiling from ear to ear.

The judge then started talking about the second part of Bruce's motion. "I'm going to dismiss the charge of 288 (a)," the judge said.

Peter Cling started to object that my lawyer had not even requested a dismissal, but had rather asked for a reduction of the crime charged. The judge looked at the assistant district attorney and said flatly, "There isn't even evidence that a crime had been committed. I'm underwhelmed by the evidence you have against this man," he continued, "after seven years!... How old is the boy now, 17, 18? I will instruct the sheriff to hold Mr. Raymond until 4 PM to allow you the opportunity to file any new charges that you may deem necessary. Otherwise, the case is dismissed."

When the deputy led me back to the holding cell, I slammed my fist into the wall and yelled, "YES! YES!" The other prisoners looked at me as if I were crazy.

At 2:30 that afternoon, the deputy walked in and barked, "F One, roll 'em up! You're going home."

After processing out and throwing on my street clothes, I went down to the basement to pick up my belt. I ran into Ron Huberman, the friend from the D.A.'s office who had arranged the meeting in 1984 with Eisenman's supervisor, Lieutenant Hesselroth. "I couldn't contact you when you were inside," he said apologetically. "John Cummings had mentioned my name as being a friend of yours. I was told to keep hands off."

At 4 PM, I walked out the doors of the Hall of Justice. It was a cold, damp San Francisco day. I spotted a news van and knew right away the TV stations were no longer interested in my story. I was innocent — and that wasn't news.

I no longer had bars between me and the rest of the world. I had won the battle, but I had a gnawing sense that I had somehow lost the war. I didn't feel the freedom that I had yearned for since that hot humid day in March a lifetime ago when I was confronted by a nervous little policeman in baggy pants. The freedom of my life in Thailand was conceptual, not physical, and the sense of my freedom was gone. The shocking realization that my government and the Thai government only allow personal freedom to exist when it suits their purposes and that my government is not of me nor for me, removed from me the sense that I am protected by that government and the feeling that I am free to be myself.

I had to re-think my reality. What had been important to me — the successful completion of an incentive program, the survival of a business, even a financially secure future — had become irrelevant. There were for me new priorities.

In a sense, I was more alive than I had ever been. Life was fragile, and I knew now I had to treat it as such, but also to continue to explore it and to savor the explorations like fine wine. The world was still out there waiting to be discovered.

I didn't need a successful business to find happiness, I needed only my sense of adventure and a commitment to myself to search for and rediscover that naive conceptual sense of freedom that had been stolen from me. I realized that would take time.

I walked out of the Hall of Justice with nothing except the clothes on my back. My life savings were gone, my sense of self-worth had been wounded and my physical health nearly destroyed. By taking away everything I owned, the government had freed me of the need to possess. I neither owned anything nor was owned by anything. But I could hear the fat lady singing and I wondered if Eisenman, upstairs in his office, could hear her too. And I thought maybe — just maybe — the nightmare was finally over.

Epilogue

A s soon as I got out of county jail, I applied for the return of my passport. I hoped to go back to Thailand and clear my name in the courts and I felt making an appearance would make a strong statement.

In May 1991, the passport office informed me my passport would not be returned until I presented documents to show that my case in California had been dismissed and there was no longer an outstanding warrant for my arrest. I obtained a letter to that effect from the San Francisco County Recorder and sent it off to Washington.

About a month later, my passport came in the mail — canceled by the U.S. Embassy in Bangkok. I went to the passport office in San Francisco and requested a new one. A clerk checked a computer and informed me that was not possible because I owed $900 to the U.S. government.

I immediately sent the passport office in Washington a copy of Marcia Pixley's receipt showing that the EMDA loan had been repaid in full prior to my departure from Thailand. But, in the meantime, a date for my appeals hearing in Bangkok was set and I had no way to travel there. For 55 weeks, U.S. Embassy officials had seen to it that I remained imprisoned as assurance that I would appear for court proceedings; now, in another dark irony, the government was refusing me valid travel documents so I could voluntarily attend my own hearing. As it turned out, Puttri had to go in my stead and tell the court I was unable to leave America. Consequently, the Thais issued a warrant for my arrest.

In August, at a second hearing, the appeals court announced that no evidence had been presented by the prosecution to cause it to reverse the decision of the lower court and my acquittal stood. The Thai warrant was rescinded.

Finally, in late October 1991, a new passport was issued and unexpectedly arrived in the mail — with no explanation.

Gradually, I tried to piece my life back together. I found work in the travel industry in San Francisco and started bicycling and walking to try to get in shape. When I had the energy for it, I searched for an American attorney who would be willing to work on contingency and sue the U.S. government on my behalf. Although there were a number of them who said they found the case "fascinating" or "challenging", they believed it would take an arsenal of law firms — and even then would prove to be a monumental task — to challenge a recent Supreme Court decision that held U.S. government officials could not be made liable in American courts for actions taken beyond the borders of the United States. If I were wealthy, perhaps this could have ended a different way.

John Cummings was eventually sentenced to 28 years in prison. He is serving time in state prison in central California.

Chat found a job at Robinson's Department Store next to Victory Monument, worked there for about a year, and then got a position in a furniture factory near Ramkamhaeng University. He writes often, recently sent the news that he met a woman whom he hopes to marry, and always ends his letters with, "I love you, Father."

Nu was forced to drop out of school after I returned to America. In January 1993, he wrote that he was rushed to a hospital with stomach pains and diagnosed with duodenal ulcers. He has apparently become quite thin and undernourished, and complains of severe pain from digesting food.

Kenji was acquitted of all charges of receiving stolen property and released from Bangkok Special Prison. He returned to the condominium and ran a tour guide service for a couple of years before moving, in late 1993, to his family home in Thonburi.

I lost all contact with Kachon. And Chat, Kenji and Nu have not seen him since 1990.

Mark Morgan was found guilty of the charges against him. The judge in the case actually told his attorney in court that he had made up his mind following the prosecution's statements and was not interested in hearing defense testimony. Morgan was sentenced to two-and-a-half years in prison in northern Thailand. In the fall of 1992, he was released and returned to Utah with his wife, Sujitra, eventually moving to the Los Angeles area.

David Groat spent two-and-a-half years in Khlong Prem Prison, and was then returned to the United States where the original case against him was dismissed for lack of evidence. However, he served time until 1993 on charges of fleeing the country to avoid prosecution. He is currently living and working in Massachusetts.

The Australian, Peter Bailey, was eventually convicted of transporting heroin for sale and was moved from Mahachai to Bangkwan Prison.

My friends in IDC, Jamie and Kuresh, were each accepted as political refugees by Norway and Germany, respectively. They were released from IDC in the fall of 1991.

Bangkok Special Prison was torn down in 1992.

One final word. My nightmare is not an isolated one. People who have been accused, though innocent, can never completely escape the stigma of the charges. As recently as last year, newspaper articles appeared in which my arrest was cited prominently but my exoneration never mentioned. In one story, The San Jose Mercury News referred to Cummings as "a Sacramento youth minister" and to me as one who "fled to Thailand" and "founded an orphanage to sexually indulge (myself and my) friends." There are many horror stories similar to mine. One of the more recent ones involved a young woman named Kelly Michaels who was the subject of a report on CBS' "60 Minutes" ("The Girl Next Door") and in the National Review ("Ordeal by Trial"). She worked at a day care center in suburban New Jersey and was convicted of raping dozens of children with knives, forks and spoons. After her arrest, she came to believe two things — (1) that what was happening did not feel real and (2) that someone would realize the absurdity of the charges against her and say, "We're sorry, there's been a terrible mistake".

The FBI searched for physical evidence at the day care but found none. Children had presumably been raped with knives, but examinations revealed no scars. Michaels submitted to a lie detector test and passed. But prosecutors manipulated interviews with children and investigators offered "badges" if the kids agreed to help them.

"In some of the earliest tape recorded interviews, the children denied that any abuse had taken place," reported Mike Wallace of "60 Minutes". But, in response to the denials, one investigator said to a child, "How come you don't want to tell me, and all your friends already told me?"

In this case and in my own (and no doubt in some others of which we are not yet aware) investigators seem to be short of the same moral responsibility they claim their suspects lack and were quite willing to bend truths and ignore facts to get what they wanted. After all, finding someone innocent of such charges is not nearly the career boost that a conviction might be.

Kelly Michaels was sentenced to 47 years in prison during the same period I was being beseiged, during what Wallace referred to as a time of "national hysteria over child abuse". With the help of Dorothy Rabinowitz, an editorial page writer for the Wall Street Journal, and civil rights attorney Morton Stavis, Michaels filed an appeal. A New Jersey appeals court ruled that she had been unjustly convicted — after she had spent five years in prison! — and an appeals court judge said, "The prosecution is required to follow the law in the prosecution of a case. And the prosecution is not privileged to violate a defendant's rights."

Steve Raymond is currently working as Director of Sales for a large San Francisco hotel.

Index

325

Index

Footnotes

1   Matichon newspaper, February 12, 1989, pages 1-2.

2   Bangkok Nation, March 3, 1989, page 1.

3   Bangkok Post, March 3, 1989, page 3.

4   The Bangkok Post ran a full two-page story justifying the practice of bribery. Entitled "Why police need bribes to fund battle against crime", it cited maintenance costs, expenses incurred while tracking clues and underpaid employees. October 28, 1990, pages 8-9.

5   Bangkok Nation, March 4, 1989, page 2.

6   Bangkok Nation, March 6, 1989, feature section (AIDSwatch), page 1.

7   Bangkok Post, March 7, 1989, page 1.

8   Bangkok Nation, March 7, 1989, page 1. United Press International also put a story on the wires dated March 6, 1989 titled "FBI seeks Americans held in Thai child sex ring" in which Bangkok Metropolitan Police Commissioner Lt. Gen. Manas Krutchaiyan said Raymond was re-arrested "on charges of sexual abuse of children in the United States."

9   Letter of March 15, 1989 given to Ken West and signed by Consul Ed Wehrli at the American Embassy. Although the letter denied any part by the Embassy in Raymond's arrest, an earlier letter (cited herein in greater detail) dated March 6, 1989 to Police Lt. Gen. Manas Krutchaiyan from David Copas Sr., security attache at the American Embassy, contradicts Wehrli's assertion.

10   Bangkok Post, August 6, 1989, Post Bag section.

11   Letter of March 6, 1989 from David Copas Sr., security attache, American Embassy, to Bangkok Metropolitan Police Commissioner Lt. Gen. Manas Krutchaiyan requesting Raymond be held without bail, even though he is described as "a suspect only".

12   Oakland Tribune, August 2, 1984, pages B-1, B-2.

13   Letter of January 1990 (exact date indecipherable) from Dr. Komain Phatarabhirom, Prosecutor General, to Consul General David Lyon.

14   Letter of April 10, 1990 from Consul General David Lyon to Harriet McNamara, president of Enjoy California Enterprises.

15   Letters to Sen. Bennett Johnston (April 25, 1990), Sen. John Breaux (April 20, 1990), Sen. Alan Cranston (undated), Harriet McNamara (April 10, 1990), Barbara Seymour (May 23, 1990) and Bruce Nickerson (February 8, 1990).

16   Letter of June 26, 1989 from Consul General David Lyon to Steve Raymond.

17   Letter of March 1, 1990 from Consul General David Lyon to Justice Sopon Ratanakorn of the Court of Appeals.

18   Letter of March 8, 1990 from Kanok Indramborya, secretary of the Court of Appeals, to Consul General David Lyon.

19   Letter of March 22, 1990 from William Wharton in the U.S. Department of State to Richard Atkins, International Legal Defense Counsel. In the same letter, Wharton wrote that the Office of Citizenship Appeals was "preparing Mr. Raymond's case for submission to and decision by the Assistant Secretary of State for Consular Affairs" — almost six months after the passport hearing at Khlong Prem Prison.

20   Bangkok Post, May 7, 1990, Outlook section, pages 25, 28.

21   Jack Anderson syndicated column, January 31, 1990, (San Francisco Chronicle, page A-21).

22   San Francisco Chronicle, February 18, 1990, Sunday Punch section, page 3.

23   Toronto Globe & Mail, July 17, 1990, page A-8.

24   Bangkok Nation, June 26, 1993, Focus section, page 1.

25   Playboy Magazine, June 1992. See also "False Allegations of Child Abuse" by Dr. Lee Coleman and Pat Clancy published by the American Bar Association.

26   Letter of July 16, 1990 from Howard Ruff to Chester Newey.

27   Time Magazine, February 3, 1992, pages 44-49.

28   Puttri would reiterate this in subsequent letters to Consul General David Lyon (August 24, 1990) and to Congressman Gary Condit (August 20, 1990 and October 24, 1990).

29   Letter of October 5, 1990 from Elizabeth M. Tamposi of the U.S. Department of State to Steve Raymond.

Steve Raymond is the sales and marketing director for the *Renoir Hotel* in San Francisco. He is the fourth of five children and the son of parents committed to social causes. His father, a Methodist minister, was a pacifist and did anti-war counseling. His mother has worked continuously in community and regional organizations to end racial inequality and social injustice. Following a stint in the Air Force and graduation from Sonoma State University, Raymond became a tour escort for an incentive travel company in San Francisco, where he also became an activist in the Harvey Milk Democratic Club. A few years later, he founded his own company, *Destination Tour Services*, and, following its success, opened an office in the Pacific Rim in Bangkok. After several seasons of modest growth, he was abruptly arrested and spent two years in a Thai prison, where he began a detailed diary that would form the basis of *"The Poison River"*

Mal Karman is an award-winning screenwriter, playwright and novelist. His co-authored teleplay, *"Wasted: A True Story"* won the Paul Newman-Joanne Woodward Scott Newman Award, a Silver Medal at the New York International Film Festival and a National Academy of Television Arts & Sciences (Emmy) award. He is also the winner of a Diane Thomas screenwriting award, a California Arts Council playwriting grant, and three national journalism awards. Karman is the author of two previous books, a political thriller, *"The Foxbat Spiral"* (Dell/Delacorte Press), and the best-selling *"Naked Came the Stranger"* (co-authored with 15 friends for Lyle Stuart Publishers) which landed on the New York Times lists for 16 weeks. His original stage play, *"The Bones of Simon Bottle"*, had its world premiere in San Francisco in 1991. On the big screen, he has written on numerous feature films in the U.S. and Europe. Previously, he was a freelance journalist and a film critic for several publications including Francis Coppola's *"City Magazine"* and received individual national journalism awards for his writing on sports, news and features. He has been an editor at *Newsday*, the *Oakland Tribune* , the *San Francisco Examiner* and the *Pacific Sun* and was a foreign correspondent for *Newsday* in Scandinavia. He presently divides his time between the San Francisco Bay Area and Marina del Rey in southern California and is at work on a new novel.

New Amsterdam Press

Mail Order Department FE

Suite 245

945 Taraval Street

San Francisco, CA. 94116

the Poison River

Please send me _____ hardcover copies of "The Poison River" @ $22.95

Please send me _____ softcover copies of "The Poison River" @ $14.95

Please include a free list of titles _____

I am paying by:

personal check _____ credit card _____

My credit card number is _____ Card expires _____

Signature _____

Name _____

(Please Print)

Address _____

A percentage of all profits is donated to AIDS research

• • • • • • • • **MAIL THIS COUPON TODAY** • • • • • • • • •

FREE SHIPPING & HANDLING*

with this coupon

* with orders prepaid by personal check within continental U.S.
(allow 4-6 weeks for delivery). California residents add 8.75%
sales tax. _____

New Amsterdam Press

Mail Order Department FE

945 Taraval Street (Suite 245)

San Francisco, CA. 94116